Studies in International Social Policy and Welfare

Edited by DR STEWART MacPHERSON, *Department of Social Administration, University of Nottingham, UK* and PROFESSOR JAMES MIDGLEY, *School of Social Work, Louisiana State University, USA*

This challenging series is designed to encourage the publication of books which deal with social policy issues in an international context. It will present new insights by highlighting the experience of different societies with regard to common problems. A major feature of the series will be its use of material from both non-industrial and industrial countries.

Titles in the series will be thematic in that they will explore current issues or theoretical propositions without relying exclusively on developments in any one country. Case studies of welfare programmes in particular countries will be avoided unless they are of special interest or draw conclusions of wider theoretical significance.

The series will make an important, innovative, contribution to the study of social policy by publishing books which make coherent, consistent use of international material for an international readership.

Series titles:

Comparative Social Policy and the Third World
Stewart MacPherson and James Midgley

Modern Welfare States
Robert Friedmann, Neil Gilbert, Moshe Sherer (eds)

Five Hundred Million Children
Stewart MacPherson

Forthcoming:

The Welfare State in Capitalist Society
Ramesh Mishra

The Crisis in Welfare
Brian Munday (ed.)

Five Hundred Million Children

Poverty and Child Welfare in the Third World

Stewart MacPherson
Department of Social Administration
University of Nottingham

WHEATSHEAF BOOKS · SUSSEX

ST. MARTIN'S PRESS · NEW YORK

First published in Great Britain in 1987 by
WHEATSHEAF BOOKS LTD
A MEMBER OF THE HARVESTER PRESS PUBLISHING GROUP
Publisher: John Spiers
16 Ship Street, Brighton, Sussex
and in the USA by
ST. MARTIN'S PRESS, INC.
175 Fifth Avenue, New York, NY10010

British Library Cataloguing in Publication Data

MacPherson, Stewart
  Five hundred million children : poverty and child
  welfare in the Third World.—(Studies
  in international social policy and welfare;
  3).
  1. Child welfare—Government policy
  —Developing countries
  I. Title   II. Series
  362.7′09172′4   HV713

  ISBN 0-7108-0176-9
  ISBN 0-7108-0240-4 Pbk

Library of Congress Cataloging-in-Publication Data
  MacPherson, Stewart.
    Five hundred million children: poverty and child welfare in the
  Third World/Stewart MacPherson.
        p.   cm.
      Bibliography: p.
      Includes indexes.
      ISBN 0-312-01262-4: $35.00
    1. Child welfare—Developing countries. 2. Poor children—
  Government policy—Developing countries.   I. Title.
  HV804.M33 1987
  362.7′042′091724—dc19   87–24067
                                                                CIP

Typeset in Times 11/12 point by Witwell Ltd, Liverpool

Printed in Great Britain by Mackays of Chatham Ltd, Kent

For Jack Lucy and Kuri Dom

Contents

Tables

Figures

Acknowledgements

This book has come out of both teaching and research interests. I would like to thank students on a number of courses, at Nottingham and in Papua New Guinea, for their interest and their contribution. My thanks also go to John Orley of the World Health Organisation in Geneva; involvement with his project on the well-being of children has given much-needed impetus to work on a number of occasions. The completion of the book would have been very difficult indeed without the technical skills and patience of Chris Isaacs; I am very grateful. Andrea, Cate and James have again given me more support than was reasonable to ask; I hope the result justifies it.

Introduction

This book appears as part of a series entitled *Studies in International Social Policy and Welfare*. It follows the spirit of that series in dealing with issues of social policy in a broad international context and attempting to promote the development of a more genuinely global perspective in the subject. The first book in the series—*Comparative Social Policy and the Third World* (MacPherson and Midgley, 1987)—dealt with these issues across a broad front. That book, and my *Social Policy in the Third World* (1982), examined welfare issues, and the nature and role of social policy, in relation to the wider development context.

Here, themes explored in those books are pursued in very much more detail, with regard to poor children in developing countries. This focus enables specific welfare issues to be discussed in some depth, and for a range of interwoven topics to be examined together. The core of the book is a concern with welfare and its relationship to patterns of development. Concentration on the poorest children is an expression of the belief that social policy is fundamentally concerned with poverty and inequality; the scale of child poverty is such as to demand attention. Most of the book is concerned with issues affecting younger children in particular. In social policy virtually all boundaries are arbitrary; in this case very many artificial boundaries have by necessity been drawn, and there are good objections to them all. In concentrating on younger children the book is to some extent reflecting a widely held view that the relatively greater vulnerability of young children puts their needs more clearly into the responsibility of social policy. In dealing with children from birth to around 10 or so, the book tries to show common themes in social welfare and social development across a range of needs. The welfare of older children, and adults, is of course marked by essentially similar patterns in terms of social policy response in the context of development and underdevelopment.

These overarching questions were the subject of substantial discussion in the books referred to earlier; that material is not repeated in this book, which seeks to do three things. First, to establish and examine some of the most significant child welfare problems in relation to the poorest children in developing countries. Second, to illustrate and substantiate, by examining specific child welfare issues, some general propositions regarding the relationships between welfare and development. Third, to begin to indicate the possibilities for social policy of new developments and approaches to the achievement of greater welfare in the context of poverty. The last of these is done in terms of contemporary responses to the welfare of children, but in examining such responses in relation to existing patterns of social policy, lessons may be drawn for other aspects of the total welfare effort. But, to repeat the point, such boundaries are essentially arbitrary and destructive of full understanding. What this book seeks to do above all is to focus attention on young children so that much more detail of social policy action and inaction can be seen. But it is hoped that the book will be seen in context; the most important determinants of child welfare lie outside social welfare policies and programmes, in the dynamics of development and underdevelopment. As I have argued elsewhere, it is the articulation of social policy with those forces which we must see as the framework for our explorations of particular themes.

Chapter 1 looks at the rights and needs of the very poorest children. Not all these children are in the very poorest countries; of the more than 500 million who are estimated to be below the absolute poverty line, many live in countries which are relatively better off. For these children the most fundamental human rights are denied by poverty. The chapter examines questions of rights and of the role of the state in child welfare. It goes on to chart the range and nature of needs in developing countries; there are general themes despite great variation in conditions between countries.

In Chapter 2 the relationship between the welfare of children and the economic aspects of contemporary development and underdevelopment is examined. It is only in recent years that welfare considerations have come to take a prominent part in the formulation and implementation of overall development strategies. In particular, the chapter looks at the impact of the recession of the late 1970s and 1980s on the welfare of the poorest children.

Chapter 3 examines the growth of programmes concerned directly with the welfare of children through coherent social policies and organized social programmes. It first examines the emergence of formal social welfare and then considers recent trends in social policy, in particular the gradual emergence of approaches marked by concern with basic needs, community participation, and greater recognition of the realities in which policies and programmes must operate.

The general themes outlined in earlier chapters are pursued in Chapters 4 and 5, which deal with health and day care for young children. For poor children survival itself is most often a significant victory; a good deal of attention is paid to a number of specific interventions which, as part of a social policy for child welfare, can dramatically increase the chances of survival and reduce levels of illness. Day care for well children is closely linked with the most important health initiatives but can in itself be a vital part of positive child welfare policy.

Formal social services have a relatively low priority in the majority of developing countries and it is against that background that Chapter 6 looks at child welfare legislation and at substitute care for children, which dominates formal provision in most countries. In Chapter 7 the needs of poor children with disabilities are set against the provision made in developing countries. The almost universal neglect of these children, and the inappropriate nature of those services which do exist, is set against the potential of community-based rehabiliation as an example of an approach to child welfare. As with many other topics in the book, this highlights the contrast between policies such as this and conventional social services. We begin to be concerned not so much with service delivery but with approaches to aspects of social development.

This theme is explored further in the final chapter, which seeks to illuminate some of the links between social development, social policy and the abuse and exploitation of children. The chapter concludes with a brief overview of the nature of social policy for the welfare of poor children, in relation to the relatively few aspects of that vast topic which this book is able to cover.

1 The Rights and Needs of the Poorest Children

Whereas mankind owes to the child the best it has to give
Now therefore,
The General Assembly
Proclaims this Declaration of the Rights of the child to the end that he may
have a happy childhood and enjoy for his own good and for the good of
society the rights and freedoms herein set forth, and calls upon parents,
upon men and women as individuals and upon voluntary organisations,
local authorities and national Governments to recognise these rights and
strive for their observance by legislative and other measures progressively
taken in accordance with the following principles [from 'The Declaration of
the Rights of the Child', UN General Assembly, resolution 1366 xiv, 1959].

The most recent United Nations convention on the rights of
the child defines a child as 'every human being to the age of 18
years unless, under the law of his/her state he/she has reached
his/her age of majority earlier'. This book will put attention
on the younger child without wishing to diminish the scale and
range of problems affecting older children. As we shall see, in
very many parts of the book there are a number of difficulties
with even such broad chronological definitions as that used by
the United Nations. Not least, during the period that we might
call 'childhood' the child's needs, activities and relationships
with adults change dramatically as the child grows older. It is,
in fact, argued by some people that the suffering of children is
more serious when it involves immature young children and
infants rather than older teenagers. Some, indeed, argue that
our sole concern should be with the very young as they are so
much more vulnerable than older children and cannot protect
themselves.

In the great majority of developing countries most children

assume a wide range of adult responsibilities before the age of legal majority. But an emphasis on the chronological age of children does draw our attention to several features of child welfare. First, children are essentially victims of adults; second, children are by definition weaker and more vulnerable than adults—their suffering is both greater and more clearly the responsibility of adults. Third, the legal status of children means first of all that their rights are subject to the actions of adults and the remedies for their suffering lie in the actions of adults, but also that as children they are denied access to decision-making processes, they lack power. They are thus far less able to protect themselves from abuse, far less able to change the conditions in which they live. For these and very many other reasons a great deal of attention has been paid, and must be paid, to the notion of the rights of children and the duty of adults to protect and enhance those rights. There is suffering among children in all societies, and in some of the societies which are materially most wealthy suffering appears to be growing. But this book is concerned with the poorest of children; in global terms there are children who are extremely privileged, both absolutely and relatively. There are many others whose conditions are adequate, tolerable, and allow for personal growth and development: There are yet others who are forced to live in degrading and intolerable circumstances, whose conditions of life are such as to cut off or stifle their development and their personal growth. It is with the poorest and most vulnerable children in the poor countries that this book is concerned.

Before moving on to look at the global picture it is important to see something of the background to the notion of the rights of children. The concept of the rights of the child has not had a very long history of recognition in either legal or social terms. Prior to the nineteenth century the legal expression of the harsh reality of the life of most children was the idea of the child as a human chattel. The child was essentially the property of the parents (essentially of the father) and owed to the parents total subservience and obedience. Parents enjoyed an absolute legal right to the child's services and earnings and had full control over the child's property and person. As Pappas notes in a recent review of child protection legislation:

children throughout the world, and in all jurisdictions, were neglected, abandoned, abused (sexually and otherwise), sold into slavery, mutilated and even killed with impunity. Infanticide is reported as a frequent phenomenon in European countries, and also in Great Britain persisting well into the 19th century. The law even provided positive reinforcement for parental authority in the form of severe sanction by the State for filial recalcitrance, including in some instances even the death penalty [Pappas, 1983: xxviii].

The more modern approach to the notion of the independent rights of children in legal systems thus did not really begin to emerge until the nineteenth century and certainly in Europe can be seen to be linked to the social reforms that followed industrialization and urbanization. Fundamental to this shift was the emergence of the independent legal personality of the child. In those countries which had greater wealth at their disposal, this legal change was accompanied by substantial improvements in the area of children's rights in practice. Throughout this book we will see the enormous achievements that have been made in many countries which have very low levels of material wealth. But it remains the case that a great deal more must be done both within countries and internationally because feudalistic notions and practices still persist and the plight of the child in very many of the poorest countries of the world is very severe indeed. But although social practices, cultural practices and legal issues are of fundamental importance, as too are other details of social welfare administration, the children of the world suffer most from the harsh realities of the social and economic systems in which they are trapped. They are in the very great majority of cases the victims not of their parents or the other adults around them but of patterns of development, underdevelopment and social change.

Historian Phillipe Aries has suggested that in medieval Europe children were hardly distinguished from adults, being regarded essentially as adults in miniature (Aries, 1962). Rates of sickness and death among children were high and children were awarded no particular status or protection as a general rule. Childhood, Aries argued, was thought to be a relatively unimportant transitional period of physical and mental immaturity, which ended at a fairly early age by the assumption of adult responsibilities. As suggested earlier, with the coming of industrialization, urbanization and changing patterns of social and family life in the nineteenth century, children gradually became the focus of family life, increasingly separated from adults and viewed very differently by them. The most important shift was that children came to be seen as innocent and weak relative to adults, in need of the guidance of adults and the care and control of adults. But authority was still vested in the male parent; the father in Europe had more or less complete freedom to treat his children, and his wife, as he saw fit. The state offered almost no protection against child abuse.

But with the rapid development of industrial society the state began to interfere in very many ways in family life and in the relationships between adults and children (Meyer, 1983). Meyer argues that it was the demands of industrial production that brought pressure for a compliant and diverse labour force, in which the establishment of acceptable patterns of adult conduct and the preparation and training of children for work were fundamental. Thus the state became involved. A number of factors brought the separation of children from adults at work, weakened paternal authority over children and further enabled statutory control. In the latter half of the nineteenth century children became the prime objects of this statutory intervention, and as part of a claim to the protection and promotion of the physical, moral and religious welfare of children a series of restrictions were placed on the length of working hours, on the establishment of compulsory education and later on the separate treatment of children in the judicial system.

Since the end of the nineteenth century there has been steady growth in a movement for children's rights. The early history of that movement owes a great deal to the work of Eglantyne Jebb, founder of the Save the Children Fund (Minority Rights Group, 1985). Beginning with work among children whose lives were devastated by the First World War in Europe, she was later one of a group who laid the foundations for 'The Declaration of the Rights of the Child'.

This was adopted by the General Assembly of the League of Nations in 1924. In 1959 a revised declaration was adopted by the United Nations. As we shall see, more recent amendments have extended the range of concerns of the United Nations declaration and a new convention has been prepared, but the original remains central to all discussions of children's rights and child welfare throughout the world.

UN Declaration of the Rights of the Child (1959)

The right to affection, love, and understanding.
The right to adequate nutrition and medical care.
The right to full opportunity for play and recreation.
The right to a name and nationality.
The right to special care, if handicapped.
The right to be among the first to receive relief in times of disaster.
The right to learn to be a useful member of society and to develop individual abilities.
The right to be brought up in a spirit of peace and universal brotherhood.
The right to enjoy these rights, regardless of race, colour, sex, religion, national or social origin.

But, of course, this declaration and many others like it are concerned with generalized principles and moral entitlements and they do not allow in themselves the establishment of enforceable rights for children. UN declarations are not legally binding and there are no procedures against those who violate their provisions. There are some rights in the UN declaration, such as the child's right to understanding, which clearly cannot be guaranteed under any circumstances. For our present purposes we are concerned with the most fundamental rights to welfare—to housing, to nutrition, to recreation, to health and to protection from abuse.

THE CONDITION OF CHILDREN IN THE POOREST COUNTRIES

Poverty and deprivation in all their dimensions are shared by populations of all ages, but some groups are very much more vulnerable to their effects than others. Because of their greater needs, children, and particularly young children, are placed at far greater risk by poverty. The incidence of poverty and deprivation in developing countries has been widely discussed and very many attempts have been made to measure its incidence (MacPherson and Midgley, 1987). As we shall see, recent economic trends have brought a considerable worsening in the conditions experienced by many of the poorest people in the world and not least by the poorest children. In the poorest countries resources are so scarce and conditions so bad that to talk of rights in the terms of the UN declaration becomes almost a mockery. The absolute poverty of the poorest countries is compounded for children within them by an unequal distribution of even the scarcest resources.

The impact of poverty and deprivation on the welfare of children can be illustrated by the use of a number of different indicators. The annual UNICEF publication *The State of the World's Children* is now established as the major source of information in this area. Reporting on trends across the world in the fight for child welfare, UNICEF brings together statistical evidence. Beginning with the 1987 report, UNICEF are now using an index of infant and child mortality—the under-5 mortality rate (U5MR). The countries of the world are ranked in *The State of the World's Children* according to the level of this index. Taking this as the measure of a country's ranking in international terms marks a distinct break with much conventional practice in which countries have been ranked according to economic performance and not according to the welfare of their populations. Tables 1.1 to 1.6 give basic data on the conditions in which the vast majority of the children of the world are living.

In the last forty years the total population in the world has more than doubled, from 2 billion to just under 5 billion. Three-quarters of that number live in the countries ranked by the UNICEF method as having very high, high or middle under-5 mortality rates. This group is more or less synonymous with those countries generally regarded as 'developing countries'. So when we talk of the developing countries, we are talking of nearly two-thirds of the world's population, and in that population are more than two-thirds of the world's children. Table 1.1 gives some basic indications of the state of the world's children today compared with the situation twenty-five years ago. Two features stand out above all: First, the appalling conditions that so many of the world's children still suffer; second, the dramatic improvements that have taken place over this period in the basic conditions of life. Indeed, throughout this book this fundamental and tragic contrast will recur time and again. On the one hand, there are very many ways in which conditions have improved and are continuing to improve, but on the other, we are faced with appalling conditions in very many countries.

It is only since the beginning of the 1980s that we have had statistics with which to compare the condition of children in the various countries of the world. UNICEF and the United Nations together prepared the first internationally standardized set of infant mortality estimates and projections. These were first published in the UNICEF report *The State of the World's Children 1982–83* (UNICEF, 1982). The new under-5 mortality rate (U5MR) is again the result of collaboration between UNICEF and the UN, and 'it is hoped that the under-5 mortality rate will be adopted by countries for national and sub-national analyses and presentation over the next few years so that it quickly becomes the standard form when used in discussing child mortality' (UNICEF, 1986: 126). In terms of death alone it now appears that of the 14.5 million infants and children in the world dying each year, nearly 5 million are above the age of 1. This is a higher proportion than was previously estimated. Current projections put the fall in infant and child deaths from 14.5 million to around 10 million at around the end of the century, but in that projection there are considerable variations. Above all it would seem that the number of infant and child deaths in Africa will be no less in the year 2000 than it is today—about 4.3 million every year. So Africa, which now has just under 30 per cent of infant and child deaths, is projected by the end of the century to account for over 40 per cent of all those deaths.

In Table 1.1 the under-5 mortality rate demonstrates very clearly the great differences between the countries of the world. In that group of countries having very high under-5 mortality rates, that is over 175 per thousand, very many are from the continent of Africa. But even the poorest countries have made dramatic gains in the twenty-five years since 1960,

Table 1.1: Countries of the world: basic indicators, 1960 and 1985

Country	Under-5 mortality rate		Infant mortality rate (under 1)		Life expectancy at birth (years)	Total population (millions)
	1960	1985	1960	1985	1985	1985
Very high U5MR countries (over 175 per 1,000)						
Afghanistan	329	380	215	189	48	16.5
Mali	302	370	210	175	43	8.1
Sierra Leone	302	397	225	175	35	3.6
Malawi	275	364	206	157	46	6.9
Guinea	259	346	208	153	41	6.1
Ethiopia	257	294	175	152	41	43.6
Somalia	257	294	175	152	41	4.7
Mozambique	252	352	174	147	46	14.0
Burkina Faso	245	388	220	145	46	6.9
Angola	242	346	208	143	43	8.8
Niger	237	320	191	140	44	6.1
Central African Rep.	232	308	183	137	44	2.3
Chad	232	326	195	138	46	5.0
Guinea Bissau	232	315	188	138	44	0.9
Senegal	231	313	180	137	44	6.4
Mauritania	223	310	185	132	45	1.9
Kampuchea	216	218	146	145	46	7.3
Liberia	215	303	180	127	50	2.2
Rwanda	214	248	146	127	48	6.1
Yemen	210	210	214	128	50	6.8
Yemen, Dem.	338	210	214	128	50	2.1

Bhutan	297	208	186	134	47	1.4
Nepal	297	206	186	134	47	16.5
Burundi	258	200	152	119	48	4.7
Bangladesh	262	196	156	124	49	101.1
Benin	310	193	185	115	45	4.1
Sudan	293	187	170	112	49	21.6
Bolivia	282	184	167	117	52	6.4
Tanzania	248	183	146	111	52	22.5
Nigeria	318	182	190	110	50	95.2
Haiti	294	180	197	123	54	6.6
Uganda	224	178	133	108	50	15.5

High U5MR Countries (95–174 per 1,000)

Pakistan	277	174	163	115	51	100.4
Oman	378	172	214	109	54	1.2
Lao PDR	232	170	155	116	53	4.1
Zaire	251	170	148	103	51	29.9
Cameroon	275	162	163	99	52	9.9
Iran	254		169		58	44.6
Togo	305	160	182	98	52	3.0
India	282	158	165	105	57	758.9
Cote D'Ivoire	320	157	200	105	52	9.8
Ghana	224	153	132	94	53	13.6
Lesotho	208	144	149	106	50	1.5
Egypt	300	136	179	93	59	96.9
Zambia	228	135	135	84	52	6.7
Peru	233	133	142	94	60	19.7
Libya	268	130	160	90	60	3.6

Country	Under-5 mortality rate		Infant mortality rate (under 1)		Life expectancy at birth (years) 1985	Total population (millions) 1985
	1960	1985	1960	1985		
Morocco	265	130	163	90	60	21.9
Indonesia	235	126	139	79	55	166.4
Congo	241	122	143	77	48	1.7
Kenya	208	121	124	76	54	20.6
Zimbabwe	182	121	110	76	57	8.8
Algeria	270	117	168	81	61	21.7
Honduras	232	116	144	76	61	4.4
Tunisia	255	110	159	78	62	7.1
Guatemala	230	109	125	65	61	8.0
Saudi Arabia	292	109	170	78	62	11.5
Nicaragua	210	104	140	69	62	3.2
South Africa	192	104	135	78	55	32.4
Turkey	258	104	190	84	63	49.3
Iraq	222	101	139	73	63	15.9
Botswana	174	99	119	72	56	1.1
Viet Nam	233	98	156	72	60	59.7
Madagascar	181	97	109	63	61	10.0

Selected countries (ranking of 130)

Country	Under-5 mortality rate		Infant mortality rate (under 1)		Life expectancy at birth (years) 1985	Total population (millions) 1985
Papua New Guinea (65)	247	94	165	68	53	3.5

Brazil (67)	160	91	116	67	64	135.6
Philippines (71)	135	78	80	48	63	54.5
Mexico (72)	140	73	92	50	66	79.0
Colombia (73)	148	72	93	48	64	28.7
Thailand (79)	149	55	103	44	63	51.4
China (81)	202	50	150	36	69	1,059.5
Sri Lanka (82)	113	48	70	36	69	16.2
Malaysia (87)	106	38	73	28	68	15.6
Yugoslavia (94)	113	31	92	23	71	23.2
USSR (95)	53	29	38	24	72	278.6
Chile (96)	142	26	114	22	70	12.0
Jamaica (98)	88	25	62	20	74	2.3
Poland (104)	70	21	62	19	72	37.2
Cuba (105)	87	19	62	15	74	10.0
USA (114)	30	13	26	11	75	238.0
UK (119)	27	12	23	10	74	56.1
Hong Kong (122)	65	11	44	9	76	5.5
Netherlands (125)	22	10	18	8	76	14.5
Japan (127)	40	9	31	6	77	120.7
Sweden (130)	20	8	16	6	76	8.4

Source: UNICEF 1986: 128–9.

as can be seen in the table. Whether such gains will continue to be made is not entirely certain, however; as is discussed in Chapter 2, the recent recession has had seriously adverse consequences for the poorest countries in the world.

Table 1.2 illustrates very clearly the massive significance of the welfare of the populations of the developing countries. Developing countries have over three-quarters of the world's total population and 85 per cent of its under-5 population. Any consideration of child welfare in the world must pay most of its attention to children in developing countries; 98 per cent of the deaths of children under 5 are in the poorest countries. The table also shows how 99 per cent of all maternal deaths are in developing countries; the relative neglect by students of social welfare of the conditions in developing countries is difficult to comprehend and impossible to justify.

Table 1.2: Developing countries' share of world population, 1986

	World	Developing countries	Share
	(millions)	(millions)	(%)
Total population	4,837	3,663	76
Under-5 population	575	489	85
Births	129	111	86
Child deaths (under-5)	14.4	14.1	98
Maternal deaths	0.5	0.494	99

Source: Derived from UNICEF 1986: 109–10.

In considering social welfare and social policy in global terms, the indicators in Table 1.3 give us some basis for thought. Comparing conditions in developing and 'industrialized' countries is of course extremely difficult and the comparisons must not be taken too far. But as is clear in the data in Table 1.3, the differences in social conditions, in the basic quality of life, are so vast that subtleties of statistical comparison pale into insignificance. These comparisons are not presented to suggest that the patterns of life in industrialized countries are there as a goal for the developing countries to strive towards, but to underline the gulf in living conditions among the peoples of the world. Any discussion of social welfare must surely come to terms with this gulf (for a discussion of social indicators and the patterns of global inequality, see MacPherson and Midgley, 1987). Average life expectancy at birth in developing countries has risen dramatically. In China it is now 69 years—the same level as in the United States in the late 1950s. In Africa as a whole, life expectancy at birth has risen from 38 to 51 years since 1950. So, although the gulf between the rich countries and the poor countries is enormous, there have been significant changes. Of course, these indicators give only the broadest and crudest outline picture of the conditions of life in poor countries. There are vast differences within regions and within countries, vast inequalities in condition and experience which are hidden by indicators such as these. Later chapters will explore some of these dimensions, particularly in relation to health.

The data in Table 1.3 underline the gulf between the rich and the poor in terms of the resources which are available to them to deal with issues of welfare. Industrialized countries overall have gross national product per capita which is twelve times higher, and as the table shows, the rate of growth of that per capita wealth is higher in the industrialized countries than in the poor countries. With vastly greater problems, the poor countries are indeed having to run faster in order to stand still. The seemingly impossible gulf between resources and the problems facing the poorest countries is clearly made infinitely more difficult by continuing population growth. There is considerable variation between the countries of the poor world in their rates of population growth but an overall rate of 2.6 per cent is still extremely high. Declining death rates, particularly among children, and birth rates which are still relatively high, mean a very young population; thus across the developing world the number of children is not only large but is growing very fast—both absolutely and relatively. But again there have been dramatic changes, particularly in recent years. Birth rates, although still high, have begun to fall. In South and South-East Asia, where family limitation programmes were taken up earliest, and where economic development has had the greatest effect, birth rates were reduced from 36 to 31 per thousand population between 1950 and 1986. In China,

Table 1.3: Indicators of health and wealth: developing and industrialized countries compared, 1986

	Developing countries	Industrialized countries
Under-5 mortality rate	130 per 1000	18 per 1000
Infant mortality rate	85 per 1000	15 per 1000
Population	3,663 m.	1,174 m.
Population growth rate	2.6%	0.8%
Adult illiteracy	38%	2%
Secondary-level enrolment	36%	87%
Measles immunization	26%	76%
Polio immunization	37%	66%
DPT immunization	40%	62%
TB immunization	49%	58%
Anaemia, children U5	51%	12%
Anaemia, pregnant women	59%	14%
Anaemia, women 15–49	47%	11%
Maternal mortality (1983)	494,000	6,000
Maternal care	48%	98%
Prenatal care coverage	68%	100%
Infant care coverage	17%	63%
Low birth weight babies	18%	7%
Safe water	57%	96%
Sanitation (1985)	29%	77%
Daily per capita supply (1984):		
calories	2,495	3,451
protein	60 g	103 g
fat	43 g	132 g

Source: Derived from UNICEF 1986: 123.

birth rate fell from 45 per thousand to 19 per thousand in that period. But even with dramatic success in terms of reducing birth rates and family size, developing countries have young populations and will have such populations for many decades to come.

Table 1.3 also indicates the gulf between the rich and the poor countries in terms of education. Only 2 per cent of the populations of industrialized countries are recorded as illiterate, but nearly two-fifths of the adult populations of the poor countries are unable to read and write. Again, an indicator such as this tells us a lot but fails to tell us a great deal more. Literacy rates have more than doubled, from 26 per cent in 1950 to about 62 per cent in 1985, but the changes have not been evenly spread. There are extreme differences between urban and rural areas, but above all between women and men. Nearly two-thirds of all illiterates are women. The same gross inequality can be seen in school enrolments. The percentage of children 6 to 11 years old who attend primary school has risen to nearly 70 per cent. Table 1.3 shows that 36 per cent of secondary-aged children are enrolled in school; this is four times the proportion in 1950. But again these figures hide very great inequalities indeed, above all between males and females. These inequalities are of fundamental importance in themselves and, for example, in the links between education, literacy and patterns of family limitation and family size.

Later chapters discuss immunization coverage for children, but of those conditions for which figures are given in Table 1.3 it is polio, diphtheria, whooping cough/tetanus (DPT) and tuberculosis for which there have been the most significant advances in recent years. Protection against measles, which is in fact the most serious of these conditions in terms of child deaths, has not made similar advances. The prevalence of anaemia, indicated in three separate ways in Table 1.3, is now recognized as a very good general indicator of morbidity, especially of children and women. That over half of all children in developing countries are indicated as anaemic is a clear sign of the general state of health. The rates of anaemia among pregnant women show dramatically the effects of poverty; an overall rate of 59 per cent includes within it situations in which virtually all pregnant women are anaemic. The implications of anaemia in pregnancy for the health and welfare of those women and their children are very serious indeed. That nearly half of all women between 15 and 49 should be found to have anaemia is again an indication of the poverty which overshadows the lives of the vast majority of the world's people and which falls most heavily on women. The figure in Table 1.3 for maternal mortality shows almost half a million women every year dying through childbirth; this is clearly linked with both economic conditions and the lack of health facilities. Less than half of women in developing countries have access to maternal care and services of any kind compared with 98 per cent of those in industrialized countries. The figure for prenatal care coverage is very much higher and at 68 per cent shows a dramatic increase in recent years. But after the birth of the child the pattern of care is very much weaker indeed. As can be seen, less than 20 per cent coverage is available for infant care in developing countries.

The availability of safe water supplies has been recognized as among the most significant factors affecting health, particularly the health of children. The rise to nearly 60 per cent in the proportion of populations in poor countries having access to safe water has been dramatic, but this rise has until very recently been almost entirely among those people living in towns and cities. In rural areas, water supplies have for many become worse rather than better. The same is true for sanitation; adequate sanitation is vital for health, and the lack of sanitation profoundly affects the spread of disease and the condition of whole populations, and most dramatically of children. There have been considerable improvements, but the towns and cities have gained most, and in many rural areas conditions have worsened rather than improved. These issues will be discussed in later chapters, as will issues of nutrition raised by the food supply indicators in Table 1.3.

THE NEEDS OF CHILDREN

There are many factors that affect the welfare of children in developing countries. But the most important of all is the context of poverty in which they lead their lives. It is poverty which emerges again and again as the predominant theme in explanations and analyses of those conditions which affect children so adversely. Table 1.4 gives some indication of the scale of absolute poverty, based on World Bank data. Since the early 1970s, researchers associated with the Bank have been attempting to estimate the incidence of poverty on a global scale (MacPherson and Midgley, 1987). The figure of

1,299 million is the most recent estimate of those people who are living below the most rigorously defined of poverty lines— essentially a starvation level of poverty. As with earlier estimates of the incidence of absolute poverty, this has a number of features. First, it is clear that poverty is concentrated in the most economically weak countries and particularly in the countries of Southern Asia and sub-Saharan Africa. But it is also clear from these figures that there is a vast amount of poverty of the worst kind in countries with relatively higher per capita incomes. For example, Kenya and Malaysia are shown in the latest figures to have more or less the same proportions of their populations in absolute poverty, but Malaysia has a GNP per capita some six times higher than that of Kenya. It is not just the level of economic development that determines the incidence of poverty but the way the fruits of that development are distributed.

Table 1.4 shows very clearly that a very large proportion of the world's poorest people are living in those countries reckoned by both conventional and more recently adopted indices to be among the relatively better off. This distribution of poverty clearly complicates the issue immensely and underlines yet again the clear relationship between patterns of need and patterns of underdevelopment. Most of the world's poor people live in Asia and particularly in the countries of Southern Asia; indeed, just four countries in that region— Bangladesh, India, Indonesia and Pakistan—contain almost two-thirds of the world's poorest people. But Africa, with a very much smaller population, has almost as high a proportion of its people in absolute poverty. The next very clear feature of the figures in Table 1.4 is that the overwhelming majority of the world's poorest people live in rural areas. The poverty of the cities and towns in the Third World is appalling and visible—the poverty of the rural areas is equally appalling but very often less visible. Nearly 1,000 million of the very poorest live in the rural areas of developing countries.

Table 1.5 focuses on the child populations of the poorest countries and confirms the distribution between urban and rural areas. Nearly two-thirds of all children under 16 are in the rural areas of the poorest countries. But as the table shows,

Table 1.4: Population below absolute poverty level: very high, high and middle U5MR countries, 1985

	Total population (millions)	Urban (%)	Urban (millions)	Rural (%)	Rural (millions)	Total (millions)
Very high U5MR countries	462	30	31	65	234	265
High U5MR countries	1498	27	162	42	378	540
Middle U5MR countries	1692	21	185	38	309	494
Totals	3652		378		921	1299

Source: Calculated from data in UNICEF 1986, Tables 1, 5 and 6 (derived from World Bank figures for the incidence of absolute poverty).

Table 1.5: Child populations in poorest countries, 1985 (millions)

	Under 5			5–16			All ages		
	Urban	Rural	All	Urban	Rural	All	Urban	Rural	All
Very high U5MR countries	19	67	86	30	105	135	49	172	221
High U5MR countries	86	130	216	162	243	405	248	373	621
Middle U5MR countries	92	85	177	242	224	466	334	309	643
Totals	197	282	479	434	572	1006	631	854	1485

Source: Calculated from data in UNICEF 1986, Tables 1 and 5.

the proportions living in urban areas are very much lower in the countries with the worst conditions, that is the group of countries with very high under-5 mortality rates. In those countries about one-fifth of all children are living in towns and cities. So again the picture is complex; when discussing the children of developing countries we are discussing an immensely complex population, ranging from those living in the remotest areas of the poorest countries on earth to those in equally remote areas of some of the most highly developed cities of the world. The differences in geography and physical environment are immense but, as we shall see, the realities of experience are very often extremely close.

Table 1.6 gives figures on a similar basis to those in Table 1.5 but only for that population under 16 years of age. These estimates of the number of children below the absolute poverty level must be treated with extreme caution. They cannot convey either the true scale of the needs of children or the full realities of absolute poverty measured at this level. These estimates suggest that of all children under 16 about one-third, or 536 million, are in absolute poverty in those countries with very high, high or middle under-5 mortality rates. There are of course very many children in poverty in those countries with low under-5 mortality rates and very high GNP per capita. But it is the group of 536 million which forms the principal focus of this book. It is these children who are the most desperately poor and the most desperately in need. All social policies and all efforts to achieve social welfare must surely attempt to meet the needs of these, the poorest and the most vulnerable of all populations. This is not to argue that social policy should be directed exclusively to this group, but it is to argue that all social policies should take account of poverty on this scale and should seek to improve the conditions faced by a third of all children in developing countries. The pattern of absolute poverty for children is complex: Of the 536 million children in absolute poverty, about one quarter are in the countries having very high U5MRs, just over 40 per cent are in the high U5MR countries and the remainder in the countries with middle U5MRs. So the great majority of the world's poorest children are in countries *other* than those with the most desperate social conditions; this reflects above all the distribution of the world's population.

Comparing the figures in Table 1.6 with those in Table 1.5 we can see that the proportions of children in absolute poverty are quite different in the different groups of countries. In countries with very high U5MRs (comprising virtually all the countries of sub-Saharan Africa, together with a few other poor countries) nearly 60 per cent of children are estimated to be in absolute poverty. For the group with high U5MRs the figure is about 35 per cent, with about 30 per cent of the children in the middle U5MR group below that level. Overall, of the whole 536 million, about 28 per cent live in urban areas; so, over 70 per cent of those in absolute poverty are living in rural areas. In relation to very many of the issues dealt with in succeeding chapters this fundamental fact will be seen to be of primary importance. In discussing the world's poorest children we are discussing, despite rapid urbanization, primarily a rural population. In the very poorest countries (the very high U5MR group) 88 per cent of the children in absolute poverty live in rural areas, and in the high U5MR group 70 per cent of these children live in rural areas. About one-third of the 536 million desperately poor children in developing countries are under 5 years old, the remaining two-thirds between 5 and 16. As we will discuss in later chapters, these age bands are essentially arbitrary and especially at the upper end begin to mean very little in many circumstances.

The context in which we must consider social policies for the welfare of children in developing countries is one of poverty. This is the factor that emerges again and again in analyses of the whole range of needs, policies and programmes. In all the countries with which we are concerned there is poverty of resources in relation to wants and needs, and this is much more than simply low absolute levels of economic production and development. It is a poverty related to services, to infrastructure and to the quality of life which people are enabled or allowed to live. It is above all related to the patterns of development and underdevelopment with which the poorest countries of the world are faced (MacPherson, 1982; MacPherson and Midgley, 1987). As has been widely argued, poverty linked with underdevelopment is

Table 1.6 Estimated number of children below absolute poverty level, 1985 (millions)

	Children under 5			5-16			All ages		
	Urban	Rural	All	Urban	Rural	All	Urban	Rural	All
Very high U5MR countries	6	43	49	9	68	77	15	111	126
High U5MR countries	23	55	88	43	102	145	66	157	223
Middle U5MR countries	19	32	51	51	85	136	70	117	187
Totals	48	130	178	103	255	358	151	385	536

Source: Calculated from data in UNICEF 1986, Tables 1, 5 and 6.

not overcome or necessarily ameliorated with improved GNP and per capita income. It requires policies and programmes which break out of conventional approaches to development. As suggested earlier, an otherwise wealthy country with impressive indicators of economic performance can contain within it high levels of both absolute and relative poverty—not just poverty of material resources but of services and opportunities. There are very many countries in the developing world characterized by extreme internal inequality. On the other hand, there are countries which despite very low levels of material wealth, have produced social programmes geared towards a basic infrastructure of social programmes which make that country rich. But it is poverty in the widest sense, and the social implications of that poverty, which provide the prime context in which child welfare must be considered. In all the situations with which we will be concerned there is extreme economic destitution, together with deprivation resulting from a lack of social policy and programmes geared towards the needs of the poorest and towards the needs of children in particular. In many countries, even if income levels were raised very greatly both for rural and urban populations, the conditions faced by the majority of children would not necessarily improve. That poverty is linked with inequality, and inequality which is in many cases worsening, as has been amply demonstrated. Inequality is not simply in terms of access to the economic rewards of development but is more specifically associated with social policies and social welfare measures. In the great majority of the poorest countries, access to social welfare services is grossly unequal, both between urban and rural areas and between poor and rich. Unless policies are pursued to reverse trends such as these there will continue to be a greater concentration of services and programmes among the better-off groups. The result will be, as Gokhale suggests, 'that "development" continues to cater for isolated pockets of affluence ignoring the needs of the infinitely vaster deprived population' (Gokhale, 1979: 278).

The industrialized and relatively rich countries have between them just under 300 million children. The poor developing countries have around 1,500 million and this number is continuing to grow. Over the last twenty to thirty years there have been enormous improvements in the conditions of life for a large proportion of the world's population and for the world's children. But at the present time the poorest countries, and the poor in the better-off countries, are faced with consequences of a period of economic recession which have only just begun to be felt. As we shall see in the next chapter, the effects of recession on children have been especially severe. In the 1980s, economic growth, in the past seen as the answer to virtually every problem in the developing countries, has come to a halt or even gone into reverse in over half the countries of Africa and Latin America. We are concerned here with child welfare; the policies and programmes which affect the welfare of children are spread across a range of sectors and deal with a host of needs. Children in developing countries live in very different circumstances; generalization is dangerous, and misleading in many cases. The remaining chapters will attempt to search out some common themes across the whole range of child welfare needs and responses. But, as noted earlier, the vast problem of absolute poverty among the children of developing countries—the more than 500 million children living below that level—must remain the focus of attention.

The chapters which follow examine a number of issues in social welfare and social policy, and in all of them it is clear that not just poverty but inequality, and the perverted social and economic relationships engendered by underdevelopment, are at the heart of the social dilemmas of social policy in the Third World. But with all this, the extreme deprivation and poverty affecting so many, and with the responses in terms of social policy being so constrained by the forces of underdevelopment, there must be room for the conviction that positive action is possible. As the following chapters demonstrate, despite the enormity of the problems and seeming impossibility of progress in many of these aspects of children's lives, gains have been made and continue to be made even in the most adverse circumstances. It is perhaps this above all which is the central theme of this book: the hope of advances in social policy and social welfare in the most adverse conditions of all.

2 Approaches to Child Welfare Policy: The Economic Context

This chapter is concerned to examine in more depth and detail the relationship between the welfare of children and the economic context of development and underdevelopment. The chapter is concerned to explore some themes suggested in Chapter 1 in terms of the effect of the contemporary recession on the welfare of the poorest children. It is only relatively recently that welfare dimensions have come to take a prominent part in consideration of overall development strategy; in recent work on world economic recession we can see that these considerations have now taken a more central place in the total range of problems and issues considered in analyses of development and its consequences.

CHILD WELFARE AND ECONOMIC CONDITIONS

In an important recent study Richard Jolly and Giovanni Cornia have brought together materials documenting the impact of the world recession on the welfare of children, and in particular on children in the poorest countries of the world. As they note in their introduction:

In all that has been written about world recession, the preoccupations have been overwhelmingly and narrowly economic. The analysis has focused on inflation and interest rates, debt and trade deficits, unemployment and declining incomes. Few have investigated the human consequences in more than a superficial manner. Not a single international study has analysed the recession's impact on the most vulnerable half of the world's population—the children [Jolly and Cornia, 1984: 1].

It is important to note that they point out that even those concerned most closely with welfare, in the fields of health, medicine, social work, education and so on, fail to look at social welfare issues in a wide context. This has been shown elsewhere (MacPherson, 1982) in terms of the underdevelopment of social policy in Third World countries. As Jolly and Carnia argue, a narrow approach to children's problems ignores the deep causes of the unsatisfactory conditions. It puts attention on individual symptoms rather than social symptoms, and furthermore on individual explanations of causation rather than social explanations. As many analysts in the social welfare field have argued, this leads to inadequate policy formation and action. Even when there is emphasis on social causation it is often only within a national frame of economic and political conditions and is only rarely connected to the international network of linkages. In developing countries, neglect of these linkages has seriously undermined the quality of analysis and action in terms of social welfare. In conditions of economic recession this neglect is even more obviously wrong. The effects of world economic conditions on child welfare are now more severe and the issues engendered by them have become even more urgent in recent years. The nature of the world recession, its extent, duration and the interconnections of its consequences for all countries of the world are well established. But for those countries which are weakest and poorest in the world economic system, those consequences are greatest. Where resources are most limited, the impact is greatest. Within the poorest countries the impact of decline in economic conditions is likely, other things being equal, to affect the poorest and weakest most of all.

It was a lack of evidence on the specific inter-connections between economic conditions and welfare which in 1972 led UNICEF to begin a study of the impact of world recession on the welfare of children. The pattern of these linkages is complex and at present is only imperfectly understood. But early work on the UNICEF programme, especially that by Dudley Seers, established three major linkages which, it was argued, were likely to dominate the relationship:

The impact on household income, via changes in employment, wages and prices; the impact on rural peasant incomes, via changes in agricultural incomes and consumer prices; the impact on government expenditures, especially on social services [Jolly and Carnia, 1984: 1].

The UNICEF study was based around a series of country case studies, which together were intended to provide some indication of how the recession has affected children in different areas of the world. Twelve countries were chosen in order to give a wide geographical distribution and to represent the broad range of different socio-economic circumstances. Tanzania, for example, was included as a least developed country, with low income and a high infant mortality rate together with high dependence on external trade and finance. India, on the other hand, although characterized by low income and high infant mortality rate, was included as a country with less dependence on external trade and finance. Countries such as Brazil and Nigeria, also included, have high infant mortality rates but are counted as middle-income countries. Others—Chile, Costa Rica, Korea, Cuba—also have conditions which give them a middle-income ranking but have low infant mortality rates. Finally, Sri Lanka was included as a country with a low income but a low infant mortality rate, despite a high dependence on external trade and finance. These countries also vary in the nature of their political systems and the kinds of social policies and programmes that they have pursued over recent years. For example, three middle-income Latin American countries were included which had followed very different strategies; Chile had pursued a free-market strategy, Costa Rica is well known for having adopted what might be called a welfare state approach, and Cuba, which has for several decades followed a socialist approach to development.

From the late 1970s through into the 1980s the world economy has been in turmoil, in the first years of the 1980s in particular there were very sharp reductions in rates of growth in output in almost all developed economies of the world. The nature of the linkages in the world economy has meant that virtually every developing economy has contracted in turn. Out of about ninety developing countries for which information was available in 1984, fifteen showed negative per capita growth rates of GDP in 1979, thirty in 1980, forty-two in 1981 and fifty-one in 1982; the number is still rising (World Bank, 1985). As noted earlier, it is Latin America and Africa which are the most seriously affected regions, with the African countries south of the Sahara being the most seriously affected of all. In those regions and elsewhere it is of course the countries most dependent, through trade in primary commodities and finance, on the health of the industrial countries which have suffered most. The impact of the world recession is multiplied as it is passed down from the industrialized countries to the poorest countries, and within the developing countries themselves it is amplified, hitting the very poorest the hardest. It is most often women and children in those communities who are most severely hit of all.

To summarize the ways in which children have been affected as income falls and cutbacks have spread, Jolly and Carnia presented the evidence from twelve case studies according to the availability of financial resources for children; availability of services; changes in child survival and welfare; and behavioral changes. Family income is perhaps obviously the main way in which the impact of the recession is transmitted to children. In very many parts of the world, average real family incomes have fallen, often very sharply.

In Brazil, income per capita fell by over 4 per cent in 1981, by 2 per cent in 1982 and by 7.5 per cent in 1983, while in Costa Rica it fell by almost 21 per cent over the three years and in Chile by 15 per cent in 1982 alone. Overall per capita income in sub-Saharan Africa, where the recession has been compounded by the effects of drought, wars and the longer-term set-backs of inflation and oil price increases, fell by an estimated 12 per cent between 1981 and 1983. Together with falling family incomes, government services for children have been cut in very many countries; this is the other major way in which the economic recession has affected the welfare of children. It has been noted that because social welfare programmes for children are usually not protected by powerful interest groups, and are still very often regarded as 'uneconomic', they most often suffer first, and dispro-portionately hard from any forced reductions in expenditure (MacPherson and Midgley, 1987).

Table 2.1: Brazil: population and economic indicators. 1960 and 1980

Indicators	1960	1980
Population		
Size (millions)	70.1	119.1
average annual rate of growth (%)	2.9	2.5
% in urban areas	45.2	67.7
% aged 0–15	42.7	37.4
% aged 65+	2.7	4.3
% of labour force:		
in manufacturing	8.6	15.7
in agriculture and mining	54.0	29.9
Economic indicators		
GDP (US $ billion)	66.8	274.3
per capita (US $ per year)	951.9	2302.6
Imports (US $ million)	1,293.0	22,955.0
Exports (US $ million)	1,269.0	20,132.0
Manufactures as % of exports	3.0	39.0
Average annual rate of inflation (%)	44.5	42.8
Share of income (%):		
of richest 1%	12.0	17.0
of richest 5%	28.0	38.0
of poorest 50%	17.0	13.0

Source: Macedo, 1984: 35, 36.

THE BRAZILIAN CASE

Brazil is considered a middle-income country by international standards; it had an annual GNP per capita estimated at US $2,300 in 1980. But it is frequently cited as a highly unequal society. Macedo shows how, in terms of the welfare of Brazilian children, this unequal social system expresses itself in high rates of infant and child mortality and low standards of nutrition, health and education. These low rates of welfare are concentrated in the lower-income classes, in especially impoverished regions of the country and in particular areas of the richer regions (Macedo, 1984). Some of these indicators of welfare are shown in Tables 2.1 and 2.2. Macedo argues that the current recession has occurred on top of persistent poverty and has thus made an already serious

Table 2.2: Brazil: basic welfare indicators

Indicators	1985
Population (millions)	136
Population urbanized (%)	73
Absolute poverty (% of population):	
Urban	N/A
Rural	N/A
Infant mortality rate (%)	67
Under-5 mortality rate (%)	91
Life expectancy (at birth, years)	64
GNP per capita (US $, 1984)	1720
Low birth weight infants (%)	9
Access to drinking water (%):	
Urban	86
Rural	53
Total	76
Immunization coverage (% of 1 year olds):	
TB	64
DPT	64
Polio	86
Measles	75
Primary school enrolment (%) (1982–4, gross rates):	
Males	106
Females	99
Adult literacy (%):	
Males	79
Females	76

Source: Derived from UNICEF, 1986, Tables 1–6.

socio-economic situation even worse. To a considerable extent current problems are seen to have their roots in the policies of the past, and in particular in an almost exclusive attachment to economic growth as the fundamental objective of government policy. Macedo's assessment of the period from 1964 to 1973 gives us a clear picture, typical of very many developing countries:

The government's social policy during the 1964–73 years failed to pursue a growth strategy with more trickle down effects for the people. This failure is symbolised by the worsening of the income distribution and by living conditions that remain unsatisfactory for a large part of the population. Social achievements could have had a wider scope if quality, efficiency and efficacy and equity considerations were brought into the picture. Now that rapid economic growth has come to a halt, the consequences of the 1964–73 government social policy will be underscored as the emerging additional problems brought about by the crisis will be dealt with by a government social apparatus that is ill prepared to cope with the new realities of a transformed socio-economic structure [Macedo, 1984: 37].

From 1973 to 1983 recession conditions worsened in Brazil, and Macedo states that the distributional impact of the crisis was on the whole regressive. As he argues, people who lose their jobs are mostly in the lower half of the income distribution. Those who own assets are in the upper half and gained from the high real interest rates that accompanied the crisis. During that period in Brazil there was a reduction in the supply of food, apart from manufactured food, and food prices increased above average prices. Movements such as this in the cost of living are cruelly regressive, given that the share of family budgets spent on food increases at lower levels of income. On top of these effects there were severe contractions in public expenditures on health and education; these affected the poor more than other groups.

A study of Sao Paulo looked, as did the rest of the UNICEF project, at the specific effects on children of the recession and its consequences. A number of indicators were used to assess these effects. First, there were so-called 'outcome' indicators—these were of health conditions, infant mortality rates (IMR), child death rates (CDR), low birth weight rates (LBW) and indicators of morbidity. In addition, there were 'process' indicators covering such things as school attendance, immunization coverage, indicators of 'behavior' such as child delinquency and abandoment, and 'input' indicators which were related to government expenditure and the availability of public services and housing.

In Brazil, as elsewhere, establishing the impact of the recession on welfare was extremely difficult in practice. There was first of all the basic problem of establishing which indicators to use, locating suitable and sufficient data on those indicators, and making this data workable. But a much more important issue was that it soon became clear in the Brazilian study, and in others, that there was a considerable time-lag between economic crisis and its specific welfare effects on vulnerable populations. A good example of this was the infant mortality rate data; in Sao Paulo the infant mortality rate had been falling consistently for very many years; Macedo gives figures from the end of the nineteenth century. This consistent trend was related to improvements in health, education, living conditions and per capita income, as well as to scientific advancements in medicine and increased provision of health services. Assessing the trends over many years, Macedo suggests that IMR is largely the result of factors which work with medium- and long-term effects. It is for this reason that he suggests that 'as the recession continues it is not unlikely that IMR will rise again in the future' (Macedo, 1984: 42).

Essentially similar conclusions were reached in relation to child death rates. But for low birth weight evidence was found to suggest a deteriorating situation, although Macedo was unwilling to attribute this to the current recession, given the nature of the available data. However, the evidence available on morbidity did allow firmer conclusions; there was more ill health, and in particular of conditions such as those related to malnutrition and anaemia.

In reviewing the series of indicators Macedo found virtually nothing but gloom. Virtually the only positive sign was that shown by the indicators of immunization, a major programme in Brazil during the period in question. But on every other front the picture presented is one of decline or stagnation, with very poor prospects. In sum, Macedo concluded that:

The lack of a consistent effort to cope with the effects of the crisis as it affects people in general and children in particular, overwhelms these few instances in which some action has been taken. The scope of the problems that are emerging is clearly beyond the impact of the measures thus far undertaken [Macedo, 1984: 49].

Thus in Brazil, previously heralded as a centre of an economic miracle, and often cited as an example to be followed by other countries in the developing world, the impact of the recession in recent years has been very severe and will continue to be felt for many years. Macedo puts the case for a comprehensive set of child welfare indicators to be used on a regular basis to monitor social conditions. The lack of such comprehensive indicators is not restricted to Brazil; there are very few countries in which child welfare is regularly monitored.

The Brazilian case illustrates a number of important themes, not least the difficulty of assessing with precision the impact of economic conditions. It is true that in general infant mortality rates continue to improve in many countries, particularly middle-income ones. But as in the Brazilian example this may be the result of the capacity of systems to buffer the effects of crises in the short term. There are clearly time-lags between the beginning of economic decline and actual deterioration in child welfare becoming apparent. Given the difficulties in available data, the recording of this deterioration may take even longer. None the less, it is the case in most countries that deterioration is gradual, and even in countries where infant mortality rates continue to fall in general, there can be a worsening of nutritional and health status among mothers and children in particular. For example, in Sri Lanka there was a substantial increase in malnutrition between 1975 and 1982, while in Costa Rica the number of children treated for severe malnutrition doubled between 1980 and 1983 (Foxley and Raczynski, 1984; Gunatilleke and Kurukulasuria, 1984).

The welfare of children is both directly and indirectly affected by the availability of appropriate services and by the active pursuit of social welfare programmes. The availability of specific services and the adoption and implementation of wider social development programmes are severely affected by adverse economic conditions. The effect of the recession is complex but in general terms it seems to be clear that in virtually every country social welfare programmes for children generally suffer quickly and disproportionately from any forced cutbacks in government expenditure and service provision. The ways in which services and programmes are affected differ widely. In some countries there have been absolute declines in the amount of such services being offered. For instance, in northern Zambia the number of child clinics has declined since the mid-1970s (Green and Singer, 1984: 121). In Chile there has been a substantial decline in the provision of housing for poor populations, in the supply of safe water and in sanitation and sewerage services for low-income areas (Foxley and Raczynski, 1984, 67–8). In very many countries one response to severe economic restraints has been the introduction of charges for welfare services previously available free. Although there may not be an absolute decline in the amount of such services being provided, the introduction of such charges limits availability to the poorest, putting an effective barrier between them and the services they need. Similarly, very many poor countries have for many years had subsidies on basic-need items, in particular food. These have been reduced in many countries as the effects of the recession have been felt.

In many circumstances there have been cuts in social expenditure resulting not in a quantitative decline in services but a decline of the quality. In the Tanzanian case, school enrolment ratios have contined to rise despite a very severe economic situation, but so too has the teacher–pupil ratio. Deterioration in the quality of education is compounded by a dramatic fall in the availability of books and other teaching materials. But Tanzania's experience is not unique; it is very difficult not to conclude that there has been a general and widespread contraction in both the quality and quantity of child-related services across the developing world. This has taken place in a situation where those services are needed as a matter of extreme urgency and the growth of need is constantly accelerating.

THE TANZANIAN CASE

As noted in Chapter 1, of all the poor nations of the world those of sub-Saharan Africa are the poorest and most severely affected by economic conditions. They are characterized by low levels of skilled workers, dependency on primary product exports, small industrial sectors, poor levels of food production, large rural populations and child dependency ratios that are virtually one to one. Tanzania has for many years been outside the mainstream of African countries as it has pursued an alternative path to development, beginning in the 1960s under the direction of Julius Nyerere (Table 2.3). In common with the vast majority of other sub-Saharan countries, Tanzania was handicapped from the beginning by both its poverty and its late independence, both of which have been seen to hamper development and above all to limit the country's ability to withstand external economic shocks. It is now clear that the problem in a majority of African countries is no longer that of trying to adjust to very slow rates of growth in per capita production, or perhaps trying to adjust to relatively temporary external economic changes and shocks. It is now the case that these countries must distribute among their populations the effects and consequences of very severe declines in per capita output which have continued for several years and show no signs of early reversal (UNICEF, 1984). When real resources fall, it is the rural poor who have tended to be the most vulnerable, even where basic government policy is both egalitarian and biased to the rural population, as in Tanzania. Tanzania shares with the other countries of Africa the enormous problems brought by shortages and high prices of food. Green and Singer report that malnutrition 'has probably grown at least as rapidly overall in urban as in rural areas—as has absolute poverty' (Green and Singer, 1984: 116).

It is not only in those countries devastated by famine that children are suffering from malnutrition in very large numbers. Across the whole of sub-Saharan Africa rising prices for food have brought widespread calorie deficiencies and a decline in the availability of protein foods. The shift is both to less-balanced diets and less food, both for children and for their mothers. Other goods too have been subject to enormous rates of inflation; such simple things as soap, basic clothing and blankets are in much shorter supply than in the past. In urban areas lack of resources and rising prices have led to worsening of housing standards, especially in the poorest areas and most of all in the settlements lacking basic services. Green and Singer argue that a result of these trends has been a rise in the environmental risks to children's health (Green and Singer, 1984). Echoing the Brazilian example, they argue that the combination of a worsening good supply, decline in the quality of shelter, rising prices for household goods and poor access to water and basic services, must mean that there will be severe effects on the health of children as well as on their physical and intellectual development.

They also put great emphasis, as in the Brazilian case, on

Table 2.3: Tanzania: basic welfare indicators

Indicators	1985
Population (millions)	22.5
Population urbanized (%)	22
Absolute poverty (% of pop.) (1977–84):	
urban	15
rural	25
Infant mortality rate (%)	111
Under-5 mortality rate (%)	183
Life expectancy (at birth, years)	52
GNP per capita (US $, 1984)	210
Low birth weight infants (%)	14
Access to drinking water (%)	
urban	88
rural	39
total	46
Immunization coverage (% of 1 year olds):	
TB	53
DPT	46
polio	46
measles	58
Primary school enrolment (%) (1982–4, gross rates):	
males	91
females	84
Adult literacy (%):	
males	90
females	80

Source: Derived from UNICEF, 1986, Tables 1–6.

the deficiencies of quantitative data which might serve to demonstrate these effects. In many ways the lack of data is worse in sub-Saharan Africa; the quality is low in more instances, and there are much longer time delays in the production of statistics. But more important than this, Green and Singer note that 'the positive trend in IMRs, CDRs and life expectancy apparently was initially resistant to reversal by the crisis' (Green and Singer, 1984: 117). In sub-Saharan Africa as with other areas of the world we are reminded that the enormous deteriorations that we have seen over the last few years are quite possibly warning signals of an even more serious crisis ahead, particularly if economic recession and policies in response to that recession continue to affect the poorest populations as they have already done. One of the most consistent themes in the reports of recent years is that the worst effects of the recession on children may still be to come. The context in which Tanzania's particular experience must be considered is one which holds out very little promise:

The recent past, present and short term future evolution of the state of Africa's children cannot be described as other than grim. External events— often but not always exacerbated by imprudent domestic policies, including delayed response, have swamped the majority of sub-Saharan African economies. Nutrition, shelter, clothing, education, health care and pure water quantities and qualities are declining for a majority of Africans, especially the rural and urban poor, many of whom had very little margin above ill health and destitution even before 1980 [Green and Singer, 1984: 117].

Tanzania is a low-income economy which had in 1984 a GNP per capita of US $210. Its total population in 1985 was estimated at 22.5 million, making it one of the bigger African states. It is, however, a very large country and its population, still predominantly rural, is not densely settled. Over the period from 1965 to 1984 Tanzania recorded an average annual growth rate in GNP per capita of 0.6 per cent. From 1980 to 1984 there was a decline in GNP per capita; a figure of -4.6 per cent average annual rate was recorded (UNICEF, 1986: 138). For very many years Tanzania has pursued social development policies aimed at improving the basic living conditions for the majority of people in the country. It is still the case that the basic social indicators show Tanzania to be among the four or five top sub-Saharan countries and above the average figures for low-income developing countries. Taking adult literacy as an example, in 1970 48 per cent of males were literate and only 18 per cent of females; in 1985 90 per cent of males were literate and 80 per cent of females. These figures are higher than for all other countries in Africa and are above the upper-middle-income country average. The figure of 80 per cent for female literacy is particularly striking, first of all in contrast with the vast majority of other similar countries but also in terms of its fundamental importance for child welfare, both directly and indirectly. Figures for primary school enrolment are similarly impressive. Gross enrolment ratios at the primary level rose from 33 per cent in 1960 to 91 per cent in 1982–4 for males and from 18 per cent to 84 per cent for females (UNICEF, 1986: 134).

As an indicator of health service provision, Tanzania recorded 70 per cent of its total population with access to health services in 1980–3, with 66 per cent of the rural population having such access. In the terms used to categorize countries in Chapter 1, Tanzania is a 'very high U5MR country'. The comparable figures for access to health services in other such countries show Tanzania to have achieved remarkable results in this aspect of its development programme. The median for high U5MR countries was 67 per cent of total population with access to health services, and 39 per cent rural; for middle U5MR countries the figures were 68 per cent and 47 per cent respectively. Tanzania had better levels of access to health services than even the median U5MR countries for which figures were available (UNICEF, 1986: 132–3). But the impact of economic constraints may be seen in another health indicator—immunization. In 1980–1, 58 per cent of 1-year-old children were fully immunized for polio and 58 per cent had received the full DPT immunization. In 1984–5 these percentages had both fallen to 46 per cent. Although at these levels Tanzania is still ahead of virtually every other sub-Saharan country, the decline is a powerful testimony to the effects of economic conditions. From 1960 to 1978 Tanzania made very considerable progress in very many areas and particularly in respect of health, education and water supply in both urban and rural areas. But from the mid-1970s on, Tanzania has been assaulted by a series of massive external economic blows:

As a result, Tanzania is today in the middle of debilitating economic crisis, one which threatens the living standards and the basic needs fulfilment of much of the Tanzanian nation. Unless some way is found of restoring economic activity to its previous levels and/or resuming economic growth, improvements in health, education, sanitation and nutrition will not be possible and even present achievements in these fields may come under severe threat [Green and Singer, 1984: 122].

In Tanzania, basic-needs services have continued to receive

priority in government expenditure allocations and have amounted to between 25 per cent to 30 per cent of this expenditure. The volume of social services and programmes for basic needs has not in fact declined; indeed, as was noted earlier in some instances these provisions have continued to increase. Primary school enrolment and access to health services are examples of this, as is the provision of safe water supplies. Since the 1960s Tanzania's priorities have been geared towards basic human needs, pre-dating the more general acceptance of this strategy in recent years. Tanzania's priorities can be seen clearly within the social sector. For example, rural health services have taken a larger share of total health expenditures, and the ratio of para-medical health workers to doctors has risen sharply; by the end of the 1970s there was one dispensary for every 6,700 rural people and one health service worker for every 1,600. But, as noted in relation to immunization, the effects of the recession have been felt very severely. As resources decline, needs do not; in this context it is the maintenance and continuation of existing capacity which becomes vital. There is a cruel paradox here: The problem is worse in those countries which have made the greatest progress towards building a wide base and an extensive range of provision in terms of basic services for rural populations. They may have trained a large number of people to operate these services but now find that not just the quality of service but even the existence of such services is threatened by economic conditions, a lack of basic resources and import control.

For Tanzania, and the other countries of sub-Saharan Africa, direct evidence of the impact of recession on children is hard to find. But we can refer to some existing statistical information. Average calorie availability fell from about 117 per cent of requirements in 1977 to 93 per cent in 1983. Real wages fell about 50 per cent between 1977 and 1982 and consuming power of rural households fell in real terms by about 15 per cent over the same period. During the late 1970s and early 1980s school fees were reintroduced in Tanzania, although there were means-tested exemptions for poorer families, and charges for medical services were introduced or increased. Green and Singer give one particular indication of possible trends in child welfare; in 1978-9 there was a study of under-5 mortality by income class. The highest income class had an infant mortality rate only one-tenth that of the lowest wage earning group, their pre-tax household incomes being ten times as high. Green and Singer conclude that declining real incomes are likely to reverse the falls in infant mortality rate and child death rate and the rise in life expectancy.

The Tanzanian case demonstrates very clearly the dramatic impact of the world recession on the poor countries. The experience of developing countries over the past twenty to thirty years has been that even modest redistribution, out of resources which were growing, has been very difficult. Attempting to raise household incomes and improve the level of services for the poor and especially of the very weakest groups, including children, in the face of steadily falling resources, may be seen as virtually impossible.

It is clear that across the developing world there has been a decline in incomes and resources for children. This decline has taken place in virtually every developing country and in many cases is now extremely severe. There has been in addition a substantial general decline in both the quality and quantity of basic-needs services and programmes; in cases such as health and education, such declines will have long-term effects. Although the evidence is scarce, due primarily to inadequate data systems, it does seem that so far the impact on child survival is more complex. In many countries death rates for children have increased where household incomes have been reduced and the cuts in social provision have been particularly harsh. As we saw earlier, infant mortality rates and some other social indicators of infant welfare, have continued to improve—although at very much lower rates. This is, of course, misleading. In most poor countries there is a continuing serious deterioration in indicators of nutrition, of health status and of education provision and achievement. It is now clear that if this process is not reversed, it will lead to very much more dramatic deteriorations, which will then make themselves felt in higher rates of infant and child mortality. The economic crisis which has been crippling so many of the world's poorest children is not over, and in very many countries policy in general is now almost completely dominated by attempts to react to this crisis. Malnutrition rates are rising in many African countries and in parts of South America. Infant mortality rates are now rising in some countries including Barbados, Brazil, Ghana and Uruguay (UNICEF, 1984).

In a number of countries the proportion of low birth weight babies has increased and in some countries diseases have reappeared, yellow fever in Ghana and malaria in Peru, for instance (UNICEF, 1986: 93). But such evidence as already exists is severely limited by the simple lack of information. For many of the poorest countries, and particularly for the poorest areas within them, it is simply not possible to document the decline in standards of living and loss of lives for children which may already have taken place and be continuing. Despite the common suffering of the poorest children, the countries of the Third World are very different in terms of their national levels of income, the nature of their economies and the kinds of adjustment policies they have implemented in response to the economic crises. There has not therefore been a uniform pattern to the effects of recession. Those countries with middle and higher GNP per capita have an inherently greater capacity to resist the impact of crisis which ought to be reflected in their social indicators. In some this greater economic strength does seem to prevent a worsening of social indicators, in others national wealth has been no protection for the weakest among their populations. In terms of household incomes, the majority of agricultural and rural people in developing countries may be more subject to changes in national policies and in the conditions affecting agricultural production than they are to fluctuations of the international economy. However, this is not true if they are engaged in export-related production. But they are, of course, severely affected by changes in the pattern of services and declines in government and other expenditure on welfare. For some poor countries the effects of the world recession have been very much less severe than in others. In large, mostly rural economies like India, relatively insulated from the world economy, recent experience has been somewhat different than elsewhere.

THE INDIAN CASE

In a recent assessment of trends in the welfare of children in India, Mundle argues that the global recession has not affected the status of Indian children directly, thanks to the basic insularity of the country's economy. But it has severely constrained the ability of the government to maintain or expand child-related programmes in real terms (Mundle 1984). The 1981 census in India showed a population of 685 million growing at an annual rate of 2.5 per cent; approximately 260 million are children under 15 years old. Nearly three-quarters of the Indian population is rural and so the vast majority, both children and adults, are exposed to the effects of world recession essentially to the extent that India's agriculture depends on external markets. Exports account for about 3 per cent of value added in agriculture. But the situation is much more complex than this; rising oil prices and a low level of exports have given India a serious balance of payments problem and, together with government deficits, has led to strong pressure on government to curtail various development programmes and social welfare services, including those specifically related to children.

As elsewhere, the data available in India to measure the status of children is inadequate and often confusing. For example, this is so in relation to attempts to measure poverty and nutritional status among children. In general terms, there can be no doubt that the overall nutritional status of Indian children is extremely poor, with 'between 50 per cent to over 70 per cent of all children across different states suffering from inadequate calorie intake and around 10–20 per cent of children suffering from protein deficiency as well' (Mundle, 1984: 129). There are considerable differences between the different regions of India, but in general Mundle was able to conclude his assessment of the evidence regarding child nutrition with the view that there has been a distinct improvement over the country as a whole during the 1970s. But he puts considerable stress on the fact that in a number of states the situation had either not improved or had got worse.

He also emphasizes very strongly that the absolute level of living at which the improvements had been registered remains abysmal. This is reflected in the infant mortality rates, which are still far above 100 per thousand live births for the country as a whole, although during the 1960s infant mortality rates distinctly improved. Mundle's assessment is that, during the 1970s, this improvement continued, if only slightly. The evidence of declining infant mortality rates, taken together with trends in life expectancy at birth, can be taken to confirm that the living standards of the broad mass of India's children were improving during the 1970s. The same basic pattern, of very low absolute rates, together with marginal improvement, may be seen in relation to adult literacy. As discussed earlier, the literacy of mothers must be seen as one of the crucial factors affecting the welfare of children. In addition, literacy may be seen as in itself a goal of development and a component in welfare. Rates of literacy in India improved during the 1950s and 1960s, and this improvement was maintained during the 1970s. But the absolute level of literacy, still at only 43 per cent (Table 2.4), remain extremely low. Female literacy rates are still very far below those for males, but they are improving at a faster rate.

Mundle compared the proportionate and absolute share of actual government expenditure going to child-related programmes during the fifteen years from 1969. The programmes covered by this analysis were education, health, family planning, water supply and sanitation, social welfare and other programmes, including nutrition. He found that the share which child-related programmes took of total expenditure had fallen during the period, but notwithstanding this decline absolute expenditure had increased in real terms. From 1969 to 1974 this increase was 44 per cent over the previous five-year period; the rate of increase subsequently fell, but real increases of 11 per cent in 1980–1 and 22 per cent in 1981–2 were recorded. Public sector intervention has a major impact on the status of children. On virtually every measure, absolute poverty remains a massive problem in India, and levels of living for a huge proportion of the predominantly rural population are still, in Mundle's words, 'abysmally low'. But, the evidence seems to suggest that India's relative distance from the linkages of the world economy have given it some measure of protection. From extremely low

Table 2.4: India: basic welfare indicators

Indicators	1985
Population (millions)	759
Population urbanized (%)	26
Absolute poverty (% of pop.) (1977–84):	
urban	40
rural	51
Infant mortality rate (%)	105
Under-5 mortality rate (%)	158
Life expectancy (at birth, years)	57
GNP per capita (US $, 1984)	260
Low birth weight infants (%)	30
Access to drinking water (%):	
urban	80
rural	47
total	54
Immunization coverage (% of 1 year olds):	
TB	65
DPT	51
polio	37
measles	–
Primary school enrolment (%) (1982–4, gross rates):	
males	100
females	68
Adult literacy (%):	
males	157
females	29

Source: Derived from UNICEF, 1986, Tables 1–6.

levels of living, India does seem to have maintained a pattern of slow general improvement in child welfare, although there are enormous disparities between different regions of the country (Table 2.5).

It is clear from what has been discussed in this chapter that basic information is inadequate to allow generalizations across the whole developing world about the net impact of economic recession. But it is clear that in all poor countries the weakest groups tend to suffer most, and that across the world the consequences of worsening economic conditions during the late 1970s and early 1980s have been severe. As countries have attempted to respond to these changes in economic

Table 2.5: India: inter-state variations in infant mortality and related variables

State	Average IMR (1975–7)	Female literacy (1981)	SDP per capita*
Kerala	52	64	1,000
Jammu/Kashmir	66	–	825
Karnataka	81	28	1,038
Maharashtra	94	35	1,455
Punjab	104	34	1,688
Tamil Nadu	108	34	997
Haryana	113	22	1,514
Himachal Pradesh	114	31	1,165
Andhra Pradesh	123	21	897
Assam	128	–	848
Orissa	141	21	834
Gujarat	146	32	1,236
Rajasthan	146	11	973
Madhya Pradesh	146	16	790
Uttar Pradesh	181	14	727

Source: From Mundle, 1984: 135.

* State Domestic Product (rupees, 1975–6 prices)

conditions, the welfare of the poorest children has in many instances been further threatened. The adoption of so-called 'adjustment policies', very often as part of agreements with the IMF and other international lenders, has been closely associated with declines in government expenditure, the falling quality of services generally, and pressure on the standards of living of the poorest. But to a considerable extent the impact of external economic forces on child welfare can be subject to national social policy; this is not only a question of the consequences of economic inevitability. None the less, with few exceptions the countries of the Third World are locked into the system of international economic linkages dominated by the Western industrial economies. Imbalances resulting from the recession have created long-lasting alterations in the nature of the economic context. Trade has slumped, the value of primary products has fallen, the flow of aid—never very large—has slowed, and lending has been reduced. The poor countries also have to grapple with the consequences of huge debts accumulated in the 1970s and before.

During the late 1970s and 1980s the burden of this debt was made much heavier by very high interest rates and the policies pursued by the industrialized countries. A growing number of the poorest countries have been forced to adopt 'stabilization and adjustment' policies as a condition of IMF lending. To date the most visible consequence of such policies in the majority of these countries, has been a decline in welfare. There are those who suggest that adjustment to new economic conditions can be achieved without massive suffering; both moral and human resource arguments are used in support of this position. The managing director of the International Monetary Fund put the human resource argument quite clearly in 1986:

Support [for programmes of adjustment] will be progressively harder to maintain the longer adjustment continues without some pay-off in terms of growth and while human conditions are deteriorating.... Human capital is after all the most important factor of production in developing and industrial countries alike. The forms of adjustment that are most conducive to growth and to protection of human needs will not emerge by accident. They have to be encouraged by an appropriate set of incentives and policies. They will also require political courage [Labouise, 1986, quoted in UNICEF, 1986: 92].

The outlook for the economies of poor countries is bleak. It is possible for these countries to implement economic and social policies which allow both economic growth and development and protection of the weakest, while at the same time enabling some progress in social welfare. But present evidence does not suggest that the majority of countries are pursuing such approaches. In most, the typical adjustment package is one which is dominated by restrictions on government expenditure, lowering output, reductions in employment and reduced levels of investment. All this means that the conditions in which social policies and social programmes for child welfare are formulated and imple-mented are even more hostile now than they have been for many years.

3 Approaches to Child Welfare: Social Policy

Saving children is a collective task here, made possible because people believe, for the first time, in what they are doing. They believe and they create: In unleashing their creative energy, the community discovers it can turn words into acts.

It is not easy. In spite of the international solidarity, there are not enough doctors and hospitals. In Managua, infants with signs of some abnormality are kept two to a crib; and in the child surgery wards, children who have just been operated upon are sent home after three days.

But the material difficulties which abound and are compounded by the unremitting war, seems insignificant in the face of others: No magic wand can wave away the legacy of inefficiency and fatalism. For centuries this country has been taught to obey, not to think, to endure history, not to make it. All this was organised so everyone would be resigned to the life he or she led and accept misfortune and early death the way the winter rains and the summer suns are accepted.

The lightning literacy campaign in 1980 demonstrated from the start that revolution is an enthusiasm more powerful than hardships, but living within the same country today, and fighting against one another, are the country that was and the country that will be [Galeano, 1983: 109-10, writing of Nicaragua].

Everything that happened in the village was as closely related and interwoven as the ribs of a straw basket. It wasn't a surprise to hear that you had missed an important lesson on health, or the weaning of children, which had been given at the Women's Sewing Club ... But most important of all, wherever people gathered, they discussed their lives and everything that was going on in their village... It was these informal talks that enabled people to know who to choose if they wanted a chairperson, say, for the feeding scheme, or for the next village committee or health committee or who should go for training at Goromonzi as a village health worker and so on ... Chizuva realised it really was like a stream, with no divisions in the flowing water [Mungoshi, 1983: 122, writing of Zimbabwe].

This chapter seeks to establish the framework of social policy action in response to child welfare needs. First of all, some issues in the consideration of 'welfare' itself, then some aspects of the history of formal social policy responses in poor countries, are examined, and lastly some themes in social policy for child welfare are discussed. The nature of welfare in the context of development and underdevelopment has been examined elsewhere (MacPherson, 1982; MacPherson and Midgley, 1987). Essentially, it has been suggested that the fundamental concerns of development itself come very close to containing the essence of the pursuit of welfare. Development cannot be defined to universal satisfaction; but it is clear that the concept embodies notions of desirable social and economic progress and at its heart must have concern with the human condition. Indeed, many attempts to grapple with the definition of development have placed considerable emphasis on notions such as 'the realisation of the potential of human personality' (Seers, 1972). Development has come to mean, above all, improvement in living conditions, and certainly in recent years there has been a significant shift in the way such improvement has been conceptualized. Earlier attention to economic growth and material conditions is now balanced by considerably more attention being paid to the quality of that economic change and to social dimensions. Development as a set of societal goals is clearly concerned with reductions in poverty, with the provision of socially useful occupations, and with the achievement of a more equitable social system. It has also been seen to be concerned with the provision of education in the broadest sense and with participation. As an organizing concept development involves change perhaps more than anything, and indeed in the context of the poorest countries profound transformation of economic and social systems has been and continues to be a major aspect of the lives of their populations. Increasingly, discussions of development have placed more and more emphasis on the small-scale community level and on the individual. As the balance of attention has shifted away from solely economic criteria and economic activities towards not just social criteria and social activities but to the smaller scale and individual dimensions of these activities, then we have witnessed a significant change. There are solid grounds for suggesting that in its more contemporary usage, the concept of development is very close to that of welfare. To the extent that welfare focuses more clearly on the needs of individuals, it does so within the context of development itself. Focusing on the individual, and the relationships between individuals and the social context, may put development issues out of focus, but it does not separate welfare and development.

But, although this consonance of meaning may be said to exist at the conceptual level, the position in practice is very different. As we shall see, welfare was historically taken to describe a very limited set of activities and concerns, and the same remains true to a considerable extent today. But just as we have seen that the term 'welfare' itself, although having perhaps an individual focus at its heart, has wide-ranging concerns, so any consideration of welfare institutions must be equally wide ranging. We must examine social institutions which deal with all aspects of welfare. It will not be enough to look only at those which label themselves as 'welfare institutions'. This is of particular importance in the context of development, since the distinctions which might be made between economic and social development activity are very much less clear. Indeed, in very many cases programmes which seek integrated socio-economic development are based on the eradication of these boundaries altogether. Our concern with the welfare of children essentially defines the field; the focus on individual needs defines it further. Thus, although most attention will be paid to specific aspects of organized health services and to social welfare services specifically designed to respond to the needs of children, these institutions do not form the outer limits of our concern. A constant theme will be the notion that it is patterns of development and underdevelopment, with their associated social and economic changes, which affect, perhaps most profoundly of all, the welfare of children.

THE GROWTH OF SOCIAL POLICY

Social policies and programmes in poor countries have been shaped, and continue to be shaped, by the forces of underdevelopment (MacPherson, 1982). Both the range and the nature of these policies and programmes have been seen to be crucially affected by the forces acting on poor countries both from outside and from within themselves. The roots of both underdevelopment and of contemporary patterns of social policy have been seen to lie in the historical experience of the poor countries, and for very many of them in their colonial experience. Formal, organized provision for welfare can be seen to be associated with the penetration of the money economy and with formal administrative systems in general. For the great majority of the world's poorest countries this penetration was associated most visibly and most forcibly with colonial rule. In traditional societies the community of the household, the wide-ranging extended family and other larger social groups, had welfare as one of their essential activities. All these had roles as agents for the provision of individual care, for material support or for the satisfaction of other individual and social needs.

The kinds of economic and social change engendered by colonial rule affected profoundly not just basic economic systems but also their social relationships. The traditional organization of welfare was undermined by these patterns of change; the support of individuals was in a variety of ways separated from the responsibility of the immediate household and the extended family. The kinship-based community, although remaining extremely powerful in its welfare role, became less and less able to cope with the demands put upon it as economic and social change dislocated patterns of life. The growth of organized social policies and programmes can thus be linked both with the patterns of economic and social change and also with the incursion of individualistic values. Taken together with the aggressively centralizing tendencies of the colonial state and its associated institutions, these forces gave considerable further impetus to the progressive detachment of welfare from the family and community. But social policy had a very minor role during colonialism; there was above all an emphasis on the maintenance of law and order, and the primacy of economic development. Welfare programmes as such were seen in general as peripheral and residual. In most colonial territories the primary responsibility for the welfare of indigeneous populations was left with missions and non-government organizations. Overall the level of such services was low.

The nature of the colonial administrative system itself gave to the emerging welfare institution a character which has remained to this day. Such administrations tend to be highly bureaucratized with a great degree of centralization. Colonial administrations were essentially designed for control, they were organized above all to maintain order and to transmit downwards policies formulated at the top. For the limited range of social welfare activities established under colonial rule there was a common adherence to imported Western approaches. The permeation of values, attitudes and beliefs, both personal and professional, may be seen as a vital aspect of social policy history. After the Second World War, when colonies began to gain independence, there was some increase in social welfare activity. To a considerable extent this was related to economic expansion, and emphasis was given to health and education, particularly of the actual or potential workforce. There was of course considerable variation in the level of resources available within colonial economies and to newly independent governments. But the great majority of these countries shared a common feature in that their economies were organized primarily for the export production of primary products and unfinished goods. At independence and in the years following, existing social policies, which were strongly established in terms of systems of administration and staffing, were not amenable to radical reorientation. Indeed, most countries pursued, within the severe limits which their economies imposed, policies of expansion in terms of their existing social programmes. Reflecting as they did a minimal conception of welfare in general and a pattern of social provision which reflected the unequal nature of colonial society, these policies were modified very little in the majority of countries. The continuing dominance of new class interests in the allocation of social resources lends weight to the notion that one of the most important factors in determining the present living conditions of the poor was the under-development of social policy.

UNDERDEVELOPMENT AND SOCIAL POLICY

It has already been argued that the concept of development itself is fundamental to any discussion of social policy in the poor countries. In the past, although the term was very frequently used, it was rarely defined with any rigour. Across a wide range of poor countries and for many years, development was taken to be synonymous with a set of social and economic changes which would lead countries towards the model of society and economy given by the Western industrial nations. It was only in the last two decades that such conceptions began to be counter-balanced by alternative views. Approaches to development in practice, which labelled themselves 'modernization' and which put almost complete emphasis on economic growth, began to be counteracted by views which acknowledged the essential normative nature of development and which emphasized the basic needs of the majority of poor people as being the primary goal of development activity. This shift should not be overemphasized, however; as Chambers has pointed out very eloquently, despite a great deal of rhetoric concerned with development for the poorest, the practice has in many cases remained unchanged (Chambers, 1983).

There may be reference to underdevelopment and to the illusory gains from so-called modernization, but it is widely reported that the essential nature of the development process is one which perverts good intentions, constrains action and misdirects the gains of change. I have argued elsewhere that in order to fully understand the reality of contemporary poverty in the poorest countries, the nature of underdevelopment must be considered. Above all, underdevelopment must be seen as an extremely powerful and continuing set of processes. These processes have different specific effects in different societies, but underdevelopment has a common impact in engendering those forms of economic and social change, both within developing countries and between those countries and the industrial nations, which foster and maintain relations of dependency. Thus, although particular forms may vary, in general terms the political economies of the poorest countries can be seen most clearly in their relationship to external forces. As will become clear in later chapters, one of the most important aspects of this perspective is that it makes clearer the apparent paradoxes thrown up by societies in which worsening mass poverty goes hand in hand with vigorous economic growth and social change. In terms of social policy, this perspective also allows more understanding of the contradictions between needs which are perceived to exist among majority populations, and patterns of social policy and social programmes; these not only fail to meet needs in quantitative terms but provide services which are visibly inappropriate.

The concept of underdevelopment has been widely used in relation to those countries with the poorest populations. Chapter 1 showed something of the extent of mass poverty in developing countries. The term 'underdevelopment' is, in many instances, used in a descriptive sense to encompass the range of deprivations suffered by the poorest. Lack of food, lack of shelter, a hostile and worsening environment, little or no health provision, no education and declining employment are all features which are emphasized in very many accounts of poverty in the Third World (MacPherson and Midgley, 1987).

As the concept is used here, underdevelopment is a continuing process, expressed in specific patterns of dependency within and between countries. It is these relationships which are the major determining factors in forming patterns of social need and of social policy response. As will become clear in relation to child welfare, the essential nature of social problems is determined by the economic and social forces related to the major changes affecting the poorest countries. In terms of response it is not just that resources are low in absolute terms, although they are desperately low. It is also that the distribution of resources is perverted by the power relationships related to dependency; what scarce resources exist are moved away from the points of greatest need. Continuing underdevelopment may be seen also in social policies and programmes. Reliance on external perceptions and prescriptions may be seen as part of underdevelopment. Indeed, it may be suggested that welfare activity, perhaps more than many other aspects of social development, is characterized by underdevelopment in this sense. Inappropriate policies are maintained, and extended against the evidence of need; social programmes continue to operate in ways which benefit the entrenched interests of the more powerful.

Concentration on the nature of internal dependency allows examination of relationships between different geographical areas to be explored, as well as between social groups. As we have already seen, patterns of poverty are marked by great inequalities, most visibily between town and country, class and class, but also between different regions of the same country. One of the most important aspects of dependency analysis is that the poorest and the most prosperous are linked together in international systems. The poverty of those most impoverished and seemingly most marginal, is essentially bound in with the wealth of the most privileged. This theme will recur in the chapters which follow; it is in the patterns of inter-relationship between the poor and the rich that we find the clearest explanations for continuing poverty.

There are of course very many other factors affecting patterns of need and welfare response. Midgley, for example, has argued that 'the dependency paradigm ... paid almost no attention to culture' (MacPherson and Midgley, 1987: 136). Midgley's argument that neglect of the cultural dimension seriously weakens analysis of Third World development is a strong one. That much dependency analysis is grossly oversimplified cannot be denied. Evidence of the relatively greater sophistication of more recent work may be seen for example in development anthropology, where both the theoretical and methodological insights of anthropology have been married with perceptions from other disciplines. Some of this work allows understanding of the huge range of particular social formations which characterize the developing world (Grillo and Rew, 1986). Work such as this enriches considerably the analysis of Third World development but does not necessarily contradict dependency as a fundamental explanation. There can be no doubt that oversimplified monocausal explanations which allow virtually no room for variation and differentiation did appear in the heyday of underdevelopment and dependency analysis. But there was much work which achieved a more completely formed result, accepting at the same time cultural differences and the essentially common set of forces linked to economic relationships and their political expression.

These issues have been debated extensively in the literature and will not be pursued here. In later chapters one aspect of culture which will be explored is the way that welfare needs are met in traditional societies, and continue to be met outside formal welfare institutions. Indeed, this is a major theme. Social change brings enormous pressure on traditional welfare systems and may pervert existing relationships. But it is the case in the poorest countries, as indeed in all countries, that a huge proportion of welfare remains with individuals, families and social groups and is not the direct responsibility of organized activity. Continuing underdevelopment may undermine or even destroy traditional patterns of care, reciprocity and understanding, but these continue to be of absolutely vital and fundamental importance, although their shape may change.

It is obvious that no account of social policy and social welfare in developing countries can be made without reference to patterns of obligation and care which are in response to the needs of individuals, in this case to the needs of children. In relation to the care of children, the position of women in society is clearly absolutely fundamental. Although women share in common inequality, exploitation and even oppression, the particular cultural forms in which women live their lives are many. In practice, it is the collision between the forces of underdevelopment and the specifics of cultural formations that produces the social dynamics with which we are most concerned. As we shall see, at the very simplest level we are concerned with patterns of extended family support for children in a variety of circumstances, but situations become very much more complex than this. The relationships between men, women and children in both customary and modern law will be seen to have significant effects. So too have property relations, whether related to law or not, again between men and women and their children. Once property is considered, then the crucial interrelationships between subsistence production and production for the market begin to have major significance, not least for the welfare of children.

Reference was made in Chapter 2 to the importance of female literacy and the education of women in general to the welfare of children; this will be discussed in later chapters, but at this point it underlines the massive significance of cultural difference in determining the specifics of particular welfare situations. Clearly, it is not only the realities of low resources and perverted economic systems which determine the level of welfare; cultural factors clearly affect the particular impact of these forces on particular communities and individuals within them.

It is clear then that we are dealing with situations of almost infinite complexity; we can do little more than point to the extreme dangers of oversimplified explanations and attempt to avoid such explanations. Both these points—the importance of cultural factors and the need to pursue specific cultural factors within a wider theoretical context—are illustrated very clearly in Sharma's work on women in urban households in northern India (Sharma, 1986). In the realities of northern India, Sharma argues for the reconstruction of the household as a unit of study, but informed by the theoretical perspective of feminism. She does this for a number of reasons but above all because, however unacceptable the position of women within households, it must, she argues, be recognized that 'in India, as in most other third world countries, there are few if any alternatives to a family based household at present' (Sharma 1986: 197). Sharma's work, in common with many other recent studies of women in poor countries, shows very clearly not just the great extent of women's work but its invisibility. Women are responsible for a great range of tasks, a large number of which are essentially concerned with welfare.

In India, as in many other countries, there are few institutional sources of support outside the household and its immediate circle of kin. There is little public welfare provision in the form of state insurance schemes, pensions, and unemployment benefit, and the free health services provided by the state are severely over-burdened. In crises such as sickness, widowhood, or loss of livelihood, individuals (both men and women) have to rely on whatever resources the household can muster internally, or else upon the external sources of aid and information which its members have been able to cultivate and maintain—kin networks for the most part, but also neighbours and other contacts ... the maintenance of social resources is, in the long run, almost as important as the maintenance of material resources [Sharma, 1986: 4].

As we shall see, formal social welfare institutions and social policies in the poorest countries have been heavily influenced indeed by external example. A good deal of social policy research in poor countries has shown how dependent social policies are on conceptions of welfare drawn from the industrialized states. A number of texts have shown in considerable detail how services for health, education, housing, social work and other programmes reflect Western approaches in considerable detail. Not only are the administrative systems similar, the professional orientations very close, but replication of even quite detailed legislative provision is not uncommon (Midgley, 1981; MacPherson, 1982; MacPherson and Midgley, 1987). Across a wide range of social policies it has been argued that social policy analyses and prescriptions imported from the West have been not just inappropriate but have constrained progress in very serious ways.

The processes of cultural diffusion are complex. Any serious analysis of the transfer of Western social policy ideas and practices to the poor countries would have to explore a wide range of both historical and contemporary forces. Perhaps the most vicious and insidious factors are those linked with 'the psychology of oppression' (Fanon, 1967), which argues that colonialism and other forms of Western domination had, as part both of their effects and of their mechanisms for continuation, the destruction of self-esteem. Colonized peoples, oppressed and dependent, were convinced both of the superiority of Western culture and in many instances of the inherent worthlessness of their own. Subjugation of indigeneous culture and denigration of its values were common. The emulation of Western ideas and belief in their superiority is still found, frequently linked of course with the propagation of Western interests. In the context of organized social welfare, a generalized desire to take Western ideas and practices was given massive impetus by the fact that staff in most countries prior to independence, and in many cases after independence also, were expatriate. These professional and semi-professional staff, recruited from the industrial countries, shared at a fundamental level the values and notions embodied in Western social policies and pro- grammes. Thus the direct transfer of approaches to social policy is not difficult to understand.

However, the perpetuation of an essentially colonial legacy long after independence is much more complex and certainly cultural diffusion must be seen to have a major role. It is now nearly a quarter of a century since the majority of colonies gained political independence. But the patterns of influence and of continuing underdevelopment in social policy mean the picture is a complicated one; there are now very many external agencies attempting to influence the policies and programmes of developing countries directly, and indirectly maintaining the flow of covert transfer. Countries such as Britain and France have lost their colonial empires but maintain very extensive relationships at all levels. They have been joined since the Second World War by the United States and the Soviet Union in particular. A huge number of international organizations, both government sponsored and non-govern- ment, are extremely active in social welfare fields. In relation to social work services Midgley suggested that these agencies are extremely important in continuing to transfer essentially Western approaches to social work to developing countries (Midgley, 1981). He put the case that these approaches with a very heavy case-work emphasis, were of little relevance to the problems being experienced in poor countries. Essentially, the same arguments apply in the field of social security. As with other social welfare programmes, total coverage is low, and relatively small proportions of Third World populations are covered by social security schemes, but the nature of these schemes is of significance to an understanding of the development of social policy as a whole. Across the Third World it is clear that Western approaches to the organization and administration of social security have been extensively implanted (Midgley , 1984). In this case the inappropriateness of such programmes is particularly vivid in contrast to the needs of the poor majority, and the benefits to relatively small and privileged groups especially clear (MacPherson, 1987).

It is not just the historical growth of social welfare programmes which can be illuminated by the insights of underdevelopment, dependency and cultural diffusion. As later chapters will show, in considering contemporary social policy dilemmas it is clear that the contradictions which appear so often in current welfare responses may be seen to be heavily influenced by factors such as those we have discussed here. The remainder of this chapter examines social policy in relation to child welfare against this background.

CHILD WELFARE POLICY

Before discussing emerging policy responses, it is necessary to attempt some definition of the boundaries of activity with which we are concerned. This is of course always problematic with regard to welfare, but in relation to child welfare in developing countries there are some very severe difficulties. The narrowest conception of child welfare is one which would make the topic synonymous with the activities of government departments, or non-government organizations with agency functions, having child welfare as their named responsibility. There are very many such departments in developing countries, almost always the legacy of colonial administration, as discussed earlier. These departments are concerned primarily with the execution of statutory responsibilites for child welfare, the provision of substitute care and the administration of regulations designed to protect children from abuse. In this way they are similar to equivalent departments in industrial countries, and are essentially social service and social work oriented. The functions they perform are vital and, it will be argued later, can be performed in ways which are much more appropriate to the contemporary circumstances of developing countries. But in general terms we cannot restrict the concept of child welfare simply to the ambit of these activities. In any context, but with particular force in poor countries, we must see child welfare as an aspect of development itself. Thus we are concerned essentially with all those aspects of policy which bear on the well-being of the child. Of course, such a notion is open to the charge that just as a social-service-oriented definition is ludicrously restrictive, so this is outrageously wide and meaningless. But a case can be made for putting the well-being of children as a point of focus for consideration of development policies and of the organized activities of government and other institutions. This is not to argue that the totality of child welfare is the product of the activities of such institutions. But in social policy terms we are concerned above all with the role of such institutions in relation to the total welfare effort.

A broad policy for child welfare must inevitably be concerned with health but also with the protection of rights and advancement of individual social welfare as represented by social services. There are many arguments for having as wide a perspective as possible while retaining a close focus on the needs of children. There are very many aspects of the development process, for example the extension of cash cropping, migration from rural to urban areas, attendance of children at institutions of formal education, and so on, which have very profound welfare implications. Too narrow a concentration on the activities of specific sectors will miss a whole range of such impacts on child welfare. Furthermore, such a narrow range will continue the production of incomplete and unbalanced policy responses, for the importance of all sectors of activity must be seen to lie not just in the consequences of the change they engender but also in the potential for the enhancement of welfare which their activities may hold. As an example, a department of agriculture may be heavily involved in the planning and implementation of rural resettlement schemes—for instance, ones which are concerned with export crop production—but may have no institutional concern whatever with the welfare of children involved. It is not just in nutritional terms that the direct involvement of such departments may be relevant to child welfare. The totality of children's lives will be affected by very many aspects of such schemes, but it is likely that unless child welfare needs are made explicitly clear, they will not be seen as an objective. Trying to put child welfare into the development process in this way is really doing no more than putting particular emphasis on the most vulnerable of all those who are the ultimate purpose of all development activity.

Just as a narrow focus in terms of particular sectors may be seen to be seriously limiting, so too is an approach which is concerned exclusively with children. While it is true that the needs of children and the welfare of children should be among the most central objectives of social policy, it is also true that those needs and that welfare are affected very much by what is happening to other groups in the population. The most important here has already been referred to; the welfare of women is directly relevant to the welfare of children in very many ways, and indirectly in very many more. If programmes and policies for children are pursued in isolation from those concerned with women, they are likely to fail. But the significance of this wider perspective is more than simply one of success in terms of implementation of programmes. It is crucial that child welfare is seen within the context of the totality of welfare at the much more profound level of the fundamental principles which are to guide and shape policy for welfare in the most general terms. Pursuing the point further, programmes for the welfare of 'mothers and children', however generously interpreted, will also be severely limited if they do not take into account the position of women *vis-à-vis* men and the social structures which express the position of men. We are faced here with a serious problem but at the same time with the potential for exciting and creative policy development. The problem, both at the level of analysis and in practice, is that there must be boundaries; without some outer limits to the areas of our concern in terms of social policy, we can make no headway in identifying specific issues and specific responses. On the other hand, there are dangers in overemphasizing this problem; the issues of central concern are usually only too painfully apparent. The most pressing needs of children and the progressive enhancement of the well-being of the lives of all children are the goal of policy. The diffuseness of boundaries and the very wide range of potentially relevant activity become the source of creative policy development and innovative programmes and projects.

We shall see again and again that virtually every discussion of specific child welfare policy returns us to these central themes; it is in consideration of development itself, of the well-being of whole communities, and of the relationship between social policy and such development that we must look for the solution to specific issues.

This is not to underestimate the difficulties of achieving coherence in terms of policy and planning for child welfare. It is always the case that attempts to formulate action across, as well as between, sectors is difficult. But there are specific needs which children have which can provide a central core of concern to which other needs may be related. The indicators discussed in Chapter 1 of this book give us a starting point for the formulation of an approach to child welfare.

THE RIGHTS OF THE CHILD

It is nearly thirty years since the General Assembly of the United Nations declared on 20 November 1959 Resolution 1386xiv, 'The Declaration of the Rights of the Child'. If we consider this declaration and the problems in the achievement of these rights, the boundaries of our topic may be more clearly demarcated. The UN declaration referred to its own 'Universal Declaration of Human Rights' in which it had been proclaimed that everyone was entitled to rights and freedoms without distinction of any kind. But the child was seen to be a special case whereby because of 'physical and mental immaturity [the child] needs special safeguards and care, including appropriate legal protection before as well as after birth'. The preamble contains the powerful principle that 'mankind owes to the child the best it has to give' and the declaration proclaimed the aim that children 'may have a happy childhood'. The declaration embodied a number of very important principles:

Principle 1
The child shall enjoy all the rights set forth in this Declaration. Every child, without any exception whatsoever, shall be entitled to these rights, without distinction or discrimination on account of race, colour, sex, language,

religion, political or other opinion, national or social origin, property, birth or other status, whether of himself or of his family.

Principle 2
The child shall enjoy special protection, and shall be given opportunities and facilities, by law and by other means, to enable them to develop physically, mentally, morally, spiritually and socially in a healthy and normal manner and in conditions of freedom and dignity. In the enactment of laws for this purpose, the best interests of the child shall be the paramount consideration.

Principle 3
The child shall be entitled from his birth to a name and a nationality.

Principle 4
The child shall enjoy the benefits of social security. He shall be entitled to grow and develop in health; to this end, special care and protection shall be provided both to him and to his mother, including adequate pre-natal and post-natal care. The child shall have the right to adequate nutrition, housing, recreation and medical services.

Principle 5
The child who is physically, mentally or socially handicapped shall be given the special treatment, education and care required by his particular condition

Principle 6
The child, for the full and harmonious development of his personality, needs love and understanding. He shall, wherever possible, grow up in the care and under the responsibility of his parents, and, in any case, in an atmosphere of affection and of moral and material security; a child of tender years shall not, save in exceptional circumstances, be separated from his mother. Society and the public authorities shall have the duty to extend particular care to children without a family and to those without adequate means of support. Payment of State and other assistance towards the maintenance of children of large families is desirable.

Principle 7
The child is entitled to receive education, which shall be free and compulsory, at least in the elementary stages. He shall be given an education which will promote his general culture, and enable him, on a basis of equal opportunity, to develop his abilities, his individual judgement, and his sense of moral and social responsibility, and to become a useful member of society. The best interests of the child shall be the guiding principle of those responsible for his education and guidance; that responsibility lies in the first place with his parents. The child shall have full opportunity for play and recreation, which should be directed to the same purposes as education; society and the public authorities shall endeavour to promote the enjoyment of this right.

Principle 8
The child shall in all circumstances be among the first to receive protection and relief.

Principle 9
The child shall be protected against all forms of neglect, cruelty and exploitation. He shall not be the subject of traffic, in any form. The child shall not be admitted to employment before an appropriate minimum age; he shall in no case be caused or permitted to engage in any occupation or employment which would prejudice his health or education, or interfere with his physical, mental and moral development.

Principle 10
The child shall be protected from practices which may foster racial, religious and any other forms of discrimination. He shall be brought up in a spirit of understanding, tolerance, friendship among peoples, peace and universal brotherhood, and in full consciousness that his energy and talents should be devoted to the service of his fellow men.

For the majority of children in developing countries, and particularly for the poorest, the rights enshrined in the UN declaration are an impossible dream. It was argued earlier that development should have as a central objective the needs of children, ensuring their health and survival, their normal development, guarding their rights and protecting them from abuse. To the extent that this is not done, there is an enormous waste of human life and potential, but in addition there is a massive level of suffering which denies the very concept of welfare itself. The lives of the poor are marked by malnutrition, ill health, poor housing and unequal and exploitative economic, legal and social systems. Natural disasters and the disasters of engineered change affect these populations more harshly, not least because even the most essential services are rarely available. For many millions of children, then, personal development is held back by the conditions in which they live. We must of course take considerable care in generalizing the notions embodied in documents such as the UN declaration. Attempting to establish universal norms is in itself hazardous. There are not universal patterns of child care—not least because the concept of childhood itself differs between social and cultural settings; later discussion of legislation relating to child welfare will take up this point.

A specific example of the way childhood itself varies dramatically in its nature may be seen in terms of employment. In the rich countries only very few children are engaged in full-time paid employment and virtually all are in full-time education. In the poorest countries virtually all children are working to some extent and very many work full-time outside the home from an early age. Similarly, the concept of childhood itself is by no means universal in its definition. It has already been noted that in the West this idea, of the early years as having some special quality, and the child being sharply differentiated from the adult, came essentially with industrialization. The way children are regarded varies enormously between cultures, and their position with regard to rights and duties will reflect that conception of the child and childhood. Thus there may well be conflicts between notions such as those embodied in the UN declaration, and existing conceptions of the child.

Many of these points will be explored in more detail later, but for the moment it should be emphasized that there is considerable risk in pursuing this argument too far. There are very few cultures which do not acknowledge the relative weakness of the child and cherish the growing child, whatever the specific duties that child is asked to perform. There is clearly much difficulty in the implementation of rights expressed in the form that the UN declaration uses; closely tied to social welfare practice in the industrialized countries, the fundamental universality of some of these may be masked by the prescriptions offered. All this directs our attention to the necessity of child welfare policies and programmes which are firmly located within the context of particular social systems.

CHILD WELFARE ISSUES

All children, wherever they live, need the opportunity for healthy development of mind and body. Their well-being is dependent upon the satisfaction of a number of basic needs, and these are essentially the same wherever they live. The first and perhaps most obvious requirement is that children at all ages require adequate food. We have already seen that in many developing countries there are large proportions of the child populations inadequately fed, with a variety of factors creating this malnutrition. The ill-effects of malnutrition are numerous: severe malnutrition will bring impeded development with long-term consequences; lack of food may well affect brain function directly, resulting in poor learning ability, apathy, lack of energy and poor protection from disease. A poorly nourished child is more vulnerable to infection. Very often lacking access to clean and safe water, the most vulnerable children will be prey to infectious diseases and in extreme danger if they have not been protected by immunization or vaccination. Children exposed to infected water and unprotected by immunization are much more likely to suffer serious and long-term consequences from illness, particularly when this is compounded by malnutrition.

Clearly, then, all children have basic physical needs but they have many other important requirements if they are to grow up and realize their full potential. The improvement of physical health, desperately needed, is not necessarily enough on its own. If more children can be protected from disease and illness, and if those children can be better fed, their health will improve dramatically; but even if this happens, and their material conditions are improved, there are very many problems which still beset the child population. Better physical conditions and material prosperity do not necessarily reduce the incidence of psycho-social problems; better standards of living may make satisfactory family and community life more possible or even more likely, but they do not ensure it.

The most basic needs of children are for physical survival, for food, clean water, immunization, and protection against the worst abuse. But if we are to regard child welfare as a positive dimension of development, and to regard the development of the individual child—as a member of the community—as the focus of social policy, then we need to look wider than basic physical survival. From birth all human needs are related together in complex ways. For this reason it is important to look beyond basic physical needs and to consider psycho-social needs of the most general kind in order to provide a context for later consideration of child welfare programmes and policies. The World Health Organisation has proposed a fourfold classification of psycho-social needs of children (World Health Organisation, 1982). Studies in many developing countries came to similar conclusions with regard to these needs—the need for love and security, for new experiences, for praise and recognition, and for responsibility. The first of these needs is met by the child experiencing from birth onwards a stable, continuous, dependable and loving relationship with parents or parent-substitutes. It is through these relationships, first with parents and then with other adults, that the child acquires a sense of personal identity and worth. There is therefore a pattern of development closely related to that concerned with physical health. For the young child in particular there is a need for security and stability in the web of relationships; consistent and dependable attitudes and behaviour are as important as the security of a familiar place and known routines. The need for love and security is one which is essential for the development of the whole child. So too is the need for new experience. Particularly during early childhood children must take on new experiences in order to develop. The most important way in which this is done is through play; play is so important for learning that it must not be treated as if it were a waste of time. Through play children are helped to acquire physical control of their bodies, to explore objects, words and sounds, and to foster their imaginations. Thus in any community play for children will be vital for their development, the denial of such opportunities to young children having very serious effects on their growth. In any society, childhood is a period which requires an enormous amount of emotional, social and intellectual learning.

Closely linked with the need for love and security and for new experiences, this learning is fuelled by the incentive of praise and recognition, particularly from those adults with whom the child relates. The fourth fundamental need, the need for responsibility, is clearly linked with the process of learning throughout childhood. Children must gain a measure of personal independence as they move towards adulthood, beginning with simple matters such as feeding, dressing and washing and moving through to much more complex personal and social responsibilities. As we shall see, issues of responsibility arise not only in consideration of legal provisions but also with regard to the proper role of both community and the state in child welfare.

But consideration of this very fundamental need for responsibility in the psycho-social development of children does underline the very delicate balance that there is between the independence and self-expression of the child and the responsibilities of others to protect, direct and guide the child. Such considerations as these may seem to be peripheral to child welfare in the poorest countries. But these needs are universal, and in many circumstances it is against the bench-mark of their satisfaction that social conditions and their consequences must be tested. There are very many specific needs which must be satisfied in order to ensure healthy physical development of children and to allow a social environment which will enable them to flourish. But behind all these is the essential point that child welfare is concerned with the development, to the maximum possible degree, of the potential of every child; in considering the welfare of the poorest children in developing countries, we are not discussing children who are somehow different in their needs—their needs are the same, but the chances of them being met are very much less.

It has already been suggested, and the data in Chapter 1 underlined this, that the basic physical conditions necessary for adequate child development are frequently not met in developing countries. For the very poorest children material conditions may be so poor that they lead short, hard lives without dignity or self-respect. Children face very many threats to their well-being, especially in the earliest stages of their lives. Rates of infant mortality and morbidity are very high; deaths from diarrhoeal diseases alone are almost 5 million every year amongst small children. Malnutrition and the relatively small number of preventable diseases take in addition an enormous toll.

Changing economic and social conditions put communities and families under stress. Not only will existing capacities for ensuring the welfare of children be undermined, but new demands will be placed on traditional forms of child care. Not the least of these will be demands for cash income. It is this which is most often behind the most extreme abuses of the rights of children. In all poor communities, but perhaps most visibly in the growing cities of the Third World, families may be forced to give up their children into circumstances where the little money they may earn is frequently at the cost of neglect, abuse and exploitation. In the most serious cases even very young children may be separated from their families, temporarily or permanently, and left to fend for themselves. But in vastly more cases the interaction of economic forces with social systems attempting to maintain traditional patterns of child care has been destructive of child welfare. Just as the oppression and exploitation of women may be hidden within the household and the family, so too may the suffering of children. In many circumstances young children, particularly girls, may be working extremely long hours in very difficult conditions within households. Again, the difficulties of drawing boundaries between family responsibility and the responsibility of the wider social system for child welfare is highlighted. What is clear, and will be discussed in later chapters, is that contemporary change is worsening these situations for many children. It is also clear that in the great majority of developing countries, despite sometimes extensive legislation protecting children from abuse and exploitation, the role of the state and agencies acting for it, is limited. Even the worst abuse cannot be contained by social services and other institutions in the poorest countries. The inadequacy of social welfare services, both in absolute terms and with respect to the kind of services provided, is a major theme of the chapters which follow; in no poor country are child welfare programmes and social work services anything but totally inadequate.

For child welfare policies as a whole, then, there are three fundamental objectives. First, the protection of the child from outside threat. Second, to ensure the normal and full development of every child both in physical and psycho-social terms. Third, and clearly linked to the second, assisting and enabling children to become fully integrated into their society. These will not in practice be separate; a programme which teaches children at school about nutrition and health education, will also have within it elements of teaching children greater social responsibility. An emphasis on these basic principles does draw attention to the fact that all policies and programmes can be measured against child welfare objectives. Whether social policies and programmes are explicitly labelled as concerned with children or not, the essential elements of child welfare may be used as a test of their value and consequences.

In the discussion so far there has been an implicit assumption that where community and family structures are more or less intact, the welfare of children is secure. This is clearly not so. In some circumstances children will be neglected and abused within the family; it can never be taken for granted that children are receiving the love and care that they need. But beyond the undoubted problems of individual failure to care for children within particular families, there are more generalized issues. Communities differ with respect to the value that they place on individual children. In some societies female children may be neglected, or even killed, in circumstances where they are seen to be of relatively less economic benefit to the household. Recent evidence that medical techniques allowing the sex of a child to be known before the birth have resulted in the abortion of females is a graphic illustration of this. There are other groups of children, the physically and mentally handicapped for example, who may also suffer discrimination and neglect. In these cases there will be very severe difficulties in attempting to reconcile protection of the weakest and most vulnerable children with the need to develop and sustain programmes for the welfare of children as a whole, within the framework of dominant attitudes and values.

No social policy can be considered in isolation from attitudes and values; customary practices and traditional values will crucially affect both priorities and the nature of programmes. This is clearly the case in relation to child welfare, as the socialization and care of children is of such massive significance in every culture. So, as we will see, there are many circumstances in which it is the practices, attitudes, values and beliefs of the specific community and society which give rise to some of the most serious child welfare problems.

Female circumcision is a very clear example of this, but so too are many other more widespread practices in the poorest societies. There is no simple answer to the difficulties thrown up by the clash of perceptions and values which so often mark attempts to pursue the welfare of children. In terms of basic child welfare needs, objectives are essentially universal, but it must be central to social policy in general and child welfare policy in particular that the nature of the specific community and society is paramount. The particular forms in which overarching policy objectives may be expressed as projects must be shaped in the context of the whole range of attitudes and values. These will include the roles of mother and father, and the nature of the wider kinship group in which the child lives; the specific concept of childhood, the roles of children and their relationships to each other and to adults; the nature of both formal and non-formal education; the extent and nature of child labour, both in formal and informal terms; above all existing conceptions of children's needs and how they should be met.

In November 1982 the Inter-Parliamentary Union held a conference on Policies, Programmes and Legislation for Children in Yaounde, Cameroon. This was in co-operation with UNICEF and both the content and conclusions of the conference illustrate very well the themes developed in this chapter (Inter-Parliamentary Union, 1983). There were delegates from twenty-three African countries, but in spite of 'the wide climatic, political, economic and cultural diversity of the continent' (p. 13), the conference proceedings concluded that 'the problems of children are very similar throughout the continent and for that reason, despite different socio-political regimes, African States have common objectives and interests in this regard' (p. 13). It was noted that children under 15 represented between 40 per cent and 50 per cent of the populations of African countries and that women and children find themselves the most vulnerable sections of the population. Dealing with the question of definition, the delegates paid particular attention to the fact that in Africa 'it is difficult ... to consider children as a clearly differentiated age group. Where there is such differentiation, it varies according to the society concerned ... The term "children" according to international organisations means a population from 0–15 years of age' (p. 15). Those responsible for health pointed out to the conference the very high mortality and morbidity rates in Africa and paid particular attention to diarrhoeal diseases and the six major endemic diseases of tuberculosis, measles, poliomyelitis, whooping cough, tetanus and typhoid. In addition, serious malnutrition was seen to be a greater problem for children in Africa. Health facilities were judged to be far from providing a solution to the problem in most countries. They were, it was suggested, 'inadequate to meet population demand; because of the failure to adapt them, they are unable to provide the preventive primary care that children need' (p. 15).

Considering education and culture, the conference pointed to serious imbalances between rural and urban areas and the 'obvious inadequate adaptation of the African school'. Discussing non-formal education, the conference was clear about the relationship between this and child welfare:

Traditional education, disrupted by the numerous changes taking place and by unduly rapid and sudden modernisation, has to some extent lost its regulatory role. The break between past and present has occurred fairly quickly. The rights and duties associated with age groups in traditional society make for easy assimilation into the rural environment. The participation of children in the economic and social life of the community in rural areas is apt to be replaced in the towns by early employment, without proper pay, and sometimes by early prostitution [Inter-Parliamentary Union, 1983: 16].

Considerable attention was paid to the situation of mothers, and to the role of women in general. Acknowledging that the development of the child is closely connected with the living conditions of mothers, the conference emphasized that the higher the educational status of the mother, the higher the chance of survival of her children; the better the nutritional status the mother has, the better the physical and mental development potential of the young child; the less fatigued and harassed a mother is, the more likely she is to provide a healthy environment for her children. Delegates were told that in Africa 70 per cent of food production, 50 per cent of animal husbandry and 100 per cent of food preparation, household tasks, and the care of children are carried by women and girls. A clear link was stressed between the heavy workload of women, their health and the welfare of children.

The conference examined the 1959 'Declaration of the Rights of the Child' in the African context and concluded that targets for meeting even the most basic of these had 'only a relative practical value and cannot be realised or attained in the same way in the different countries' (p. 18). In policy terms, delegates formulated three questions which they felt should be asked of national policy for child welfare. First of all, what policy is there to protect children against premature death, morbidity and lack of adaptation? Second, what polices are there to train children and prepare them for life? Third, are there policies to help children become assimilated into adult society, to express themselves in it and to take part in its evolution? In its conclusions regarding policy priorities the conference quite clearly followed recent trends:

The solutions to these problems are to be found in the broad context of overall development ... [policy] cannot simply address what are termed the social services (education, health, social welfare, etc.) but should above all be directed towards the satisfaction of these and other essential needs [Inter-Parliamentary Union, 1983: 18].

In specific terms it was recommended that as top priority there should be a minimum of facilities to meet the essential needs of children, youths and women in the least privileged parts of rural and urban areas. These essential needs were seen to be access to clean drinking water, essential drugs, primary health care, education, sufficient and balanced food, decent housing and a healthy environment. In order to achieve these goals national efforts were called for which decentralized administration, utilized community resources through participation both in terms of defining needs and choosing means, and improving the condition of working women. Arguing strongly that as problems are interrelated, then policies and programmes must be complementary and not be introduced in a scattered and uncoordinated fashion, the conference pointed to the compartmentalization of actions and the excessive centralization of planning systems. Although most African

countries had planning systems, it was felt that in general
'national development policies do not yet contribute efficiently
to the protection of children and young people' (p. 19).
National commissions for children, youth and women were
recommended to prepare national policies for children to
monitor their implementation, co-ordinate research and
evaluate programmes. This conference was only one of very
many that have been held in different parts of the world in
recent years; it is typical of conferences of this kind. The
emphasis on interrelationship between issues is a common
theme, as too is the general thrust towards decentralized,
community-based programmes involving participation. That
the role of women was seen as central to any consideration of
child welfare is also a feature of more recent debate in this
area. In identifying a lack of nationally co-ordinated child
welfare policy in Africa, the conference again was typical of
those held in different parts of the world. Planning systems
have in general neglected the social dimensions of development, but even where these have been given serious attention,
this has most often been expressed in terms of narrow sectoral
policies. In relation to child welfare, as we have seen, the issues
and problems demand action across a whole range of sectors
and if this is to be effective, action must be co-ordinated and
complementary. For child welfare such effective co-ordination
is rare, with responsibility for children most commonly lying
with rather narrowly defined social-service-oriented government departments.

While co-ordinated polices and programmes are relatively
scarce at the national level, where resources are allocated and
actions taken, there has been much more progress at the level
of the international organizations. UNICEF, which celebrated
its fortieth anniversary in 1986, has been the focus of work on
children. It was a UNICEF-sponsored survey in 1961 which
mapped the needs of children in developing countries and
emphasized the interrelatedness of the problems and the need
for action on many fronts at once (Sicault, 1963). UNICEF
was closely involved during the 1960s in the evolution of basic
services strategies which attempted to mobilize community-
level resources in health, nutrition, education and women's
advancement. In the last decade and particularly in the 1980s,

UNICEF has been the leading force both in the documentation of the problems facing children, and also in terms of action for the improvement of their situation. Most especially in relation to basic health, UNICEF has been the leading force in the 'child survival and development revolution' (Black 1986). Chapter 4 looks at some aspects of that revolution.

4 Health

By far the greatest emergency facing the world's children today is the 'silent emergency' of frequent infection and widespread undernutrition—an emergency which kills well over a quarter of a million children every week ... In the past, child deaths on this scale have been regarded as acceptable because they have been perceived as inevitable. Today, that perception is simply out of date. In our times, advances in knowledge, and the social organisation to put that knowledge to use, have brought the silent emergency out from the cold of the inevitable and into the domain of the preventable [UNICEF, 1986: 1].

This chapter examines some aspects of health and development in relation to the welfare of children, and in particular young children. It is in four major parts. First, some aspects of the relationship between health and development in general will be considered and the emergence of Primary Health Care will be discussed. Second, the dimensions of child health problems in the poorest countries will be explored, with particular attention being paid to young children. Third, and the major part of the chapter, there is an explanation and discussion of the major elements in the UNICEF-led Child Survival and Development Revolution. This collection of health interventions has emerged over recent years as the major focus of child welfare activity. The fourth and final part of the chapter will discuss these medical interventions in the context of Primary Health Care, social policy, and development in general.

Over the past twenty years there has been a massive shift in the way that social polices for health in developing countries are discussed. The movement towards the adoption in the late 1970s in Primary Health Care and the effects of that on policy since then have been extensively discussed (MacPherson, 1982, 1987). In social policy terms, perhaps the most important single dimension of this shift was that health came to be seen as a dimension of development itself and not a matter of health service delivery. Both in terms of understanding patterns of illness and disease, and for the formulation of policies to combat these, health was seen to be inextricably tied in with patterns of social and economic change. One of the most important elements in the 'Alma Ata Declaration on Primary Health Care' in 1978 was this recognition. Health services, and even more important, policies and programmes which aimed to improve the state of health of majority populations, have to be seen in relation to national political, economic and social structures and the goals and objectives of development in general. Primary health care was offered essentially as an organizing concept, and the definition in the Alma Ata declaration was adopted in very many countries. Although putting considerable emphasis on the development of Primary Health Care services, the 1978 declaration and subsequent World Health Organisation publications have put equal emphasis on social, political and economic factors:

Primary Health Care ... reflects and evolves from the economic conditions and socio-cultural and political characteristics of the country and its communities ... [It] involves, in addition to the health sector, all related sectors and aspects of national and community development, in particular agriculture, animal husbandry, food, industry, education, housing, public work, communications, and other sectors; and demands the coordinated efforts of all those sectors; [it] requires and promotes maximum community and individual self-reliance and participation in planning, organisation, operation and control and Primary Health Care [World Health Organisation 1979: viiii–ix].

In locating health clearly within the context of development, and in emphasizing existing inequalities in the distribution of both resources and power, the Primary Health Care declaration must be seen in the context of debates on development planning taking place during the 1970s. There was in that period a considerable questioning of existing strategies and approaches to development. Much more emphasis on the extent and nature of poverty and open acknowledgement of the need for structural changes became the mark not just of academic literature but of the reports from international organizations such as the WHO, UNICEF and others. Together with this new public awareness of the nature of poverty, and to some extent of the social and economic dimensions of underdevelopment, was the associated conviction that approaches to planning in any one sector must necessarily involve the work of others. Thus, for health, there was very much more concern with linkages between health and what was going on outside the rather narrow confines of health services. The other significant dimension of work on health was that attention increasingly focused on the most impoverished populations, reflecting a more general emphasis on basic needs.

There was, from the beginning, serious questioning of the enthusiasm for Primary Health Care (MacPherson, 1982: 111–13). But in terms of the major international organizations, and for the great majority of Third World governments, Primary Health Care emerged in the late 1970s and early 1980s as the dominant approach in statements about health problems and health strategies. There was no doubt that the perceptions embodied in this new approach had clearly come out of a realization that existing health care systems had failed the majority of people in poor countries. In its concern for basic health needs it was part of a more general trend in perceptions of development; crude economic criteria were being displaced, to some degree, by social and distributional criteria. In the emergence of this new organization concept and the practical programmes for action which were drawn up on the basis of Primary Health Care, the experiences of particular countries were influential. During the 1970s Cuba, China and Tanzania were seen as providing dramatic evidence of the possibilities of basic level transformation in social conditions. In those countries attempts through social policy and social action to achieve very far-reaching social transformations had included health as part of overall national development and change. As Primary Health Care emerged as the dominant model for health policy in the late 1970s, its approach focused on basic health needs of the majority, attempts to integrate promotional, preventive and curative health, and in particular the use of low-level health personnel, coupled with a very heavy reliance on community participation. In seeking to build health policies and programmes on this basis, it was argued that although social, political and economic contexts were of major significance, both in determining the nature of health programmes and their likely outcomes, a great deal could be achieved in terms of improving health conditions for the poorest, whatever the context (World Health Organisation, 1981).

Before moving on to examine recent activities in relation to specific medical interventions in child health, it is important to emphasize the essential character of Primary Health Care as a concept. Underlining the present discussion is the conviction that Primary Health Care is part of a particular approach to development and not primarily a way of organizing health services, or a set of techniques for mobilizing communities. It is essentially a set of guiding principles concerned with a particular dimension of development as a whole; health is not simply a factor in the development process, but an essential element in development as a goal. Some of these points will be discussed further towards the ends of this chapter after an examination of aspects of child mortality and social policy responses.

CHILD MORTALITY

As we saw in Chapter 1, about 98 per cent of infant and child deaths are in the poorest countries. Table 4.1 shows the major causes of these. The deaths of children constitute one-third of all deaths for the whole world, and in the poorest countries over a half of all deaths. Despite very substantial falls in mortality rates over the last twenty-five years, these remain very high; the rates prevailing in the poorest countries of the world are now somewhat similar to those found in the poorest parts of the industrialized nations during the nineteenth century. It has been shown very clearly that the dramatic fall in infant and child mortality in the industrialized countries, which occurred particularly during the first half of the

all, makes it extremely dangerous to draw direct parallels between the experience of early industrialization in the rich countries and contemporary change in the poorest. So, it is not necessarily the case that economic development will bring social improvement for the majority of the poorest in the developing countries. But as the rest of this chapter will show, even if it were the case that such change would inevitably take place, it would necessarily be slow. The scale of child mortality and the suffering that it brings is so enormous as to demand action. Furthermore, there are very strong grounds indeed for believing that direct intervention of very specific kinds, which reduces child mortality dramatically, can form the focus of much more far-reaching and long-range social mobilization.

It is still widely believed that the health problems of children in developing countries are dominated by exotic tropical diseases and rare conditions. This is not so; most deaths occur in the very young, before the age of 5, and most of these deaths, as Table 4.1 shows, are from a very small group of relatively simple yet savage conditions. Up to 70 per cent of deaths are caused by diarrhoea, pneumonia and contagious infections—underlying very many of these is malnutrition. In many poor communities this combination of illnesses is so common as to be accepted as a normal and inevitable part of childhood. There are perhaps three-quarters of a billion episodes of acute diarrhoea in children under 5 years of age each year, of these 5 million result in death primarily because of dehydration. Evidence from many countries shows that morbidity rates are highest in the earliest period of life, particularly in the first two years, the most vulnerable group being young children from six to eleven months. In the same way, death rates are greatest in the under-1 and 1-year age groups. Evidence from Latin America showed diarrhoeal diseases to be responsible for nearly 30 per cent of all child deaths from all causes and 69 per cent of the deaths which were due to infectious diseases (Rohde, 1983a). Diarrhoea is the condition which kills most children, especially young children; the vast majority of those who suffer diarrhoea survive, but this huge toll of 5 million is taken every year. Diarrhoea is also a major factor in the onset of malnutrition and in worsening its effects. The child with diarrhoea loses appetite and is less able to absorb food. These effects are aggravated further by the common practice of withholding fluids and food, including breast milk, from the child. Malnutrition is of course in itself a major contributory cause to very many deaths associated with childhood diarrhoea.

The majority of other major killers of young children are immunizable diseases. Of these very many go unrecognized, not only because they may not be recorded. Whooping cough, for example, is estimated to cause 600,000 deaths every year but in many countries the official mortality statistics may show relatively few cases, with deaths being ascribed to respiratory infection, possibly pneumonia. Whooping cough (pertussis) has a low fatality rate, estimated at 1 per cent. But its incidence is very high indeed. Neonatal tetanus, on the other hand, which takes around 1 million children every year, has a very high fatality rate, about 85 per cent, and so although incidence is very much lower, at around fifteen per thousand births, deaths are very many. Again, very many deaths from neonatal tetanus are unreported.

In the West, measles has for many years been regarded as a relatively straightforward illness of childhood. Yet in the poorest countries it is the most serious of all the immunizable diseases, with more than 2 million children dying with measles every year. The incidence of measles is very high indeed, approaching 100 per cent, and the fatality rate is between 2 per cent and 8 per cent; but its importance may still not be recognized. Despite the fact that in epidemics mortality can be as high as 15 per cent, and death can occur long after acute illness, cases of measles may not be seen as such or counted as such. Essentially, this is because children with measles die of diarrhoea, pneumonia and malnutrition like so many others; but where the underlying cause is measles, intervention is possible.

In the industrialized countries low birth weight as a result of poor foetal growth occurs in less than 8 per cent of births, but up to 15 per cent of babies in the developing countries are classified as having low birth weight (less than 2,500 grammes). Table 4.2 shows that this incidence of low birth weight is by no means evenly spread. Mortality rates are very much higher among low birth rate babies, with those surviving very frequently remaining malnourished. As was noted above, diarrhoea is closely interrelated with undernutrition, but so too are many other illnesses. Especially in young children, illness contributes to lack of nutrition and this in turn makes the child vulnerable to more frequent infection with more severe consequences. Measles, whooping cough and tuberculosis all have very serious nutritional impact. In countries such as Bangladesh, where children may suffer diarrhoea-related illness for 10–15 per cent of the time, weight deficits may reach over 1 kilogram per year (Rohde, 1981).

Table 4.2: Low birth weight by region, 1986*

Region	%	Number (millions)
China and East Asia	6	1.3
Industrialized countries	7	1.3
West Asia	7	0.3
Central and South America	10	1.3
Africa	14	3.6
South-East Asia	17	2.0
South Asia	31	10.5

Source: Derived from UNICEF, 1986: 116.

*   Low birth weight—less than 2.5 kg (figures based on 1982 surveys updated for 1986 birth estimates only).

It is obvious that nutrition is a profoundly important factor in child survival. In stark contrast to the consequences of undernutrition and malnutrition, studies have shown that adequate nutrition has very dramatic effects on survival rates. Well-nourished children, even in poor areas, may have mortality rates which are only marginally greater than those in the industrialized countries, while in the same areas children who are malnourished are dying at rates which are ten or even twenty times higher (Kielmann and McCord, 1978; Chen *et al.*, 1980).

There are many other diseases and conditions which contribute to child mortality, but none of them have the impact of these major immunizable diseases. This group of conditions, closely linked with nutrition, and especially with diarrhoea, account for the great majority of deaths among children and especially young children. Attention is focused on these for this reason, but also because for these things there are readily available, easily understood and dramatically effective interventions. Table 4.3 gives some indication of the power of these interventions. It is with these that the next section of this chapter is concerned.

GOBI-FF

In the last few years, many UNICEF publications have come to use the mnemonic GOBI-FF to stand for the main elements of what UNICEF describes as a child health revolution: The elements are growth charts, oral rehydration therapy, breast-feeding and immunization. The additional elements are food supplements and family planning. As we saw earlier, present demographic and economic trends together suggest that the proportion of the world's children who will be living with inadequate food, water, health care and education will remain very much the same for the rest of this century. For very many of the poorest children, conditions are set to deteriorate. The absolute number of children living and growing up with malnutrition and ill-health will increase. In common with other international organisations concerned with child welfare and social development, UNICEF has argued for a number of years for development strategies in which organized communities and trained development workers are backed by organized services and international systems. It is argued that this is the only feasible way in which basic health care, clean water, sanitation and basic education can be brought to the great majority of the poorest populations. The relationship between such strategies and social policy have been discussed elsewhere (MacPherson, 1982; MacPherson and Midgley, 1987; Midgley *et al.*, 1986). Just as social development has increasingly focused on small-scale feasible actions within local communities, so scientific and technical attention has been directed at health interventions of relative simplicity. In relation to the medical problems already identified as causing

Table 4.3: Potential annual reduction in infant and child deaths

Disease	Deaths	Interventions	Effectiveness	Potential reduction
Immunizable diseases	3.3 million to 5 million	Vaccines	80–90%	3.5 million to 4.5 million
Pneumonia/respiratory infections	4 million	Pencillin	50%	2 million
Low birth weight/malnutrition	3 million	Maternal supplements Treat infections Contraception	30%	1 million
Diarrhoea	5 million	ORT	50–70%	2.5 million to 3.5 million
Deaths	17.0 million			Reduction: 10 million

Source: Rohde, 1983a: 51 (1980, WHO figures).

the most extensive child mortality, there has been significant scientific and technological progress in recent years. The most dramatic of these has been the recognition of the importance of oral rehydration.

ORAL REHYDRATION THERAPY: THE TASTE OF TEARS

The discovery that sodium transport and glucose transport are coupled in the small intestine so that glucose accelerates absorption of solute and water was potentially the most important medical advance this century [Editorial, *Lancet*, 1978].

The basis of oral rehydration therapy lies in the fact that a person with acute diarrhoea begins to lose water and essential salts from the onset of illness. Unless replaced, dehydration will begin, and thus prevention of dehydration is the most appropriate response to diarrhoea. Rehydration is necessary in order to replace accumulated deficits, but therapy must be continued in order to replace continuing abnormal losses due to diarrhoea and vomiting, and normal fluid losses due to respiration, sweating and urination, all of which are particularly high in infants.

Fluid replacement for the treatment of dehydration from diarrhoea was used as early as the mid-nineteenth century. But for very many years attempts to use such therapy employed intravenous techniques and saline solutions. Such approaches were costly, needing sophisticated equipment and highly trained workers. It was not until after the middle of the twentieth century that the concept of replacing fluid losses by mouth began to receive serious scientific attention. In the 1960s a major breakthrough was made with the successful use of an oral solution containing glucose and essential salts to treat cholera cases with very severe diarrhoea. A major part of the scientific explanation for success of oral rehydration therapy was that the presence of sugar (glucose) made absorption easier and this process was unimpaired even during acute episodes of diarrhoea. There are very many causes of diarrhoea, working in very different ways. But it is now clearly established that whatever the causative agent or the age of the person affected, oral rehydration solutions containing glucose and essential salts are absorbed, and replace both previous and continuing losses. Oral rehydration therapy does not stop diarrhoea, or cure disease, but the diarrhoea usually continues for only a limited time, and the effects of dehydration are considerably lessened or removed entirely. As experience has been accumulated in the use of oral rehydration it is now clear that there are different responses appropriate in different circumstances. First of all, to prevent dehydration, solutions can be used which are prepared from ingredients commonly found in the home. So-called 'household food solutions' and salt and sugar solutions are both home remedies of this kind. To correct dehydration which has already taken place, it has been found that more balanced and complete glucose salt solutions are necessary; oral rehydration salts of the kind recommended by WHO and UNICEF meet these requirements. It is only in very severe and very rare cases of extreme dehydration that intravenous therapy is necessary.

Clearly, the prevention of dehydration is to be preferred of all approaches. WHO and UNICEF policy in this area is that prevention should be intensively promoted and the use of home remedies at an early stage encouraged (WHO/UNICEF, 1983). The implications of this are very many, not only for the organization and delivery of health services but also for programmes which are based on community organization for health. The two groups of home remedies have different characteristics. The first, the so-called household food solutions, are things normally available and are appropriate in many cases for early treatment of acute diarrhoea. Often these are prepared from boiled water, thus increasing safety for drinking, and are frequently found to contain sodium, and sometimes potassium; both are components of prepared solutions. In addition, household food preparations are sources of glucose, in the form, for example, of starches, and these facilitate the absorption of salts. Two examples are rice water, very common in large areas of Asia, and soups. Of the latter, carrot soup, very frequently found in North Africa, is an excellent example of such a household food solution. There is considerable work already taking place to identify other appropriate fluids in different parts of the world.

The second kind of solution, consisting of salt and sugar, has been widely advocated as part of the early response to diarrhoea. White sugar is less effective than glucose, and the lack of potassium similarly reduces the usefulness of these solutions. A very large number of different recipes have so far been suggested and many ingenious methods have been devised to ensure that they are prepared in the right proportions. Although relatively simple, these do require health workers and others to be able to communicate both knowledge about the preparation of solutions and skills for recognition by parents of the advantages and limitations of these solutions. Clearly, another serious limitations of these approaches is that in the very poorest homes the ingredients may simply not be available; this puts further pressure on the need to find even more household food solutions which have adequate properties, but also directs attention to making available pre-prepared oral rehydration salts. In terms of prevention, then, it is now clearly established that very much can be achieved through the use of very simple and in many cases home-prepared oral rehydration solutions. Child diarrhoea also requires, along with oral rehydration, appropriate feeding both during and after attacks of diarrhoea. In many communities the response to diarrhoea is a withholding of both food and fluid in the mistaken belief that this will stop the diarrhoea and ease the suffering. In fact, withholding food and fluid increases dehydration and worsens the effects of the illness.

The treatment of dehydration requires a balanced glucose/salt solution; in the relatively short time in which this approach has been used considerable experience has been gained in the use of oral rehydration salts. UNICEF, with the WHO, began to recommend and make available packets of oral rehydration salts from 1971. From the beginning these salts were prepared as universal so that they could be used to treat dehydration resulting from diarrhoea of any cause and to maintain hydration during continuing illness. In order to have maximum effectiveness as a universal solution the WHO/UNICEF salts contain sodium chloride, sodium bicarbonate and potassium chloride as well as glucose; if unflavoured the resulting solution has a taste like tears, though a little less salty. Oral rehydration salts are relatively cheap; even the individually wrapped UNICEF packets cost less than 10 cents, and quantities bought in large amounts and distributed locally in plastic bags, paper or even in leaves cost as little as 2 to 3 cents. During the 1970s there was very much evidence of the powerful impact wrought by this simple and cheap therapy.

In hospitals and clinics it was found that well over 90 per cent of patients with acute diarrhoea, including infants, could be treated with oral rehydration salts alone. The costs of treatment are substantially reduced when salts are used. In many hospitals and health centres the number of admissions has been reduced by the use of salts and the number of deaths decreased. There appear to be very few side effects from oral rehydration salts.

Given its nature, oral rehydration therapy was seen to be extremely suitable for use in primary health care services, and beyond that in community programmes concerned with primary health care in a wider sense. There were a number of reasons for this. Even when salts were used from a hospital or health centre they necessarily involved parents (mothers) directly in the care of their children. Their use enabled health workers to communicate information, not just on oral rehydration therapy but on other aspects of health education, and in particular on diarrhoea prevention and nutrition. In terms of services in the community, it has been found that basic-level health workers and parents have accepted oral rehydration salts quite readily as a treatment for acute diarrhoea. Not least among the reasons for this is that the use of oral rehydration salts has decreased the number of deaths from diarrhoea by as much as 60 per cent in many communities (WHO/UNICEF, 1983).

In oral rehydration therapy we have a very dramatic example of a clearly understood therapeutic principle, the expression of which in practical action is straightforward. The implications for child welfare are profound; social policies which fail to take on board the potential of this scientific and technological breakthrough cannot be seriously addressing fundamental welfare issues. But there are very many problems in bringing the clearly demonstrated benefits of oral rehydration to the majority of poor children in developing countries:

To realise the potential of the oral rehydration therapy breakthrough, there
will have to be an equivalent 'social breakthrough' in making the knowledge
and the means of oral rehydration therapy available to the five hundred
million mothers and young children in the poorest areas of the developing
world [UNICEF, 1982: 8].

The problem now for oral rehydration is not a scientific or
technical one, nor even a medical one; there are very many
advances that are still being made with regard to the
composition of salts and the identification of home remedies,
and these are vital, but the problem is social. People
everywhere will use this therapy for the benefit of their
children once they have access to it and its usefulness has been
demonstrated. By the end of 1985, when oral rehydration salts
were available in virtually every part of the developing world,
it was estimated that only about 20 per cent of families knew
enough about the technique to be able to use it (UNICEF,
1985: 20). Access among the very poorest is worse than this.
There has been considerable activity related to oral
rehydration therapy and many countries have adopted this
approach enthusiastically. Perhaps one of the most remarkable aspects of this is the speed with which the therapy has
gained legitimacy with the medical profession (Chen, 1983:
101). At the beginning of 1985 campaigns had taken place in
more than twenty countries and during 1984 UNICEF had
supplied seventy-eight developing countries with approximately 65 million sachets of salts. By the end of 1975 forty-one
countries had begun large-scale production of salts; in 1985
total world production by developing countries was estimated
at 200 million packets (UNICEF, 1985: 20). There can be no
doubt of the widespread enthusiasm for this therapy, but the
practical problems of implementing policies to ensure its use
are severe. Chen argues that:

Oral rehydration is not a panacea. While recognising its importance, we
must avoid over-sell. Diarrhoea is only one—granted, important—disease
amongst several major health problems. Diarrhoea is both a symptom of
and a contributor to poverty and underdevelopment. Oral rehydration
therapy should not be used as an alternative or paliative to avoid addressing
the fundamental problems of poverty. Finally, choices must be made ... the
premium today is on pragmatism. What works? Approaches to oral
rehydration will necessarily vary between different communities in different
countries [Chen, 1983: 101].

Before looking more closely at some of the problems in implementation and the relationships between policies for oral rehydration and other policies for child welfare, a few examples of successful programmes will illustrate the potential of oral rehydration in practice.

ORAL REHYDRATION IN PRACTICE

China

A survey of the Shanghai county in China in 1979 showed that although diarrhoeal disease was common, deaths from dehydration were not (UNICEF, 1984: 38). At the time, the reasons for this were not clear and it contradicted the experience of most developing nations. In 1982 the Ministry of Health in China began working with UNICEF to promote maternal and child health. During the initial research for this project, a village barefoot doctor was asked how she would treat a child with diarrhoea. She mentioned a variety of treatments, one of which was instructing mothers to give a sugar and salt solution to the child. A much wider survey of barefoot doctors in China revealed that this practice was fairly widespread. In some cases, mothers already knew that they should give their children a sugar and salt solution to treat diarrhoeal disease; the reason for the rarity of deaths from dehydration was the use of oral rehydration therapy.

The origins of this were found to be in a programme which had almost been forgotten. In 1956, a severe epidemic of diarrhoeal disease had overwhelmed the children's hospitals in Beijing. Because doctors did not have the intravenous facilities to cope, they developed an oral treatment using tablets of sodium chloride and potassium chloride dissolved in water. Before giving this salty solution to their children, mothers routinely sweetened it, just as they traditionally sweeten all medicines, thus making an oral rehydration solution. Throughout the late 1950s and 1960s this sugar and salt solution was widely promoted in health education programmes. The technique was used in the following years by many mothers and barefoot doctors, while the hospitals reverted to using intravenous therapy. Today in China many mothers are using oral rehydration therapy without depending on the health services—the ultimate aim of the campaign to promote oral rehydration.

Uganda

In Uganda diarrhoeal diseases are a major health problem, causing high rates of infant mortality and contributing to malnutrition. However, attempts are being made to spread information about oral rehydration therapy (Bukenya, 1982: 3). One such programme was started at the Kasangati Health Centre which is attached to Makerere University Medical School, Kampala. The main aim of the programme was to educate as many mothers as possible in the hope that they would pass on the message to others. To achieve this, particular attention was given to training primary health workers who would work in the community. They were taught how to recognize the signs of dehydration, and particular emphasis was put on starting oral rehydration as soon as possible. The value of the mothers' participation and the need for their own involvement in practical demonstrations of oral rehydration was also recognized. Diarrhoea was explained to the mothers in terms they could understand. They were taught to start oral rehydration as soon as possible, how to recognize any serious symptoms, and also simple hygienic measures that could realistically be carried out in the home. Because prepackaged oral rehydration salts were not available at this time in Uganda, mothers were taught by demonstration how to prepare oral rehydration fluids from locally available materials, one main guideline being that the solution should not taste more salty than tears. Cases of dehydration have decreased markedly in this area of Uganda, and the key to the success of the programme was the participation of mothers in the treatment of their own children.

With over 60,000 children dying every year and half these deaths attributable to diarrhoea, the success of this project led to a national programme. The Control of Diarrhoeal Disease Project began in 1984 with the aim of reducing the use of intravenous therapy by 60 per cent in diarrhoea-related diseases by the use of oral rehydration. In the first year, 600,000 packets of salts were distributed. Considerable attention was paid to the education of health professionals; many of them were resistant to the use of oral rehydration in place of intravenous therapy. The salts are sold widely through commercial outlets as well as being distributed through health facilities. In 1985 they were judged to be expensive by those responsible for the programme, but planned production within Uganda was expected to reduce the cost. There was concern that commercial producers were flavouring and sweetening the salts to increase sales (Katumba, 1985).

Bangladesh
Bangladesh is the country where much of the pioneering work on oral rehydration therapy has been done. Even so, 10 per cent of all the children born in Bangladesh die before reaching the age of 5 from dehydration and malnutrition brought on by diarrhoea. The country would need to produce 90 million packets a year instead of today's 17 million to supply them to all mothers of young children. The majority of Bangladeshi women are illiterate so would not be able to read the instructions on the packets, health services only reach 20 per cent of the population, and although the packets are cheap, they are beyond the purchasing power of many poor families (Abed, 1983). The Bangladesh Rural Advancement Committee recognized that a therapy was needed which every household could afford, and devised a home-made solution *(lobon-gur)* containing ingredients which are available in nearly every home. A three-finger pinch of salt *(lobon)* and a four-finger scoop of molasses *(gur)* dissolved in half a *seer* of water—a familiar local measure of 467cc—make an oral rehydration mixture which has been shown to be very effective (Ellerbrock, 1981). Almost 1,000 oral rehydration workers have been trained to go from door to door in the villages, and the most striking feature of the programme is the individual teaching (Bhatia and Cutting, 1984: 3). Over 5 million mothers had half an hour of instruction with an oral rehydration worker, who introduces seven points explaining diarrhoea treatment. Mothers are taught that it is a mistake to stop giving food and drink to the child as this only increases the danger of dehydration. The worker shows the mother how to

prepare the *lobon-gur* solution and then watches as the mother makes up the solution herself. Surveys were conducted after a month to collect samples of the home-made oral rehydration solution and to ask mothers how many of the seven points they remember: 98 per cent of the mothers can prepare the home mix correctly, and over 90 per cent remember all, or almost all, of the seven points. As Abed suggests, the 'oral therapy extension programme is essentially a teaching programme. The most important aspect is face to face instruction' (Abed, 1983: 253).

However, many of the mothers who know how to make the oral rehydration mix do not use the technique when a child actually falls ill with diarrhoea. Usage rates varied from 8 per cent to 80 per cent. The Bangladesh Rural Advancement Committee concluded that oral rehydration needed more support from husbands and male community leaders, so talks were given to the village men and the traditional healers and leaders of the community. Although average usage rates have yet to rise above 60 per cent, the committee is confident that they will continue to grow, especially now that the technique is also being promoted by a media campaign using posters, leaflets, television and radio. By the end of the decade, the committee estimates that the teams of workers will have visited three-quarters of the households in the country (UNICEF, 1985: 50).

Haiti
Haiti has long been one of the poorest and least healthy countries in the Western hemisphere, and diarrhoea was known to be associated with approximately half of infant deaths with 40 per cent of deaths occurring in the under 5s (Rohde, 1983a: 4). Although oral rehydration therapy was introduced in the mid-1970s, it was neither widely accepted nor generally available to the public. Health professions would not believe that such a simple solution could be effective. In 1980 a Rehydration Unit was established in the University Hospital in Port-au-Prince; and the subsequent decline in case fatalities, from more than 30 per cent to less than 1 per cent, demonstrated the efficacy of oral rehydration therapy, compared to antibiotics and other anti-diarrhoeal

preparations which had previously been used. Mothers brought their children to receive treatment earlier, and their direct involvement in the child's care whilst in hospital led to early home use of oral rehydration therapy. Similar units were established in other hospitals. Diarrhoeal disease control was declared to be the national health priority, and all levels of the Health Ministry were called upon to focus efforts on universal implementation of oral rehydration.

Supplies of the prepackaged oral rehydration salts were manufactured in Haiti, and to ensure availability each of the 250 health establishments was encouraged to set up selling posts within the local community. Village stores, traditional healers, community leaders, police and army posts, teachers and volunteers were recruited to stock the salts, a painted sign and colourful poster marking the site of each post. Within a year there were over 2,000 community selling posts. The technique of oral rehydration was promoted in two main ways—through the media and through community involvement. In July 1983, the president initiated the publicity campaign in a nationally televised Oral Rehydration Day, and radio messages, coloured posters, brochures and leaflets were used to spread the message about oral rehydration therapy. Strong political support encouraged many members of the community to participate in the campaign, and many people were trained to administer the salts. Over 80 per cent of parents in the poorest areas of Port-au-Prince, and 30 per cent in the rural areas, had begun to use oral rehydration therapy by 1984 (UNICEF, 1985: 25). The technique has become standard treatment for diarrhoea at all levels of the health care system in Haiti.

Jamaica
The success of an experimental study using oral rehydration therapy for outpatients encouraged the Ministry of Health in Jamaica to set up a National Diarrhoeal Disease Programme in 1980 (Elliott, 1983: 3). The result has been a reduction in mortality and in the need both for admission to hospital and the use of intravenous fluids. Oral rehydration therapy has been integrated into the primary health care system. At the health centres, parents learn how to use oral rehydration salts

and how to recognize the signs of dehydration. They are given packets for further use at home, together with advice about the reintroduction of solid food. Pamphlets, posters and radio programmes reinforce the educational message. The Ministry of Health plans to improve the health information system to obtain more reliable data for use in evaluation and in policy-making about the appropriate use of oral rehydration at home. Communication between health workers and parents at health centres is recognized as being sometimes inadequate. Giving out the salts without proper instructions has been found to be inadequate and good advice about nutrition is also essential.

Egypt
Diarrhoeal diseases in Egypt's Nile Delta were killing one child in every twenty, and the 'Menoufia intervention' in 1979 aimed to reduce this (Grant, 1983: 14). Oral rehydration promoters visited 45,000 mothers in certain villages to explain where to get and how to use oral rehydration salts to prevent diarrhoeal dehydration. The organizers of the campaign expected it to cut the child death rate by more than a third. However, at the end of the first year, the death rate was the same as in villages untouched by the campaign. An explanation for this gradually emerged. In the treatment villages hardly any of the mothers had actually tried to use the oral rehydration salts in their own homes. The whole Menoufia intervention had rested on an educational campaign which failed. Questioned afterwards, most mothers admitted that they were so uncertain about when and how to use the salts that they either did not use them at all or used them in inadequate quantities or at inappropriate times. Also, neither the communities themselves nor the local doctors had been involved in the campaign. The result was that there was neither moral support nor practical help to encourage mothers to use oral rehydration therapy when their children became ill.

In 1980 there was a second attempt to introduce oral rehydration into two villages in the Nile Delta (UNICEF, 1983: 16). Advance study revealed vital constraints, for example, that the most common kind of drinking glass used in the villages held about 200 millilitres. Therefore smaller packets of salts were needed which could be easily measured. In both villages, sachets were made available in government health clinics and volunteers visited families to check on cases of diarrhoea and advise mothers on what to do about it. In one village sachets were also sold in every store and for a year the community was blitzed with information about how to stop diarrhoea from killing children, through meetings, talks and at festivals. At the end of the year, every mother in this village had heard about ORT and three-quarters of them knew how to use it properly. People's attitudes towards diarrhoea had been changed, and mothers knew how to treat their own children. When they were asked how diarrhoea should be treated, 87 per cent of mothers suggested ORT, as opposed to only 12 per cent in the villages where there had been no special promotion campaign. Most important of all, the number of child deaths was more than halved by the oral rehydration campaign.

Honduras
The government of Honduras aimed to produce oral rehydration therapy by the same methods which have put drinks like Coca-Cola into almost every village in the Third World—social marketing. The government enlisted the help of an experienced social marketing team, the American non-profit Academy for Educational Development (UNICEF, 1984: 52). The campaign, in 1981, aimed to promote Litrosol, the brand name of the locally manufactured packets of the WHO/UNICEF oral rehydration formula. Radio was selected as the main medium for reaching most mothers, and several 60-second oral rehydration advertisements were developed for use on thirty commercial radio networks. The advertisements were short and catchy and intended to compete with high-quality commercial advertisements. The oral rehydration theme song became nationally popular and almost three-quarters of all mothers knew the words. Follow-up announcements emphasized child care during diarrhoea, encouraged administration of Litrosol and stressed the importance of continuing breast-feeding during diarrhoea (Smith, 1983: 4). However, it was found that most mothers also needed a one-to-one demonstration of oral rehydration

therapy; trained village demonstrators flew a red heart flag, the symbol of the campaign, above their homes so that mothers knew where they could go to learn how to mix the solution. Less than a year after the campaign had begun, over 90 per cent of the population knew about Litrosol and almost 50 per cent had used it at least once. After eighteen months, a survey was carried out in the homes where a child had suffered from a diarrhoeal infection in the two weeks prior to the survey. Almost 40 per cent had been treated with oral rehydration therapy. Social marketing techniques, it is claimed, can be used to promote oral rehydration therapy, and are even more successful when complemented with individual instruction.

These examples of success demonstrate very clearly that the issue facing social policy is essentially one of implementation and not one of scientific and technical knowledge. As noted earlier, the value of oral rehydration has been recognized for some years as an effective and simple substitute for more costly therapies. But, as is the case with other health interventions which are not hospital based, there are very many questions concerning the organization of programmes for oral rehydration, and in particular the integration of such programmes into existing health systems. Closely linked with this are questions concerning the promotion of oral rehydration at the community level in ways which ensure that it is part of a genuine Primary Health Care movement.

Although diarrhoea is an extremely important component in childhood ill-health and mortality, it is only one component; there are very many diseases and other factors affecting the health of children. In relation to diarrhoea itself, although the use of oral rehydration has a dramatic impact on mortality, it is only one element in a strategy for dealing with the problem of diarrhoea. Thus, while there are no doubts regarding the value of the intervention, there are those who argue that its simplicity and effectiveness should not obscure the wider problems of diarrhoeal control. Even more important, it is argued, there are serious dangers for policy and for the development of primary health as a whole if techniques such as this are implemented alone, out of context with other policies and programmes. This will be discussed in more detail later. At this point it is useful to examine some of the issues related to the place of oral rehydration therapy within the whole range of policies directed at child welfare and social development.

Cole-King argues 'there are both good epidemiological arguments for linking ORT with other programmes, as well as organisation and logistic ones' (Cole-King, 1983: 104). The most significant epidemiological arguments have already been referred to. The most important are the links between diarrhoeal disease and malnutrition, links between these diseases and other common childhood diseases, and the significance above all of the relationship between these sets of factors. It is suggested that the model most fitting for understanding causation is not so much a chain but a net or web, and this net produces 'multiple synergisms—between different diseases, between the causal factors which contribute to the diseases, and between the interventions themselves—which argue most cogently for linked strategies' (Cole-King, 1983: 105).

In organizational terms the arguments are essentially against vertical programmes which concentrate on specific interventions. Many of these programmes are justified on the grounds that a single concentrated effort can avoid the inefficiency of management and lack of control which may be seen as characteristic of existing services, or of programmes which attempt action on a number of fronts at once. But evidence from many poor countries shows quite clearly that intensive control programmes, many of them initially successful, have failed in the long run to contain specific diseases. Resurgence of particular diseases has been found where an infrastructure to sustain the efforts of the concentrated campaign is lacking. With severe restrictions on available resources the introduction of new programmes may, at the extreme, destroy existing health efforts in other fields. The practical problems of implementing large-scale programmes, and of integrating these with other development efforts, should not be underestimated.

The relationship between interventions such as oral rehydration and the drive for Primary Health Care is complex and difficult. As Cole-King points out, an argument for programmes such as oral rehydration therapy is that the poorest countries cannot wait for a primary health care system to be established, when there are feasible and dramatically effective low-cost technologies available. But, as she argues, Primary Health Care has made tremendous progress in recent years and one of the most serious problems facing those involved in its growth and development is that of overload. It has been pointed out very many times that a great deal is expected and demanded of community health workers in particular.

The need to establish priorities is clear. There are precedents for national and even international priorities in health policies and goals, but these need to be matched with community felt needs and local epidemiology, and not merely imposed [Cole-King, 1983: 107].

Both in planning terms and in relation to the management and organization of programmes, interventions such as oral rehydration present enormous possibilities but also very many serious difficulties. But it is important to note that the problems are not simply those of planning or management; the most serious objection to single disease programmes is that people find them unacceptable. Except in the very short run, what people expect are health programmes which respond to the total health needs of themselves and their children. The concept of Primary Health Care embodies, at its very heart an integrated, complete, approach to health. It is surely incompatible with primary health care as part of an approach to social development, that different aspects of health should be seen as demanding separate organizations, separate staff and separate strategies. Any community which is concerned with health, and where the mortality of children is seriously affected by diarrhoea, will want to include oral rehydration among the responses that it makes to the health problems it faces. The essential issue is how this therapy, and others, can be integrated with approaches to health in general and health programmes for children in particular.

In terms of implementation, the experiences of a number of countries suggest a variety of obstacles to success. Among the most important of these has been a lack of infrastructure for the implementation of oral rehydration programmes; inadequate health education campaigns and associated teaching methods; deficient referral arrangements for children needing more than home treatment; negative attitudes of health workers; and the vested interests of commercial organizations.

Both the positive arguments derived from the essential nature of oral rehydration, and the negative ones from the failure of many programmes, point to the Primary Health Care approach as being the most likely to succeed. If health workers, or members of the community with health training, preferably female, make regular home visits, then oral rehydration can be one item in the advice and assistance given in response to the priority concerns of people themselves. The effectiveness of oral rehydration therapy will in the long run be determined by the same factors that affect the success of Primary Health Care at community level. The more such interventions are linked with other action, for example on water supply and nutrition, the more successful and effective they will be. There is potentially some tension between the technically based single issue intervention programme and the drive for Primary Health Care as part of a community-based approach to social development. This issue will be returned to after some discussion of other specific interventions.

IMMUNIZATION

Parents empowered—and blessed—by the knowledge that their children need no longer die from diarrhoeal dehydration, or from vaccine-preventable diseases, do not indulge in schoolmen controversies about the theological niceties of development. If their children are protected against preventable deaths, their lives have 'developed' [Vittachi, 1985: 31].

Every minute eight children under the age of 5 die in the developing countries because of one of six communicable diseases. These deaths are unnecessary; in the industrialized countries these diseases—measles, polio, whooping cough, diphtheria, tetanus and tuberculosis—have been virtually obliterated by immunization. It is this basic truth which lies behind the major effort currently being put into the achievement of universal child immunization by 1990

(UNICEF, 1986). These six diseases kill about 5 million children every year and cripple, blind or cause mental damage to another 5 million (World Health Organisation, 1981). Among poor children in developing countries high incidence of these diseases is closely linked to poverty; nutritional status, housing, access to water and to health facilities are all of major importance. Immunization programmes have been carried out in very many developing countries over many years, but coverage remained very low, particularly among the poorest children. Immunization rates were very much higher in urban than in rural areas, but overall remained at less than 25 per cent in very many countries. The World Health Organisation programme on immunization (EPI) was launched in 1974 to cover the six diseases. To some extent this was linked to the successful eradication of smallpox, the last case occurring in Somalia in 1977. In order that the specific problems of immunization can be understood in relation to child welfare policies as whole, it is necessary to outline some features of these immunizable diseases.

Measles is highly contagious and commonly contracted after the age of six months by children not vaccinated. For at least the first six months infants are protected if their mothers had measles as children. In the poor countries measles is a very serious disease; it causes fever, diarrhoea and other complications, affecting children particularly during the weaning period when they are often malnourished as a result of changing from breast milk to feeding based on an adult diet. Vaccination is recommended from the age of nine months in developing countries, to avoid the high rate of very serious cases in unvaccinated children. The measles vaccine most commonly used is sensitive to heat and deteriorates quite easily. Without immunization virtually 100 per cent of children in poor countries will contract measles; complications occur in about 30 per cent of all cases, the most serious leading to pneumonia, blindness and deafness. The worst effects are found among malnourished children, with mortality rates of over 10 per cent. Measles itself is a significant cause of malnutrition and diarrhoea; it is estimated that overall about 3 per cent of children who catch measles will die from it or from its complications.

Whooping cough (pertussis) is again highly contagious and affects young children much more severely; about two-thirds of deaths are of children less than 1 year old. Vaccination is therefore required from the age of about eight weeks and at least three doses of vaccine are required over a period of at least four weeks. In developing countries, the World Health Organisation estimates suggest that four-fifths of unvaccinated children contract whooping cough, but only 50 per cent show the typical signs of the disease. Thus only half of the cases will be attributed to their real cause.

Tetanus is not contagious but results from infection through wounds. Incidence is closely related to environmental conditions and death occurs in about half of all cases—but virtually all cases occurring under 2 years of age are fatal. The incidence of tetanus is particularly high in rural areas where contacts between humans and animals are frequent and close, and tetanus vaccination relatively rare. Neonatal tetanus is particularly high where the physical conditions of child birth are poor. Deaths from neonatal tetanus can be prevented by vaccinating pregnant women who develop an immunity which they transmit to their infants, and by improving the conditions of childbirth. Tetanus immunization is remarkably effective. In the US army there were thirteen cases of tetanus for every 1,000 men wounded during the First World War, but only twelve cases out of 2.7 million wounded men during the Second World War. Six of these twelve had not been vaccinated.

Poliomyelitis is frequently referred to as infantile paralysis. It causes permanent damage, retards growth and commonly results in serious disability. Where there is a low vaccination coverage, incidence can be between twenty to thirty per 100,000 inhabitants. The oral and injectable vaccines are extremely effective.

Tuberculosis is both infectious and contagious, being transmitted from one person to another in many cases. Most of the nearly 3 million annual deaths are in developing countries where the disease is endemic in the poorest areas. Incidence is closely related to poverty and lack of health care. It is always severe but especially dangerous for children; it is recognized that immunization is particularly valuable for children living in poor conditions. Immunization is by injection.

Diphtheria is endemic in developing countries, among non-immunized populations. It particularly affects children under 5, infants being protected by anti-bodies transmitted by their mothers until the age of six months.

In recent years there have been significant advances in vaccine production. In particular, the stability of vaccines has been improved. During the 1960s and 1970s the heat sensitivity of vaccines was a major source of difficulty; since 1980 measles vaccine for example can be stored at 37°C for a week. This improvement is dramatic, as the problems of maintaining the 'cold chain' are enormous.

The case for immunization is very clear, but the logistics of delivering the service, and the relationship between immuniza-tion programmes and other aspects of Primary Health Care are much more complex. Table 4.4 gives data on the proportions of pregnant women and very young children covered by immunization. Comparisons with industrialized countries are difficult in this instance, because of course for conditions such as tetanus very low rates of incidence in richer countries means a much lower need for protection. It is clear, however, that in terms of immunization coverage, the poorest regions of the world are the worst served; these are the areas in which the poorest children live, those with the very highest risks from these diseases.

There are special difficulties with the delivery of immunization services. Transportation, refrigeration, scattered and illiterate populations, all compound the problem of delivery which is in itself complicated. Only certain vaccines can be combined, some must be given at birth, some to pregnant mothers, others require repeat doses over a period of time. Achieving successful immunization is made more difficult by the fact that innoculation may result in the child suffering a temporary fever or other symptoms which will make parents reluctant to continue immunization. This again underlines the need not just for education but for involved participation so that parents and communities are both informed and motivated regarding the benefits of programmes such as immunizations. Technological advances are being made as noted earlier and

Table 4.4: Immunization coverage of pregnant women and twelve-month-old children, by region, 1984-5[a]

Region	Vaccine coverage (%)				
	BCG	DPT	Polio	Measles	Tetanus
Africa N. of Sahara	66	50	55	46	10
Africa S. of Sahara	36	26	25	31	15
Cent. and S. America[b]	55	54	66	64	5
East Asia (ex. China)	87	78	83	35	5
South-East Asia	51	22	21	14	19
South Asia	53	43	32	5	25
West Asia	36	56	57	56	8
(Industrialized countries)	(58)	(62)	(66)	(76)	(—)

Source: Derived from UNICEF, 1986: 118, based on UNICEF and WHO estimates.
Notes:
(a)   Latest data available for each country.
(b)   Fifteen countries, Brazil and Mexico.

together with very much increased number of trained health staff, these make the practical problems of delivery more manageable. With the exception of heat-stable measles vaccine, the most significant advances in recent years have not been in technology itself but in terms of organizational capacity and in particular the training of health workers. In 1985 the director of the World Health Organisation's immunization programme argued that the supply of vaccine, and related equipment, was no longer a problem. Any country wishing to implement immunization policies, could obtain supplies. In common with other organizations in this field, in the mid-1980s the World Health Organisation put emphasis on 'demand':

For a mother in the developing world, getting a child immunized usually means giving up half a day's work and wages, travelling on foot or by bus carrying at least one young child, queueing in the sun for perhaps an hour or more, getting back home to catch up on the domestic chores, putting up with the usual slight fever and crying which keeps the family awake at night, and justifying to her husband and his mother why all this lost time and money is necessary on three or four separate occasions for a child who is not even sick [UNICEF, 1986: 51].

Making vaccination available at reasonable times and

places is important, but overcoming the very serious rates of drop-out from immunization programmes requires much more far-reaching social action. It is argued that mobilizing demand for immunization services, if taken together with political commitment and the use of a wide range of government and non-government agencies, can bring major success. In essence it is claimed that countries must mobilize all possible delivery and communication resources. The example of Burkina Faso is one of the most dramatic.

Vaccination Commando in Burkina Faso

Burkina Faso (formerly known as Upper Volta) is one of the poorest countries in the world. It has a population of about 7 million, 4.5 million of whom are under 16, with over 1 million under 5 years old. Over 90 per cent of the population live in rural areas and the under-5 mortality rate in 1985 was 245 per thousand. In 1984 the country had less than 200 doctors and only half of the very scattered rural villages had health services of any kind. The literacy rate is under 10 per cent, life expectancy at birth well under 40 in rural areas and there are no nation-wide newspapers or television networks. The reported successes of the immunization campaign are remarkable in themselves, but are startling in this context; some 2 million children were immunized at the end of 1984 against measles, meningitis and yellow fever (Burkina Faso, Ministry of Health, 1985).

Measles has always been extremely serious in Burkina Faso but mass campaigns for immunization in the early 1960s had little impact because the coverage achieved was limited. Linked with the world-wide WHO programme, an expanded programme of immunization was introduced in 1980 to be implemented through health centres and mobile teams. It began in the two largest towns and a few provinces. In 1982 an intensive simplified immunization programme began in one province; this achieved extremely high coverage. Different implementation strategies produced very great differences between provinces and between rural and urban areas. Geographical coverage remained very low, however, at around 10 per cent, virtually all of which had been achieved through mobile teams. The 1984 campaign was designed as a rapid, effective operation of short duration; it focused on easily administered single-dose vaccines against three priority diseases—measles, yellow fever and meningitis. The major stated objectives of the campaign were first to avert future epidemics particularly of measles and yellow fever and also to accelerate geographical immunization coverage since the limited coverage of existing programmes had had little impact on morbidity. Measles vaccine was to be administered to all children aged nine months to 6 years, and the meningitis and yellow fever vaccines to all children aged 1 to 14 years. If successful, this operation would allow the continuing immunization programmes to be focused on new-born children and infants: At the same time, the campaign was designed, through a process of social mobilisation, to create awareness by the population of the need to immunize all their children, a prerequisite for the acceleration of the existing EPI' (Burkina Faso, 1985: 306).

The campaign involved very large numbers of people; more than 100,000 were working full-time for up to six weeks. Most of those involved were existing health staff whose regular activities were postponed or carried out at other times. It is reported that the most spectacular aspect of the operation was the 'sensitization and mobilization of the people':

In order to carry out Vaccination Commando it was necessary to motivate, educate, mobilize and inform a population that was largely illiterate and located in dispersed villages not easily accessible by road, and sometimes beyond the reach of the press and radio. There was early and continuing recognition of the importance of a co-ordinated and intensive approach to communication activities within the campaign. The strategy adopted was based on local, person-to-person contact, simple thematic messages and the use of theatre. This aspect of the campaign extended through all of its phases—planning, resource mobilization, execution, and follow-up [Burkina Faso, 1985: 317].

In 1985 an analysis was made of the campaign coverage. Some 5.9 million doses of vaccine were administered, and it was estimated that about 2 million children in the target populations received at least one vaccination. About 90 per cent of the vaccinations were given in rural areas; overall 75 per cent or more of the target populations for the three diseases were reached by the campaign. As evidence of significant reductions in morbidity and mortality it is estimated that between 350,000 and 500,000 cases of measles may have been prevented among children aged nine months to 6 years.

There is an important and instructive relationship between this immunization campaign and the development of primary health care in Burkina Faso. Building on the gains in co-ordination and social mobilization, the country intends to extend primary health care services throughout the rural areas under the slogan 'One Village, One Health Post'. Mass campaigns, similar to that used for immunization, are planned to mobilize commitment and resources; at the village level, health posts are to be staffed by volunteer health workers appointed by village committees and supported by the community. Each primary health post is to have two community health workers, a village health worker and a traditional birth attendant. These workers will have important, specific medical tasks, but it is claimed their most important role will lie in sensitization of the community and promotion of new practices in nutrition and hygiene. All village-level health workers are to be remunerated by the village, and the Ministry of Health will provide only training and supervision (Burkina Faso, 1985: 326).

As with oral rehydration therapy, concern is frequently expressed that immunization campaigns can act as a substitute for and a diversion from the less spectacular and visible work of achieving Primary Health Care. But there is evidence from many campaigns, such as that in Burkina Faso, that they are successful in themselves very largely to the extent of their achievements in social mobilization. The involvement of large numbers of people in such campaigns, with attention focused on health and positive actions which might be taken to safeguard children, can serve as an important part of the development of Primary Health Care.

GROWTH MONITORING

Another major element in strategies to improve the health of children, particularly young children, is the mass use of growth monitoring. Focused especially on the development of child growth charts kept by mothers in their own homes, considerable attention has been put in recent years on the development of techniques associated with growth monitoring (Tremlett *et al.*, 1983). Monitoring the weight gains of young children, in conjunction with other information on their health, can be a very powerful tool in the detection of illness and in particular of malnutrition. Almost all child malnutrition is invisible, even to mothers. As was noted earlier, consistent undernutrition linked with successive illness and diarrhoea can retard growth over weeks and months, but may do so in insidious ways that go unnoticed even by parents. Properly designed and produced growth charts, on which regular weights can be entered by the mother herself, may make malnutrition visible at the point where most can be done. It is in many cases clear that child malnutrition is caused not just by a lack of food in the family but by the invisibility of the problem. This is one reason why making the problem visible can reduce the incidence and severity of child malnutrition. A child who has recently had measles or suffered diarrhoea, for example, may fail to gain weight from one weighing to the next. A reaction to this is likely to be that the child will be given more food or fed more frequently.

Figure 4.1 shows a common pattern for the growth of a poor child in the developing countries. In the very early months breast-feeding keeps the infant growing normally, but after that, when weaning begins and outside contacts increase, malnutrition and infection linked with each other begin to affect the child's growth. With each successive illness—each possibly relatively minor in itself—wiping out the small gains previously made, the child is constantly vulnerable. In this example, between six months and three years the child has gained only 1 kg. If the mother can see this problem on a clear and well-explained chart which she has in her own home, then there is some chance that progress would have been better. The significance of breast-feeding, for example, is very clear. Immunization and oral rehydration therapy could both have had a very dramatic impact in this case, where there have been approximately sixteen weight losses from infectious illnesses and diarrhoea over three years.

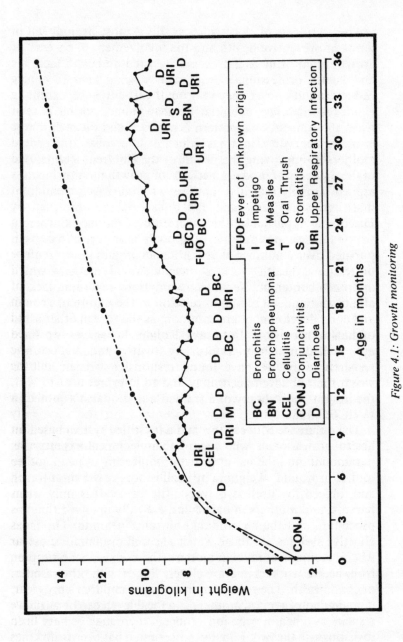

Figure 4.1: Growth monitoring

The usefulness of charts such as this is most strongly felt in terms of preventive health and the involvement of parents. If growth monitoring as a process is centred on health facilities and health professionals, with charts being kept in clinics rather than in homes, they may be of very little use, except as clinic records. The potential of growth monitoring is seen when the conventional pattern is reversed and the technology is made accessible in ways which will involve and enable mothers in improving the health of the children. Rohde, one of the pioneers of modern methods of growth monitoring, has argued strongly that it is mothers who must weigh children, mark growth charts and make use of the information. Discussing in particular the experience of Indonesia, where a very extensive programme of growth monitoring has been pursued over a number of years, Rohde argues that too often professional health workers have views of mothers which approach contempt. Negative assumptions regarding lack of ability and understanding in relation to the nature of growth and child development are common, as they are in other areas of health provision. But, says Rohde, 'whenever we have approached mothers in a culturally sensitive and intellectually respectful way, we have found responsive women able to weigh their children accurately and to interpret growth with the insight and subtlety of a trained nutritionalist' (quoted in UNICEF, 1986: 77).

The difference between this and a mystified system based on health professionals who regard their technical expertise as paramount, and the use of growth monitoring as just another tool, is profound. Weighing by itself is not growth monitoring and, indeed, by itself is of very little value. It is only when parents, and mothers in particular, are fully involved that the procedure and the records take on any meaning. The most effective systems are those which are well organized, close to where people live, involve mothers themselves, have support from health workers and are closely linked with other aspects of child health. The regular monitoring of children's progress, if it genuinely involves mothers at a local level, can be as much a social as a health occasion—indeed, there may be very little to distinguish the two. Equally important, it has been found that such approaches to growth monitoring have had important consequences for the Primary Health Care effort as a whole:

Furthermore, village based growth monitoring activities 'pull' Primary Health Care out of the health facilities and into the community itself. Villagers have begun to demand services at the monthly weighing rallies, asking for immunization, ORT, de-worming, contraceptive re-supply, vitamin A and simple curative care in the village. There, it becomes relevant, demand-responsive, and achieves high coverage of the most needy population—what Primary Health Care was meant to be [Rohde, quoted in UNICEF, 1986: 77].

Other aspects of the relationship between growth monitoring techniques and the community are of vital importance. Lovel *et al.* (1984) report on a research study in Ghana which investigated the attitudes and behaviour of mothers, health workers and other community members concerning child growth and development. In rural Ghana, as in all other communities in developing countries, mothers and fathers and other relatives, neighbours and friends, have always watched children growing and noted whether they were developing well or failing to thrive. In these communities, just as in similar communities in the rich countries, reasons for growth or lack of growth are seen and responded to. But 'this pool of community knowledge and experience has been largely ignored in the past by planners of child nutrition services and by those involved in the promotion of growth charts' (Lovel *et al.*, 1984, 276). It is not just, as was noted earlier, that the nature and benefits of growth charts and growth monitoring need to be sensitively conveyed to mothers and that they should be enabled to use these devices; there must be traffic in the opposite direction. The so-called 'modern approaches' followed by organized health services are rooted in Western conceptions of health and disease. In practice, this very frequently means that local beliefs and behaviour patterns are not just seen as irrelevant, but may in general be regarded as harmful. In contrast to interventions such as immunization, growth charts and growth monitoring are long-term devices which demand involvement of parents in the health of their children. If they are unrelated to the health perceptions of the communities in which they are used, they will be relatively useless. Health workers must learn how people in the communities they serve measure growth; the chart can be used as a basis for this learning and for discussion on child care. It is the growth chart itself which is the new device; growth monitoring itself has always and everywhere been practised. The technology of the growth chart can enable more accurate monitoring of growth and, by bringing together a number of different pieces of information which may be used in the context of regular health monitoring and treatment, can be tremendously valuable.

A survey in Ghana, carried out in a subsistence farming region in 1983, where 27 per cent of children attending clinics were below 80 per cent of the standard weight for age, confirmed the necessity of understanding existing concepts and concerns regarding child growth. Very many indicators were used by mothers and other relatives in relation to child growth; some of these were physical, others related to behaviour. The major advantage of growth charts, using weight-for-age, was seen to lie first in its greater precision but also in its ability to alert mothers to early onset of malnutrition or sickness. But as the Ghana study points out, further research on the sensitivity of traditional indicators is necessary both so that health workers can improve their understanding, and so that these methods may be integrated with the growth chart approach. Behaviour changes probably take place even before changes in weight; mothers may very often see that something is wrong before they or health workers find weight loss. A joint approach to growth monitoring is needed which integrates traditional and modern approaches, bringing together the observations and measurements made by both mothers and health workers. In this area of rural Ghana, mothers bringing their children to clinics saw growth charts as objects of value. As well as taking it regularly to the clinic, many used it at home as a reference. Overall, in excess of 50 per cent of the clinic mothers demonstrated understanding of the chart, in that they could interpret the meaning of the dots, lines and the child's weight curve. Understanding, not surprisingly, was linked with the level of formal education, but even among those with no formal schooling, over 40 per cent showed some understanding of the chart. This underlines yet again the vital importance of female literacy that has been pointed to so many times.

Yet again the use of a specific technical intervention in practice quite clearly demonstrates that the social dimensions of Primary Health Care are of vital significance. In this case we have a relatively sophisticated piece of technology, in the form of the chart itself and its contents, which can be made comprehensible and accessible to all parents. But the success of the intervention cannot simply be seen in terms of 'implementation rates, coverage rates, or acceptance rates'. Growth monitoring, as the Ghana study demonstrates, is an inherent and fundamental part of bringing up children everywhere. The value of the growth chart technology lies in its relationship to the development of Primary Health Care as a whole, and in exploring this relationship the vital boundary between organized health services and primary health care from the community is yet again exposed as a major focus of concern:

Health workers tend to refer to professional concepts and standards in monitoring growth and in educating mothers. In discussing a child's progress with the mother, more health workers need to view the child through the mother's eyes and to place greater emphasis on questions of behaviour, activity level, mood changes and other customary indicators that mothers regularly use to monitor the child's well being [Lovel et al., 1984: 289].

THE PROMOTION OF BREAST-FEEDING

As has been noted several times, the health and survival of infants and young children is profoundly affected by the patterns of their feeding. For young infants, breast-feeding is of dramatic importance. As we have seen, the young child gains both sound nutrition and protection against a number of specific diseases from breast milk. Breast-feeding has declined steeply in poor countries and considerable efforts are now being put into attempts to reverse this trend from breast-feeding to bottle-feeding. The problem is complex, involving not just efforts to improve the nutrition of mothers, persuading them also that breast-feeding is best, but also attempting to change medical attitudes and hospital practices.

In addition to these efforts, there have also been concerted actions aimed at controlling irresponsible promotion and marketing of artificial infant formulas (Chetley, 1984). In the rich countries breast-feeding, after a steep decline, has increased again in recent years; breast milk is the best food for young infants in any society. But for the very poorest children in developing countries the advantages of breast-feeding over bottle-feeding are so enormous as to make the difference between life and death. The World Health Organisation code on the marketing of artificial milk indicates the profound difficulty of the relationship between companies selling these products and those consuming them (Fig. 4.2). Low rates of female literacy mean that instructions on packets and tins of formula may go unheeded. But even where the instructions are understood, the irresistible force of poverty most often means that quantities of artificial milk used are less that they should be and it may be used for less time than it should be. In poor communities, boiling water every four hours may be a complicated and expensive enterprise. The sterilizing of equipment is rarely possible and the water itself may be unsafe. In many millions of cases poor mothers are persuaded not to breast-feed, or to abandon breast-feeding and to use artificial milk instead. They are being persuaded to spend a large proportion of small incomes to expose their children to the risk of malnutrition, infection and illness. In Brazil a study in 1980 found that among the infant children of poor parents, babies fed on artificial milk were between three and four times more likely to be malnourished (Mattai, 1983). In Egypt, a study of bottle-feeding showed the risk of infant deaths to be five times greater among children fed this way; in Chile the World Health Organisation reported that babies bottle-fed for the first three months of life were three to four times more likely to die than those who had been exclusively breast-fed; in India, bottle-fed babies have been found to suffer from twice as many respiratory infections and three times as many episodes of diarrhoea (UNICEF, 1983).

Attempts to halt the trend to bottle-feeding and to promote breast-feeding are very greatly hindered by attitudes within the health services themselves. Mattai notes that in Brazil 'doctors and public health personnel were generally indifferent to

The International Code places control on inappropriate marketing in two ways: Identifying improper practices that should be eliminated and identifying potentially harmful practices which should only take place under restricted conditions.

Practices to be eliminated:
— Direct consumer promotion including advertising, gifts and free samples.
— Any contact between company marketing personnel (such as 'mothercraft nurses') and pregnant women or mothers.
— Posters, placards and the like within health-care facilities.
— Gifts to health workers.
— Bonuses related to sales of the products.
— Pictures of infants on labels.

Practices that require restrictions:
— Information to families, health workers or on labels shall include the superiority and nutritional benefits of breast-feeding and the health hazards of unnecessary or improper use of artificial milk.
— Governments ultimately have the responsibility for ensuring that information is objective and consistent with the Code.
— Health workers may only receive samples for professional examination and research.
— Fellowships, grants, travel allowances and the like to health workers should be disclosed.
— Donated formula supplies should only be used for infants who have to be fed on artificial milk and should continue for the duration of that infant's need.
— Donations of materials and equipment may bear a company name or logo, but may not advertise specific brand names.

Figure 4.2: Features of the International Code of Marketing of Breast-Milk Substitutes (World Health Organisation, 1981)

breast feeding and inadequately informed on the subject'
(Mattai, 1983: 227). Clavano reports on a successful effort to
change both attitudes and practices within formal health
services (Clavano 1983). As she points out, one of the main
reasons why so many women abandon breast-feeding is that
the hospitals themselves encourage this; another is the
promotion of artificial milk by commercial companies and in
particular the distribution of free samples in hospital and
health centres. Baguio General Hospital is in the north of the
Philippines and in common with other hospitals in that
country, and other poor countries, new-born babies were
separated from their mothers at birth, put into nurseries and
first given powdered cow's milk very soon after birth. At the
end of 1974 there was a dramatic shift in policy and practice at
the hospital, which admits between 2,200 and 2,500 babies
every year. Standard procedures were changed and artificial
feeding completely phased out. Infants are now only separated
from their mothers in extreme circumstances. The policy
produced dramatic results and underlined very clearly the
enormous potential of breast-feeding in comparison to
artificial feeding. Death rates and infection rates were
compared for the two years before the policy change and the
two years following. The results showed dramatic and
significant correlation between breast-feeding and decreased
death and illness in infants. The incidence of diarrhoea
dropped from 27.0 cases per thousand to only 1.5; sixty-four
babies had died during the first two years, when bottle-feeding
was the predominant form, only three died during the second
period. Of the sixty-seven babies who died over four years,
sixty-four had been bottle-fed (Clavano, 1983: 90). The
Baguio success was dramatic but was restricted initially to one
hospital; such dramatic changes of policy and practice are
extremely difficult to translate into national and international
terms.

Papua New Guinea provides an example of national action
which has achieved considerable success in containing and
even halting the spread of artificial feeding. Although rates of
perinatal mortality are quite high in many areas of the
country, nutrition is not a major problem for the first six
months of infancy. It is still the case that cultural patterns

supporting successful breast-feeding, often for quite extended periods and allowing infants to feed on demand, have been maintained (Townsend, 1985). But after independence in 1975, there was increasing concern both about malnutrition and diarrhoeal disease among young children in the capital, Port Moresby. Between 1964 and 1974 the percentage of mothers leaving the general hospital breast-feeding their babies had fallen from 94 per cent to 78 per cent, and in 1975 it was found that 35 per cent of babies in Port Moresby were being artificially fed and over two-thirds of them were found to be malnourished. At the same time, only one-quarter of breast-fed babies were seriously underweight (Lambert, 1978). In the late 1960s action was begun to halt the decline in breast-feeding and to prevent the use of artificial milk from spreading to the rural areas. Advertisements for artificial milk were banned and some education campaigns on the advantages of breast-feeding were mounted. But it was soon clear that the sales of artificial milk were hardly affected by these measures and attempts to persuade those selling artificial milk and feeding bottles were having little or no effect.

In 1977 legislation was passed which made the supply of baby-feeding bottles, teats and dummies illegal, except on prescription. In principle, before health workers sign prescriptions, they are required by law to ensure that there is a good reason for changing to artificial milk and that mothers know how to mix the formula and sterilize the equipment. Indications are that the legislation has been successful in its intentions. In 1979 it was found that the proportion of breast-fed children had risen from 65 per cent to 80 per cent and the proportion of seriously undernourished infants had gone down from 11 per cent to 4 per cent. Among children who were still being fed with artificial milk, mostly with prescriptions, malnutrition incidence had been reduced by 50 per cent (Benjamin and Biddulph, 1980).

But despite the success of the Papua New Guinean approach, there are many serious problems remaining. The country is still predominantly rural and the actions of the 1970s, together with continuing work within the health services, has significantly slowed the spread of artificial feeding into these rural areas. But in the towns there are heavy pressures on women to use artificial feeding. For those working in the formal sector there are very many difficulties in arranging child care and employment in ways which allow breast-feeding. Townsend notes that 'even hospitals have so far been mostly unsuccessful in setting up crèches for children of their employees' (Townsend, 1985: 12).

Even successful control of artificial milk designed for young infants is not enough. Chetley points to efforts by the infant-food industry to promote commercially produced weaning foods for use in feeding bottles (Chetley 1983). A UNICEF report in 1982 noted that companies are suggesting the use of these products is normal, if not necessary, for infants as young as one month old. Weaning food was advertised on television in Sierre Leone in these terms, in total opposition to that country's health policy that babies should be fed on breast milk alone for the first four to six months. As Chetley suggests, 'as one set of doors are being closed, the infant food industry is attempting to open another' (Chetley, 1983: 4).

The promotion of breast-feeding is in many ways a euphemism for combating artificial feeding. Concerns here are with technical intervention; but in this case it is the intervention itself which is the essential problem. As with oral rehydration therapy, immunization, and growth monitoring, success in this area demands involved understanding on the part of parents, and mothers in particular. Programmes which attempt to shift patterns of behaviour have to contend with attitudes, beliefs and prejudices among health workers as well as populations subjected to advertising and other forms of persuasion. In the feeding of infants the use of artificial milk and bottles has a place. Positively promoting breast-feeding and returning artificial feeding to its proper place is a vital part of efforts to ensure the health and survival of young children. For poor communities in developing countries, the consequences of artificial feeding can be devastating; technical intervention unrelated to the social and economic context is very often so. Chetley quotes Dr Lambo, deputy director-general of the World Health Organisation, on bottle-feeding: 'We did willingly and gratefully accept a life-saving tool for the few, and endorsed it to be used for the many who did not need it' (quoted in Chetley, 1984: 5). Clavano puts essentially the same point rather more strongly: 'We have been able to prove that milk formula and bottle feeding is only a man-made deviation which can and should be dispensed with. We have no need for infant formula' (Clavano, 1983: 91).

CHILD HEALTH AND DEVELOPMENT

The specific interventions discussed in this chapter represent the major attacks on the most serious causes of infant mortality and morbidity in young children. What is clear from all of this is that the technology itself is of relatively minor significance. Although it is crucially important that knowledge of these techniques should be spread as far as possible, their implementation within the framework of primary health care and child welfare as a whole is primarily neither a technical nor a medical matter. If interventions such as these are part of a genuine development effort, and act to sharpen awareness and focus action in relation to long-term change, then they have very much to offer. But as we have seen, at many points there is considerable risk that the technology itself begins to define goals, and this is particularly so when health systems themselves are biased in this direction. These are tools only, and it must not be the case that patterns of development, and peoples' involvement with their own health, should be led by the imperatives of technology. In the case of children, no amount of technological intervention of the kind discussed in this chapter can combat increasing landlessness or the consequences of shifts from food production to export crop production. Long-term improvement in child health can only come through changes in social, economic and political conditions, and both the goals and processes in relation to these are frequently diffuse and difficult to identify or define.

The short-term gains from interventions such as those described in this chapter are clear, easily defined and dramatic. There can be no argument which would suggest not using these interventions, and thereby saving immense suffering and grief. The argument is not to mistake the technology for the objective:

Neat transfer of resources and technology does not necessarily bring us any closer to the realisation of a desired state. Unless one builds the human rights dimension into the development paradigm, this will not happen ... we have to think of human survival as the main aim of the development paradigm. We have also to see it as an essential condition of human creativity. And we must think of survival—like a subsistence economy—as not a negative, minimal goal but as a dynamic force projecting a positive alternative to the theory of progress and the goal of affluence, one that finds dignity in genuine equity and in diverse cultures working out their own strategies in local movements for democracy and autonomy [Kothari, 1984: 22].

INTEGRATED CHILD DEVELOPMENT SERVICES

A policy resolution adopted in August 1974 recognized the importance of organizing early childhood services: 'It shall be the policy of the State to provide adequate services to children, both before and after birth and through the period of growth, to ensure their full physical, mental and social development' (UNICEF [India], 1984: 8). The policy marked a change from the welfare programmes of the 1950s and 1960s which were judged piecemeal and uncoordinated. The ICDS initiative was intended to achieve social and economic development through child-oriented services. Aside from financial resources, the major restriction was seen to be the lack of an efficient organizational framework at the village level; the new system was linked to existing government infrastructure. ICDS was introduced in 1975 on an experimental basis, with thirty-three projects, of which about half were rural, one-third in so-called tribal areas and the remainder urban. The intention was that each project would aim at provision of a co-ordinated package of services across a wide range; this includes health monitoring, immunization, nutrition education and non-formal pre-school education. By the end of the 1970s, schemes were underway in 200 administrative areas (Singh, 1981) and by the mid-1980s more than 1,000 projects were operational.

The point of focus for the ICDS projects is the Anganwadi or pre-school child centre. The centres cover on average a population of around 1,000 in rural and urban areas and about 700 in the tribal areas. These child welfare institutions are run by Anganwadi workers; from the local community, these workers are selected on the basis of their education and then given four months' training in child care. They are all women. Their day-to-day work is run by a supervisor in charge of twenty Anganwadis altogether. The administration of the ICDS programme is organized by a child development project officer who co-ordinates health activities with staff at the Primary Health Centres. At the village level, the health aspects of the Anganwadi's work are supervised by an auxiliary nurse/midwife. Non-formal pre-school education is run from the centre with local children between 3 and 5 attending for several hours every day. No formal curriculum is operated, the emphasis is put on the worker to stimulate and arouse the children's curiosity and learning abilities in whatever manner is possible or appropriate. Education in aspects of health and nutrition are organized for all women between 18 and 45; the priority groups for this are pregnant and nursing mothers and especially those whose children seem prone to illness or malnutrition.

The Anganwadi is also a source of supplementary feeding for children in need, aiming to give around 300 calories a day, in order to bridge the gap between average intake and the twelve hundred calories a day recommended. In addition, nutrients and vitamins may be supplied to combat specific deficiencies, for example iodated salt for iodine deficiency, and vitamin A supplements.

Growth monitoring, including the use of growth charts, establishes which children are in need of supplementary feeding. All children showing signs of malnutrition are given supplements, more severely malnourished children receive therapeutic nutrition and some require hospitalization (Kapoor, 1979: 173). Recent surveys suggest that ICDS has achieved significant success in lowering the rates of malnutrition, the rates of low birth weight and child deaths. Sample studies in fifteen states showed that 85 per cent of malnourished children gained weight through the ICDS scheme (Tandon *et al.*, 1984).

Tandon and others were employed to carry out baseline surveys when ICDS programmes began in 1975 (Tandon, 1981a). Baseline surveys of 10 per cent of project area populations were carried out in order to provide the basis for future evaluations of the service. Data from 27 predominantly rural project areas showed that 66 per cent of households lived below the absolute poverty line and that the overall illiteracy rate was 60 per cent. Access to health services was poor and rates of immunization coverage were very low. For smallpox, DPT and BCG, revaccination rates were 7 per cent, 7 per cent and 17 per cent respectively for children in rural areas. These initial baseline surveys also examined patterns of nutrition; severe protein and calorie malnutrition was recorded in roughly one in six of children examined, measured as being below 60 per cent of expected weight for age. In discussion of these baseline findings, Tandon put the case for the use of ICDS in strengthening the activities of Primary Health Centres and supplementing the existing health infrastructure by the use of the Anganwadis. In a later comment, he saw the main strength of the Anganwadi to be in the fact that it not only has links with health service provision but is also connected with social welfare and educational services (Tandon, 1981c).

With regard to previous nutrition programmes, Tandon's view was that these had restricted themselves to food distribution activities and had not been part of a wider child development service. This was seen to reduce their effectiveness very considerably. Often, food supplements were taken home and used by other members of households, so not reaching the children for whom they were intended. Supplies had often been subject to disruption and frequently arrived in a state unfit for consumption. Conditions at many feeding centres in the past were judged to be unhygienic, and rarely was the distribution of food combined with nutrition, education or other health education. This lack of integration between health and education services was seen to be closely related to the poor acceptance of preventive health activities by many communities. It was felt that ICDS could achieve dramatic improvement in both the quantity and quality of services with respect to nutrition. The Anganwadi centres could be used to provide hygienic surroundings for the distribution of food supplements and these could be consumed at the centre; ensuring that the children who needed the food were eating it.

Educational activities focused on the Anganwadi centre would, it was felt, increase awareness of the relevance of preventive health measures and could affect much greater integration with health services, thus strengthening the total Primary Health Care infrastructure. Problems of supply and the quality of provisions could not be dealt with by the Anganwadis themselves but would remain as concerns of planners and administrators.

After nearly two years the delivery of services through ICDS was reviewed and the impact of the Anganwadis assessed in terms of their original goals. Baseline data was compared with new survey data from fifteen areas representing a cross-section of urban, rural and tribal area projects. The results were encouraging (Tandon, 1981c). In the project areas surveyed, immunization coverage had increased quite substantially; BCG immunization had gone up from 11.3 per cent to 49.3 percent coverage in rural areas. DPT immunization had increased from 5 per cent to 35 per cent, and the distribution of Vitamin A had risen from around 6 per cent overall to 44 per cent in rural areas and 60 per cent in the tribal areas. Food distribution also showed upward trends. The overall nutritional status of children in areas with Anganwadis showed marked improvements. At the time of the baseline survey nearly 22 per cent of children under 6 years old were found to be severely malnourished; after twenty-one months of Anganwadi activity, this figure had been reduced to under 6 per cent. The impact was most dramatic on children under 3 years old but was still considerable for children betweeen 3 and 6 years—the effects being clear in rural, urban and tribal areas.

Summarizing the Anganwadi activities for the first twenty-one months, Tandon emphasized the integration of services—nutritional, health and educational—as perhaps the most important. From the point of view of the community, the Anganwadi centre is a focus, a place where families can bring their children in the knowledge that the Anganwadi worker will be able to help them herself or call on whatever help might be necessary. The mutually reinforcing effects of the different elements in the ICDS programme make the sum effect greater than that of the separate parts. The fact that children come to the centre and spend a good part of the day there is seen to be of vital significance. Each service in the package of child-care services depends upon the support of the others. Giving a child supplementary food, for example, would be of little benefit if the child drank unsafe water or was continually exposed to poor sanitation and hygiene. Women and girls were involved in Anganwadi activities and the centres were used as the base for activities directed specifically at them. This practical linking of women's health concerns and child welfare was most important. So too, in Tandon's view, was the participation of outside academic institutions in the continual monitoring and evaluation of the project.

But not all evaluations were as positive as this. In an assessment of urban Anganwadi provision, Gupta and his colleagues found that the expected improvements in health services had not been achieved due mainly to staffing problems, unsatisfactory location and poor co-ordination between the staff and workers at the Anganwadi centre (Gupta *et al.*, 1979). Despite such difficulties, it would seem from evaluation studies and reports that the ICDS approach to integrated services for children has achieved considerable success. A great deal of this success seems to flow from the employment of women as Anganwadi workers and the fact that a wide range of child welfare activities are focused on a day-care centre from which the Anganwadi worker operates and at which children can receive both food and pre-school education.

Educational activities focused on the Anganwadi centre would, it was felt, increase awareness of the relevance of preventive health measures and could affect much greater integration with health services, thus strengthening the total Primary Health Care infrastructure. Problems of supply and the quality of provisions could not be dealt with by the Anganwadis themselves, but would remain as concerns of planners and administrators.

It does seem that it is the practical expression of the relationship between health, education and social welfare that is the essence of day care of this kind. The most vulnerable children are the youngest, particularly those from birth to 3 years old. Recent estimates suggest that the ICDS programme covers about 50 per cent of this age group overall, with good rates of coverage for the poorest (Krishnamurthi and Nadkarni, 1983). Although supplies remain a problem in many rural areas, health services coverage and immunization have improved significantly in areas where these Anganwadi day-care centres are operating. The direct impact can be seen most clearly in the health and nutritional status of young children attending these centres and those coming within their orbit. There is evidence of increased birth weights, lower levels of malnutrition and improved patterns of weight gain through infancy. In addition, the activities of these centres have stimulated the implementation of other programmes in response to local needs: water supply and sanitation, distribution of oral rehydration salts, family planning advice and services, and so on.

It is, of course, difficult to measure impact of this kind, but the available evidence does support the argument that a multi-purpose day-care centre for children has a significant impact in poor communities, where the worker is close to the community and flexible in approach and response. Even more difficult to measure directly, but perhaps more important in terms of long-term change, is the growth of community involvement in Anganwadi provision and the impact that ICDS as a whole may have on the status of women in poor communities. To some considerable extent it may be seen that heavy emphasis on food preparation, child care, domestic hygiene and other activities of this sort merely reinforce the position of women in male-dominated and child-care centred households. But this view may to some extent be balanced by another perception, which sees improvement of women's position being positively affected through both the delivery of services, not least availability of fertility control methods, and opportunities for the use of centres for activities such as functional literacy classes. Related to this is the employment of very large numbers of women in the operation of Anganwadis themselves. It remains the case that in most poor communities there are severe limitations facing women workers; but to the extent that they succeed in improving child welfare and in involving other women in the community, they can provide the basis for change. The example of one day-care centre of this type will serve to illustrate both some of the potential and some of the limitations.

An Anganwadi

In Dhandhlan, a village of around 4,000 in northern India, there are four Anganwadis. Singh describes the work of the woman running one of them (Singh, 1981). Ompati is 23, married with two children; although from a higher caste, she works in the day centre located in the Harijan area. There were no Harijan women with enough formal education to qualify for the position, and Ompati had to overcome opposition from her family and others in order to take this job, just as she had

128   *Five Hundred Million Children*

to overcome opposition when she had attended the four-month training course 200 km away.

There were just over 800 people in the area of her centre, but males out-numbered females two to one; infant mortality was very high and miscarriages were frequent. There were 150 children under 6 years, seventy-seven less than 3. Initially, there was little enthusiasm for the Anganwadi, even though a building had been erected by the local council. Considerable persuasion was needed before reaching the position in 1981 when Ompati had sixty-seven children attending the day-care centre and forty-nine women and girls in the functional literacy class and taking part in income-generating activities. The latter she felt to be particularly important as this group is the weakest in the community, very few owning any land, virtually all working as labourers. With a helper she prepares a mid-day meal and children play during the morning. At noon the children sit down for the food, some of them arriving just in time. Very many parents send children only to eat the mid-day meal and many still arrive with unwashed hands and faces. In the afternoon, women and girls use the centre for discussions of health, nutrition, cooking methods and child care. There is sewing and knitting as a group. Ompati's attempts to convince women to have smaller families have largely failed because of opposition from their husbands. She is aware that in many respects the centre has failed; its impact is only slight and many people still do not see its real purpose. But, on the other hand, she says, 'I have seen children in my area looking much healthier and their weight charts show the improvements. There are fewer miscarriages and fewer babies die in our village now. These are changes that I have seen with my own eyes' (Ompati, quoted by Singh, 1981: 22).

The Anganwadis are primarily concerned with health; a major emphasis of these integrated child-care centres is on those issues affecting the health of young children with which earlier chapters were concerned. But as day-care centres they have distinctive and important features. Above all, children attending these centres are not sick, so they serve as a focus of action and activity related to the normal growth and development of all children. It is this which distinguishes them most sharply from health facilities, which might otherwise be the only point of contact between children (and their mothers) and organized services. The essential need to perceive child welfare in positive terms, that is in terms of development, growth, improvement and the realization of the potential of every child, is vital. Health services are perceived, and nearly always operated, on the basis of pathology. They are there to deal with illness above all, and although considerable progress has been made in relating treatment facilities and other health activities, there are considerable obstacles to this. The example of the Indian ICDS programme is an important one. As later chapters will show, formal social provision for children is very restricted indeed in poor communities. Narrowly conceived in terms of purpose, very often restricted in access, and virtually always biased to the urban areas, social welfare programmes for children are almost everywhere unrelated to development (MacPherson and Midgley, 1987). In the remainder of this chapter we focus more closely on welfare provision, in an examination of crèches. Again the discussion is predominantly about provision in India, but examples later in the chapter are from other poor communities.

CRÈCHES AND THE WELFARE OF CHILDREN

That the welfare needs of young children could be met by the provision of day-care facilities has long been recognized by international organizations (World Health Organisation, 1962). Although most often closely related to the provision of health services, the emphasis in day-care provision is on the care of well children and the enhancement of their welfare. While in virtually all developing countries there has been some growth in the provision of day-care facilities for young children, this has almost always been in a form which denies access to the poorest children. Most commonly seen in terms of pre-school education, and provided on a fee-paying basis, day care has acted to further widen the gap between rich and poor in many countries (MacPherson, 1982). If we are concerned with facilities provided for the welfare of poor children, we very quickly find that these are much less extensive. In 1974, India adopted a National Policy for

Children which stated that 'equal opportunities for development to all children during the period of growth should be our aim for this would serve our larger purpose of reducing inequality and ensuring social justice' (de Souza, 1979: 249). India is not only one of the most populous developing countries but is one of the very few to have such complex child welfare provision, though all commentators agree on the inadequacy of the services. Since the mid-1970s Indian child welfare policy has given priority to programmes for crèches and other facilities relating to the care of children with working or ailing mothers. These services are of particular significance in urban areas; the special problems and needs of poor urban children are among the most serious social welfare issues facing Indian social policy. National policy which emerged during the 1970s was intended to produce an integrated approach to child welfare needs. Previous programmes and policies had been highly divided between sectors with little account being taken of the child as a whole. 'In various budget allocations, of course, the child is somewhere in the picture, like an arm here and a leg there, but of the whole child we have little evidence' (Baig, 1980: 7).

But even with the adoption of a national policy, budget allocations for child welfare remain low and commentators differ in their views on the likely outcome of the integrated approach to child welfare policy. Luthra suggested that the policy served a number of social goals and that if systematically pursued would considerably advance child welfare (Luthra, 1975.) Others argue that India's policy for children is an expression of 'mere pious hope' (Jagannadham, 1979); children, particularly poor children, will never receive justice because the problems are so vast and complex. The strategy in India has been to promote the welfare of pre-school children in two major ways. First, there was a general objective of increasing the psycho-social well-being of all children; second, it was intended to make pre-school children the focus for community involvement. The stated intention was to develop community awareness, draw on community resources of all kinds, and to build services as an integral part of Indian life—creating forces which would lead to the further expansion of the programme (Luthra, 1975). The concept of community involvement or community participation is an extremely important one and is now extensively employed in discussions of social policy and social development in developing countries (Midgley *et al.*, 1986). An approach which involves a relationship between the state and local communities in the establishment and development of welfare services is of itself significant. The contrast is with the form of service provision which dominated colonial and immediately post-colonial welfare systems—that of highly formalized, centralized and conventional social services, informed above all by remedial approaches.

In the Indian case, as elsewhere, a particular problem is that of providing for children who for various reasons need care outside their homes for part of the day. With increasing urbanization, and greater involvement of women and siblings in formal employment, many children are not able to receive care in their own homes. The creation of a system of provision for crèche services is one response to this need. Crèches and day-care centres in urban areas can increase the welfare of children and become community centres through which a number of other activities and services can be channelled, just as centres in rural areas were seen to have a developmental potential. From the mid-1970s on, the establishment of crèches in India was administered by the Ministry of Social Welfare; the Central Social Welfare Board channelled resources to voluntary agencies, which operated the crèches and day-care centres. The Central Welfare Board also regulated the operation of these facilities (Anandalakshmy, 1980).

Many hundreds of thousand of India's children are neglected during early childhood due to lack of day-care facilities. Commitment of women to formal employment and shortage of services most often pulls an older sibling (a girl) out of school to undertake child care, or forces working mothers to take small children with them to work-sites where they face added hazards. In the largest cities in India well over 90 per cent of female labourers work in the unorganized sector where employers provide no services whatsoever for them or their children (Chaturvedi, 1979). The lack of facilities for these children is seen as a major problem; failing to provide such services, it is argued, will have devastating consequences—'no amount of benefits likely to be received in adulthood can ever compensate for what the generation missed earlier in childhood' (Kulkarni, 1979: 52).

Formal legislative provisions very often bear little relation to practice, and in relation to day care in India this is clearly so. The law provides for day-care services for children of women workers in a number of categories, but very few employers fulfil legal obligations. The vast majority of working women are in unorganized employment, which goes unrecognized by census and other figures. Women working in the so-called informal economy or in small establishments are not covered by the provisions of the relevant Acts. It was estimated that in 1975 about 35 million women were working outside their homes, of whom only 10 per cent were in the formal organized sector (Baig, 1975).

As in so many other areas of social policy, the gulf between legislative intent and practical reality is great. For example, under the Contract Labour Act 1970 a contractor in India must provide a crèche wherever twenty or more women are employed as contract labour. The Act provides for a crèche to be set up within fifty metres of the working establishment and a number of standards are laid down: The room must be well lit and ventilated with at least 20 sq. ft floor area per child and a shady open-air playground must be provided; amenities such as a kitchen, bathroom, latrine and water for drinking must be arranged (Anandalakshmy, 1980). There are, however, very many loopholes; for instance, the contractor may show less than twenty women on his records. Under the provisions of the 1970 Factory Act, all factories employing at least thirty women should provide crèche facilities, but again employers simply do not fulfil their obligations. In 1973 there were only 900 factories in the whole of India providing such facilities (Baig, 1975). Provision of day-care facilities by employers, enforced by legislation, provides for only a very tiny fraction of the children of working women.

The most vulnerable children are those of the poorest families in the urban areas. But although over 70 million children live in India's cities, perhaps half of them in absolute poverty, it remains the case that nearly three-quarters of all India's people live in rural areas. Swaminathan has argued that these facts have resulted in considerable confusion within social policy for child welfare (Swaminathan, 1979). On the other hand, there is vital concern with the vast majority of India's children who live in rural areas. Linked with this is recognition of the considerable inequality between rural and urban areas. As we have already seen, on many indicators urban populations are much better served. But such generalizations mask gross differences; the children of the poor in Indian cities may be much worse off than their counterparts in the rural areas. Furthermore, as Swaminathan suggests, easy assumptions that the facilities and benefits of urban life are available to all urban dwellers may lead to serious neglect of the special problems of poor urban children. Concern with the needs of poor and underprivileged children, in both urban and rural areas, must be the essential feature of social policy for child welfare. Poor children are united in their fundamental needs as well as in the near-universal neglect of those needs. Integrated social policy initiatives, covering the mass of children, are essential, and stand in contrast to many existing social service systems. It may be argued that the consequences of poverty are worse for children in the poorest urban areas. The poor are marginal in the life of the city, although vital for its functioning. They have poor access to its advantages and are continuously reminded of their poverty and insecurity by the lavish and often wasteful life-styles of the more affluent in the same city.

Among the less well-off and the poor, there are further divisions. The very poorest are those in the least-organized sectors, of employment, of housing, and so on. They may be relatively recent migrants, with insecure employment, uncertain incomes, poor housing with few facilities and perhaps no tenure. Children will be affected by the insecurity as much as by the living conditions, the poor nutrition, the poor sanitation and the risk of illness and disease. In Indian cities, as elsewhere, the very poorest of all may be treated worst; in many instances not even the very minimum facilities are available to them, 'if they survive at all it is because of their coping skills, their pluck and their luck (Anandalakshmy, 1980: 117). If there are services available in poor parts of the cities, it is not uncommon that these are used by the relatively better-off groups in poor communities—the marginally more organized and established. Very often, those most in need of welfare services receive little or nothing. If there is a struggle for survival in a harsh urban environment, children very often are forced to bear the brunt of that struggle. In many cases the economic hardship is compounded by the impersonality and even social isolation that may come with living in the very poorest of urban communities:

In any village a man has an identity as a member of a family, a caste group, a community. In that setting no man is unknown, no act anonymous. A large city provides him the opposite type of experience. Every man is faceless, every transaction impersonal. While this can be harsh on the man it hits the woman and child with greater force [Anandalakshmy, 1980: 117]

In most traditional communities, child-rearing is a centrally important shared task of the extended family and indeed of the local community as a whole. Many families in the cities find that even to stay on the edge of subsistence, every one who can must work. The capacity of kinship systems to give support may be stretched beyond breaking point, and a larger proportion of children than ever before are in need of care during the day. The decline of the extended family in social care may be deplored, and this decline may frequently be overstated, but it is in very many instances a vivid reality. Where support is not available, and this may be especially so among the poorest, weakest and most vulnerable, the institutionalization of child care in social policies and programmes is a vital necessity. Such policies and programmes can be informed by new approaches and by sensitivity to the particular needs of local communities, but the reality of the urban situation for the very poor remains. In India, as elsewhere, rural families more often live, work and move together; children of the unskilled urban workers may wander worksites during the day and may be left unattended: 'the relaxed courtyard where the child could play under the solicitous eye of many an elder is replaced by the rubble site and the indifference of the passer-by' (Anandalakshmy, 1980: 117).

In urban areas of India particular attention has been paid to the problems of children with mothers working as labourers, very often on building sites, and crèche provision has emerged in response to the particularly harsh problems faced by these children:

Children of unskilled workers have always merged with dumped materials and earthworks on large construction sites. They camp with their parents in temporary shelters and move with them from one site to another. The exposure and the poor facilities take a severe toll on their health, and constant movement closes forever the chance of education or development [Singh, 1980: 359].

For the children of women construction workers in Indian cities, the provision of day care is of enormous significance. They may get some care, however little, when before they got virtually none. We see here a dramatic example of the pressure of economic and social forces on welfare—marginalization and abject poverty driving a wedge between mothers and children, forcing women to virtually abandon their own children during long, hard days. In cases like this, day-care facilities do not release women for employment; these women are forced into employment regardless of the availability of day care. All children, even those from families which have ample time, resources and facilities for child care and education, benefit from well-run crèches, day care and pre-school education. For the poorest children in developing countries, day care serves a much more fundamental purpose; it protects them from some of the harshest threats to their very existence, and may give them and their families some chances to change that existence. In the great majority of poor communities in developing countries the provision of alternative care is also of massive benefit to older sisters of young children on whom the burden of care inevitably falls.

Two examples will serve to illustrate the practical expression of policies to meet the need for day care. The first, in urban areas, is a mobile crèche scheme, the second a programme for day care in Pondicherry, which provides facilities in both urban and rural areas.

MOBILE CRÈCHES

The Mobile Crèches began in 1969 with the informal establishment of a small-scale project to provide day-care facilities on one construction site. It was registered in 1970 as an independent voluntary organization and despite considerable growth (there were 150 crèches in Delhi and Bombay by the end of the 1970s), it is still a relatively small programme of intensive integrated child care. From the original purpose, it quickly broadened its scope and attempted to provide integrated services in two major ways. There was horizontal integration, through the co-ordinated provision of services in health, nutrition, recreation, non-formal education, pre-school and adult education, family planning and community services by one worker under one roof. Vertically, the work of the programme was extended to deal with all age groups from birth to adolescence. As a programme, Mobile Crèches now provides a wide range of activities, with emphasis on the involvement of parents and local communities in the provision of services relevant to their children's needs. It is argued that they have evolved a structure which enables their basic objectives to be translated into practical action (Swaminathan, 1979). The pattern for the establishment of crèches and the development of child-care services based on them is essentially similar in each case. First, when a crèche is established the major objective is to reach the children and families on construction sites by initiating dialogue with contractors, so that basic amenities of shelter, water and other resources may be shared. Basic care facilities are then set up on the work site and locally recruited child-care workers are trained. So-called 'support lines' are set up, for example helping children to integrate into schools where formal education is available. A major objective of the programme as a whole and of specific crèches in particular areas is to bring these problems to public awareness and to seek legislative and other action to improve the situation of the unorganized sector (Singh, 1980).

Reports on the operation of this programme suggest that a relatively small-scale voluntary organization has achieved a considerable amount in terms of increased child welfare, community involvement and self-help. A study of crèches in Delhi suggested that mothers from very low income groups were, contrary to widely held beliefs, receptive to new ideas and practices which met the needs of their children. Crèche workers were far more effective than any other professions at bringing about changes in child-care in these communities (de Souza, 1979). Given the target populations of this programme there are very considerable problems. The poor health and sanitary conditions mean that the operation of a crèche necessarily involves a complex net of activities including clinical and preventive health, nutrition and, in many cases, basic child care. Older children also had to be provided for, which brought the evolution of a nursery and primary education programme. The absence of workers trained to deal with such a wide range of needs and activities led to the setting up of a programme for the training of staff.

The expressed intention is to assist the development of whole communities and create better living conditions for all, with provision for children as the basis. The centres intend to provide full day care with a comprehensive coverage of a whole range of needs—physical, mental and emotional. They cater for children from birth to 14 who are divided into three groups; crèches are for children up to 3 years old, day care (*balwadi*) for those from 3 to 6, and some education for those over 6 years old. Reports suggest that the daily crèche routine emphasizes cleanliness, habit formation, nutrition and affectionate interaction with adults. Clinics are held regularly at the crèches, with doctors visiting about once a week for treatment, follow-up being carried out by the day-centre staff. In principle there is a programme of structured and unstructured play for the young children, using simple low-cost games. Educational games are played to prepare children for primary education, with older children having more formal lessons. Organized play during the mornings ends with a meal at midday, the afternoons being spent in a variety of informal activities. In the evenings the centres are used for literacy classes for men and women separately, often run by the same people who work with the children during the day (Swaminathan, 1979). It is claimed that the programme is comprehensive, integrated, relevant and flexible. Its supporters argue that it caters for the needs of the poorest children in realistic ways. Mahadevan, the first chair of the organization, claimed that 'in all that we do, we keep before us the picture of poor India' (Mahadevan, 1975: 44).

The staffing of such centres is obviously vital, and in support of the in-service training it is argued that 'no professionally trained worker, with pre-conceived notions of her own, can possibly survive in our environment' (Mahadevan, 1975: 45). It was found that untrained young girls of relatively low standard of education, from backgrounds with few physical amenities, were best suited to the programme. It was suggested that their low educational level gave them a greater degree of flexibility, with their backgrounds enabling them to adjust to the poor amenities of the construction sites, and of their day-care centres. Most staff are young girls from 16 to 25 who may continue their education while they are working; because they have few family responsibilities they are able to work at low salary levels. It is claimed for the in-service training programme that better workers result. Most are recruited locally and 'the girls ... are ground through the mill of the in-service training programme. Iron enters their souls and nothing can deter them from doing a good and worthwhile job thoroughly well' (Mahadevan, 1975: 47).

Those involved in the Mobile Crèches programme stress that its effectiveness in poor, virtually resourceless urban communities demands a bias towards community-based social welfare in which a pivotal role is played by community development. It is argued that imported ideas and methods of child care are almost entirely inappropriate for the practical care of the poorest urban children in India; it does not allow for their specific needs and problems. It is claimed that the continuing development of Mobile Crèches relies heavily on problem-solving discussion in close interaction with families and local communities. Planning, it is suggested, takes place in response to concrete situations, and it is this which gives understanding of the lives of those facing the most severe hardship.

There can be no doubt that the programme has been remarkably successful both in terms of the number of crèches established and in the extension of child welfare activity in the most hostile of conditions. Not all crèche provision meets these standards, however. A study of crèches in slum resettlement areas and on construction sites in Delhi examined provision operated by a number of different organizations (de Souza, 1979). Some of these provided very good care, but others were judged to be very unsatisfactory on virtually every count. Overall it was felt that the physical conditions of these crèches, for the poorest groups of children, were characterized by 'congestion, poor ventilation, and the lack of facilities ... the psycho-social environment, too, is rather neglected and this can be seen from the inadequate play equipment and the lack of organised activities conducive to the development of the physical and mental health of the children' (de Souza, 1979: 181). The study found that only 8 per cent of mothers were dissatisfied with the facilities offered. The discrepancy between the mothers' assessment and the quality of care being offered is explained by de Souza largely in terms of 'ignorance'. He argues that the great majority of mothers were not in a position to assess the facilities or performance of the crèches because they lacked knowledge of health care and nutrition. Added to that, they spent very little time in the crèches and were unaware what was going on in them. Furthermore, he argues, these mothers were from the very lowest income groups and tended to have very low expectations, accepting anything that is offered because there are few or no alternatives. There were crèches which maintained high standards, but very many did not due to lack of resources, poor staff and low levels of literacy and education among mothers. In contrast to the philosophy evolved by the Mobile Crèche programme, de Souza found that the majority of crèches in his study operated on a concept of child welfare services in which the emphasis was on custodial care 'for the convenience of the mother rather than on developmental needs of the child' (de Souza, 1979: 181). The enormous potential of day care was recognized, but in too many cases an almost exclusive preoccupation with institutionalized custodial care prevented virtually any possibility of the realization of this potential.

Day centres do have the potential to become the focus of community action and particularly for the involvement of women. The provision of day care for the children of working women not only provides a vital service and a stable environment in which the most vulnerable children can be enabled to develop, but such centres can act as an opening for much wider community activity. But these things are by no means automatic. In the best examples, understanding of local needs and perceptions, together with high standards of child care, provide a powerful base for action. In community development terms, techniques are required which allow community self-education through analysis of problems and the identification of the means of improvement. Mobile Crèches argues that in using such techniques it has stimulated action to cut the ties of dependency on traditional services, and stimulated a process of self-development. Caro argues that state-directed social policy can learn a great deal from programmes such as this: 'the development of programmes for children begins with small, simple experiments which may eventually offer the government viable alternatives which differ from the usual approaches that have done so little to solve the problems of poverty' (Caro, 1979: 164).

THE BALWADI PROGRAMME

The Balwadi is defined as a centre for non-formal pre-school education and other activities for children less than 6 years of age with better facilities and services than in an Anganwadi. The number of children in India who require day-care and crèche facilities is huge; Rao gives an estimate of 19 million, of whom only 2 million are in urban areas (Rao, 1980: 352). As with the Mobile Crèches, the Balwadis provide day-care facilities for the children of women at work, almost all of whom are in the organized sector. In Pondicherry the Balwadi Programme began in 1966, and by the end of the 1970s there were about 200 centres, providing pre-school activities and day care to about 10,000 children between 3 and 5 years of age in the Pondicherry area. This is about one-quarter of the total population of this age group, a much higher coverage than in India as a whole. About half of the centres are in urban areas. The location of Balwadis is on the basis of the socio-economic conditions; preference being given to families from the lowest socio-economic groups. But Rao reports that although virtually every family had a low income, as a group they had much higher literacy rates than for the region as a whole, or India overall. These centres offer services in health, nutrition and education, with some activities geared towards mothers and older children. Essentially, the Balwadis are concerned to offer pre-school education and most time is spent on this. Each Balwadi is staffed by a Balsevika (a multi-purpose child welfare worker) and one helper. All workers are women and the Balsevika is responsible for selecting children to attend, conducting non-formal educational activities, administration, supervision and maintaining contact with the community (Rao, 1979: 355). The workers are full-time employees of the state government, and those in charge of the centres are high-school graduates who have been trained for eleven months. The staff are supervised by the Department of Social Welfare, with six social welfare organizers in the region to cover the 200 Balwadis.

It is argued that community support and involvement play a major role, and are among the more important criteria used for the selection of locations for establishing Balwadis. The operation of these centres depends on the co-operation of the local community, and members of the community must assist the workers in a number of ways. Typical forms of assistance include provision of accommodation, maintenance of buildings, accommodation for workers and occasional help with the preparation of food. The costs of the programme are met by the Department of Social Welfare, with staff salaries being the major item of expenditure—between two-thirds and three-quarters of the total.

An evaluation of the programme in Pondicherry was undertaken in 1979 by the Indian National Institute of Public Co-operation and Child Development (Rao and Choudhry, 1979). The study report was very favourable and pointed to several distinctive aspects of the Balwadi programme. First, it was noted that the percentage coverage of the pre-school population was high and that children from the lowest socio-economic groups were very well represented. The evaluation found that the Balwadis were not restricted merely to custodial care of the children but that as well as being looked after and provided with adequate food, the children were also given 'opportunities to participate in a variety of interesting educational and play activities'. It was also felt that the programme as a whole was well organized, administered and

supervised. But there were a number of criticisms. Although
local communities were strongly favourable towards this
programme, it was found that the degree of community
contact was very low. Only 40 per cent of mothers interviewed
reported that they visited the Balwadi regularly, and a very
small proportion attended women's meetings. The great
majority came only to deliver and collect their children. It was
also felt by those evaluating the programme that too many
centres were located in urban areas and that the health service
provision could be substantially improved. The fact that those
running the Balwadis were full-time government employees
was felt to be a significant factor in the high morale and
enthusiasm that these workers showed. The programme had
attracted well-qualified and well-trained workers who
appeared to be well respected in the community, and to be
strongly motivated. It was thought that a number of distinctive
features of the area were important to the success of the
programme. Perhaps the most important of these was the
geographical compactness of the region, which allowed good
administration, regular supplies and frequent supervision.

In this programme, then, there is evidence of the successful
implementation of a programme of day-care facilities for
young children. But these are run in a very conventional form,
with full-time salaried employees providing, on a semi-
professional basis, full-time child care for the children of
working mothers. The programme is clearly of immense value
to those women and their children; there are no charges for the
day care and the programme does not have the bias towards
high-wage earners which is typical of programmes of this kind
in many countries. There was a degree of urban bias, but again
this was very much less in the Pondicherry case than is
generally found in similar situations in developing countries.
In contrast to facilities discussed previously, these day-care
centres were organized and supervised principally through the
Department of Social Welfare. In the context of organized
social service provision, these centres would be relatively
unusual in the extent to which they provide for the lowest
income groups, but certainly not unusual in their lack of
genuine community involvement and consequently narrow
focus of activity.

This chapter has indicated some issues concerned with the provision of day care for the very youngest children. From a fundamental concern with health, and at the most basic level with survival, social policy for child welfare broadens its range to cover the developmental needs of young children. It is here that we begin to see more clearly the linkages between social policy and developmental activity as a whole. In negative terms we can see that where child welfare needs are met by the direct provision of services, however efficiently, the links between the achievement of child welfare and the achievement of social development in general may be much weakened. In later chapters this will be seen to occur at a number of other points. Other examples of day care will be discussed later, in relation to different aspects of the provision of child welfare services. Day-care provision has essentially the same specific purpose in whatever form it is organized; the immediate welfare of individual young children is its fundamental concern. But day-care provision can be much more than this as the examples in this chapter have suggested.

6 Child Welfare Legislation and Social Services

Children are the most vulnerable group in any population and in need of the greatest social care ... the State has the duty of according proper care and protection to children at all times, as it is on their physical and mental well-being that the future of the nation depends [Preamble to the Children Act India, 1960, quoted by Goriawalla and Raghunath, 1979: 260–61].

The rights of the child are amongst the most essential principles etched in the statutes of humanity. They are also the most frequently disregarded [Grant, 1983: xi].

Formal social services generally have low priority in the poorest countries and are still in general dominated by essentially remedial approaches. In most countries organized social services for children are restricted in coverage and may bear very little relationship to the pattern of urgent needs and priorities. As we have seen, services in nearly all countries have considerable urban bias and have grown in ways which reflect the dominance of Western approaches and concepts (MacPherson and Midgley, 1987). Poor countries inherited patterns of child welfare provision, very often the responsibility of non-government organizations, which were primarily concerned with residential care, dealing with children who broke the law, and administering adoption and foster-care procedures.

In a great many states contemporary legislation for child welfare still reflects the very heavy influence of the past. As social service provision concerned with child care is dominated by legislation, the nature of the law is important in affecting both the content and approach of child welfare services. All countries have laws which in principle both guard children from abuse, and more positively, ensure their welfare and development. But the rights and needs of children are neglected, the poorest children suffering most of all. In some cases it may be that the continued implementation of fundamentally irrelevant policies and programmes flows from the kind of legislation which exists and the social institutions associated with it. As we shall see, there is in particular a gulf between the kinds of formal services and institutions that imported legal provisions and concepts demand, and the problems to which these are supposedly directed. Above all, recent years have shown a rapidly growing awareness of the need to change child welfare legislation in ways which make it relevant to the total development effort; the search for relevant and appropriate law is yet another expression of the search for relevant social policy.

This chapter looks first at aspects of child welfare legislation in developing countries and in particular those which bear most directly on organized social welfare services. The second part of the chapter examines one aspect of the expression of this legislation in practice: The provision of substitute care for children. Any attempt to generalize across a wide range of social and legal systems is fraught with difficulty, but there are broad themes which may be indicated and constantly recurring issues which are of direct relevance to social policy for children.

DEFINITION OF 'A CHILD'

The definition of 'child' in legislation is essentially one of age; the definition is quite clearly of major significance in social welfare policy. Child welfare legislation is above all an expression of rights and duties in relation to the very young. In particular, such legislation is fundamentally concerned with the role of the state and its relationship to young people. A major boundary of state action in relation to children is thus formed by the very definition of 'child'.

In very many countries the age of civil majority has been

lowered in recent years, most commonly to 18; this legal definition of 'child' is one which the recently proposed convention on the rights of the child seeks to ratify (International Children's Rights Monitor, 1983). But the situation is made infinitely more complicated by the fact that ages for marriage, military service, employment and criminal responsibility vary widely, and are almost always lower than eighteen. In relation to marriage, for instance, there are still very many states which have no provision regarding a minimum age for marriage and some allow marriage at very young ages, particularly for girls. From many developing countries it is common to find discussion of the inappropriateness of many of the present legal age limits and the pressing need for these to more clearly reflect changing social conditions. In general, it is recognized that there should be some relationship between the various legal age limits applied to children with regard to different activities or responsibilities. Above all, there should be some clear and reasonable association between a particular age limit and the specific purpose it is supposed to serve in the community the child is part of (Weisberg, 1978).

A major theme, recurring in very many reports on child legislation in developing countries, is a perceived tension between the desire to protect the child and the wish to maximize rights of self-determination (Pappas, 1983). The recognition that maturation is a gradual process has led a number of states to remove some legal disabilities from children and to grant them some freedom of action prior to the attainment of full civil majority at 18. These issues clearly become more difficult in the case of older or more mature children, and in relation to child welfare services affect questions regarding the consultation of children about decisions which seriously change their lives, such as adoption and custody. There is a recurrent complaint that too little attention has been paid to this aspect of child welfare law by the institutions which carry out its provisions. In some states legal authorities have developed a concept of 'emancipation' in which a child is defined by status for particular purposes. In such situations young people are judged to have achieved *de facto* independence from parental control and thus ceased to be children in legal terms. Pappas suggests 'there is a case to be made for universal recognition of this concept and for consideration to be given to whether minors should be accorded the right to petition for emancipated status in cases of irreparable breakdown of family ties' (Pappas, 1983: xlii).

It is not intended here to pursue legal arguments such as this in detail; none the less, the issue is of considerable significance to child welfare. A particularly sharp example is to be found in discussion of child labour and the responses of social welfare agencies to the fact that very many children live independently, especially in urban areas. This issue will be explored later, but at this point it may be noted that the question of definition is by no means straightforward. Not only do legislative provisions in developing countries frequently embody outdated concepts imported from the West, commonly during colonial rule, but more important developing countries must seek to accommodate formal legal provisions with existing traditional and customary law. In the latter, a concept such as that of legal status being defined by chronological age may be alien in the extreme.

DISCRIMINATION

Legal provisions in many states continue to discriminate against particular groups of children. Internationally, this is a source of considerable concern and again the draft convention on the rights of the child seeks to eliminate discrimination. But discrimination will remain in very many states for specific social, cultural and religious reasons for some considerable time. The most significant and widespread forms of discrimination are those based on gender and those which relate to birth status. Gender discrimination is widespread and can be seen in very many forms in legislation and judicial practice. Legal provisions regarding marriage frequently treat boys and girls differently; rights to education may be substantially less for girls; it is common that inheritance laws significantly disadvantage girls; and in very many legal systems the relationships between parents and children vary substantially according to the gender of the child.

In relation to birth status, there are many instances of very serious discrimination. Related closely to religious beliefs and customary law, this discrimination fundamentally affects inheritance, maintenance, the custody of children and even the entitlement to welfare benefits in many countries. The very extensive discrimination against children on the grounds of birth status is intertwined with discrimination against women in general and with the expression of that discrimination in family-law provisions (International Society on Family Law, 1975).

CHILD CUSTODY

In very broad terms there are two themes which are clear in contemporary development regarding child custody. The first is the establishment of formal provisions governing the disposition by legal authorities of the children of divorced or separated parents. This has been especially important in recent years for systems which were hitherto dominated by traditional and customary law. Closely linked with this is evidence of attempts in very many countries to remove or to significantly alter imported legal provisions where these have resulted from a period of foreign administration (Bandiare, 1977; Azicri, 1980; Ladjili, 1980; Yorac, 1981).

The movement towards more active formulation of provision on a national basis is clear. The nature of such provision varies enormously, although some trends may be identified. One, which affects very many countries, is towards much more flexibility in legal provision and to a much less rigid adherence to invariable rules, which awarded custody as a matter of course on the basis of matrimonial guilt or the child's age or gender. In principle, the concept of 'the best interests of the child' is frequently invoked as one which guides decision-making in terms of custody. As noted earlier, discussion of this is very often seen to necessarily involve consideration of the child's own opinions and preferences. In poor countries, however, conditions may be such as to make these general propositions extremely difficult to discern in practice.

Legal provision in the People's Republic of the Congo is typical of very many developing countries: 'Family relations is certainly one of the fields of modern Congolese law which creates the greatest concern, not because it is less organized, but because it is regulated as several legal systems based on a variety of juridical philosophies' (Tchibinda and Mayetela, 1983: 191). In the Congo there are customs which vary not only between regions but within regions, from one social group to another, and these still play an important role in the settlement of family affairs and in the custody of children. Thus there are courts in the Congo which adjudicate by reference to customary law, as there are in very many other developing countries. Again, in common with very many other countries, the Congo also has statute law which is largely the law passed on by the colonial power. Tchibinda and Mayetela note that the draft Family Code, elaborated in 1975, was never completed. They further note that as a general rule the fact that men are in a much better economic situation means that, with the exception of the very youngest, children are most often left to the responsibility of the husband in cases of marriage breakdown. This is in accordance with the civil code which provides that 'children shall be assigned to the spouse who obtained the divorce, unless the court at the request of the family or a state authority and in the light of the information collected ... rules that in the best interest of the children all or some of them are to be entrusted to the other spouse or to a third party' (Tchibinda and Mayetela, 1983: 200). Such provision is clearly very similar to that obtaining in very many other countries, including many industrialized societies. But in the Congo, in common with the majority of poor countries, such law is pursued in the context of a number of competing sets of legal principles and concepts. The point should be made here that in relation to child custody, as with most other aspects of child welfare law, only a very small proportion of the population in poor countries will in fact have access to or be subject to the full panoply of formal law. In most countries the majority of poor people will settle questions of this sort outside the formal legal system but certainly within systems of customary and traditional law. But in many cases there will be situations in which both parents and children will be caught at the boundaries of these systems, subject to contradictory prescriptions from competing legal principles and values.

ADOPTION

Hoggett, in an overview of adoption law, suggests that the primary object of such law is to effect the transfer of the adopted person from one family to another (Hoggett, 1984). The law creates and legitimates the complex relationships involved, and in addition lays down procedures for effecting the transfer. Hoggett argues that the way in which the law does this will depend primarily on whether adoption is essentially a private transaction in which the state has minimal involvement or whether it is seen as a matter of concern to the whole national community, involving expert agencies and state sanction. Between these two extremes there is a spectrum of variation.

Adoption, as a means of creating by law the relationship of parent and child, is ancient; in customary adoption laws and practices this was a basic social transaction. The form it took varied between societies but it was universal. As O'Collins notes:

Adoption norms and practices reflect different attitudes to parent-hood and parenting behaviour. In many small-scale societies adoption is between relatives; not always permanent although this may be the intention at the time of the adoption; does not involve cutting off ties with the birth parents; and may involve continuing or additional inheritance and successional rights. It is clear that this is a very different approach from that of formal non-relative adoption in modern western societies [O'Collins, 1984: 289].

Essentially the same point is made by Mumba, a high court justice in Zambia (Mumba, 1981). Drawing a very sharp contrast between traditional adoption practice and the post-colonial Adoption Act, Mumba suggests that in Zambia there were traditionally two types of adoption. The first involved bringing up the children of relatives. Such children could use either their natural father's surname or they could change to that of their guardian, changes such as this requiring no formalities but being generally accepted. For the natural father there was no loss of parental right and he could still play a role as parent. In another system of adoption people with superior social rank could bring up the children of others voluntarily and without reward. Again, children thus brought up had a choice in the use of name. In this system also there was no loss of parental rights for the natural parents and they knew their children's guardians at all times, for there was no secrecy in the system. Mumba argues that 'the reasons for such adoptions are many, ranging from natural love for the children by the guardian to lack of proper support of the children by natural parents; but whatever the reasons, no animosity exists between the guardian and the natural parents of the children so adopted' (Mumba, 1981: 197).

Ahmad notes that adoption in India rarely arose out of humanitarian considerations but was 'generally resorted to by people when they were either unable or to old to beget a child' (Ahmad, 1975). 'The child adopted in such cases was mostly male, and the immediate motivation was almost always the desire to have an heir. There rarely were any adoptions simply to fulfil the desire of having additional children in the home' (p. 181). As elsewhere, the large number of adoptions that took place in India were almost always informal, in the sense that they accorded with customary law and not with imported codified law, and almost always involved close relatives. Ahmad argues that adoption was resorted to most often by foster parents for their own advantage and rarely for that of the adopted child, but goes on to suggest that under the influence of Western practice, some families have begun to adopt children out of humanitarian concern for orphans and the homeless, but the number remains extremely small. As in all other poor countries, social, economic and personal life came to be more and more affected by formal legal systems and rules. As this happened, the informal nature of adoptions 'often resulted in intense litigation after the death of the foster parents by other legal heirs who tried to secure the disinheritance of the foster child and establish their own claims to succession and property of the deceased' (Ahmad, 1975, 1982). In the Indian case, and again this is not uncommon, some groups explicitly rejected the possibility of legal adoption on religious and other grounds. And as late as the mid-1970s there was in India no national adoption legislation covering all communities and groups and providing relatively simple legal procedures.

In relation to the welfare of children in developing countries today, we are dealing with extremely complex social and legal systems. But there are common features in that the great majority of countries are moving quite rapidly towards a codification of laws on adoption, the establishment of precedents, and uniformity in matters such as succession and inheritance. This 'has affected more flexible if sometimes ambiguous customary adoption practices' (O' Collins, 1984: 291). In this aspect of child welfare policy, we see, as in so many others, the problems and difficulties caused when Western values, attitudes and legal provisions diverge from, or conflict with, traditional approaches. In this case it is almost universally acknowledged that traditional adoption customs and practices were very much more flexible and in some cases, as O'Collins suggests, their predominant feature was 'ambiguity'. If it is indeed the case that in many traditional systems 'adoption customs rest on a mental attitude difficult to conceive for those nurtured in western traditions' (Lowie, 1930: 460), there are important and far-reaching consequences for contemporary child welfare policy and practice.

The most important issue in considering legal provision for the adoption of children is the protection of those children and their legal status in comparison with other children. It is striking how many legal systems in developing countries are attempting to formulate provisions which ensure that children can gain full rights consonant with specific social and cultural patterns of the particular society, or groups within it. As noted earlier, many states have only recently enacted formal adoption legislation. Many commentators have made the point that formal adoption procedures, although perhaps necessarily less ambiguous and more restrictive than those in customary law, can be made to embody some of the values and principles of customary and traditional systems.

It is clear that where adoption law is concerned, there are considerable difficulties which result from the tensions between three sets of rights: Those of the natural parents, those of the adoptive parents and those of the child. These tensions and difficulties will exist in any context. In recent years, relatively more emphasis has been given to the welfare of adopted children, and their rights may be seen to have gained some ascendency over the rights of their natural parents. But this remains an area of law where there is considerable variation both in legislative provision and in practice. Many poor countries are introducing formal legal adoption provisions in response to rapid social change. This may be seen as an important aspect of the relationship between child welfare legislation and social policy; it is in those circumstances where social dislocation is greatest and the pace of social change most rapid that there are perhaps the greatest threats to child welfare. O'Collins makes an important observation in this respect: 'a communal sense of collective guardianship which is part of tribal custom may also mean that the concept of adoption only becomes important in terms of social dislocation. The group may normally look after its own without the necessity of a formal adoption ritual' (O'Collins, 1984: 302).

The formulation of appropriate legislation and practice in this area is extremely difficult but of enormous importance to all those involved. At present the numbers of children affected by formal adoption procedures is falling in most industrialized countries and although rising slightly in developing countries, is still very low indeed; but adoption is a vitally important concern for several reasons. It focuses attention on the nature of pre-existing systems of social care, their interrelationship with imported Western formal systems, as well as highlighting the activities of formal welfare agencies. In many countries social service workers, and lawyers, spend considerable time and resources in pursuit of formal legal adoption procedures which affect only a tiny minority of children. There may be a very strong case for the pursuit of relevant and appropriate adoption law and practice, which could be made an important part of child welfare policy as a whole.

FOSTER CARE

Foster care, as a formalized, legally prescribed form of care, is relatively little used in developing countries. Of course, outside formal systems, foster care is very widely practised indeed. In the context of poor countries it makes sense to discuss foster care only in terms of organized formal systems. These seek to place children—who lack care from relatives or the community—with specific families, under supervision. It is essentially an alternative to institutional provision and is widely seen to have enormous advantages in situations where adoption is inappropriate (the vast majority of cases). But given that formal social service provision is not extensive in poor countries, then the use of foster care placements as an alternative to institutional care is still relatively rare (United Nations, 1980). But when traditional systems of social support and provision for substitute care have begun to break down or become inappropriate, the need for legally prescribed foster care provisions becomes apparent (Jain, 1979). As with adoption, there are very many developing countries where attempts are being made to formulate socially relevant legislation for foster care; just as with adoption, the relationship between formal provisions and traditional customs and practice is central. The potential for foster care as an alternative placement for children in need of care is very great. But it requires considerable resources and imaginative legal provisions. There are very few examples of welfare systems which have successfully adopted the principles of foster care within community-based approaches to child welfare and social policy.

There are many problems with the formulation and implementation of child welfare legislation. Perhaps one of the most potent sources of difficulty is the considerable overlap between provision for children 'in need of care and protection' and children who, in breaking the law, are seen to be in need of some 'treatment', 'punishment', 'rehabilitation' or other regime (Pappas, 1983). The separation of children into these very crudely drawn categories is increasingly seen as difficult to defend in conceptual terms. In virtually all states, child welfare legislation has become much more complex and is subject to rapid change, both of these attesting to the difficulties here. Legal provision in very many countries does not draw the distinction very clearly, if at all. In practice, much of this discussion can be seen as virtually irrelevant, as legal distinctions become even more blurred and may be unrecognizable. Very often, children who need the protection of legal provisions to ensure them substitute care are 'criminalized'. The gulf between legal provision and actual practice is very often great; for the poorest children in the poor countries that gap can be so enormous as to mock any legal provision.

It none the less remains important for foster-care legislation to be carefully considered; there is enormous potential here for the development of imaginative and innovative child welfare policies and programmes which can avoid the use of institutional care.

OTHER LEGAL PROVISION

Significant laws and regulations here are those which govern the powers of state authorities, delegated agencies, to intervene where child welfare is threatened. In any society it is this set of legal provisions which determines the nature and form of social services for children. In child welfare, the great majority of developing countries are still burdened with inherited law which is in many cases inappropriate and essentially unworkable (Pappas, 1983). Several aspects of intervention by social welfare agencies on the basis of legal provision will be discussed in later chapters—the exploitation and abuse of children, child labour and responses to destitute children. It is the law in this area, and its frequently detailed associated regulations, which essentially gives social welfare workers their legitimacy and authority. It also defines their duties and the way these duties should be performed; the transmission of specific forms of social work practice via the vehicle of imported legal forms is a consistent theme in studies of social welfare in developing countries (Midgley, 1981; MacPherson and Midgley, 1987).

There are also laws and regulations, also affected by these forces, which govern the procedures and standards of those facilities which are used to provide 'substitute care'. In many instances legal provisions may insist on very specific types of facilities, and legal regulations may be of considerable significance in preventing the adoption of more innovative approaches to the provision of care (Harrell-Bond, 1977; Rao, 1979). Other aspects of child welfare legislation will be discussed in later chapters; the remainder of this chapter will examine some aspects of residential care of children in poor countries.

RESIDENTIAL CHILD CARE

Whatever the priorities in child welfare policies as a whole, and the arguments in favour of programmes located in the community, residential institutions for child care are common. There are a number of reasons for this, the most obvious that the conditions of the very poorest and most vulnerable children are such as to force the provision of some substitute care. The situation in the mid-1980s is very little different, except in degree, from that twenty-five years ago, judged to be such 'as to make necessary some kind of full-time care for children outside their families, as a last resort when all other measures have failed' (World Health Organisation, 1962). In all parts of the world, but most particularly in the cities of the poor countries, there are huge numbers of children abandoned, destitute, uncared for. In Bombay alone it has been estimated that 1,500 are abandoned each year. For a host of reasons, increasing numbers of babies and young children are without care; parents die, mothers of illegitimate babies abandon them in the face of social hostility and prejudice, but total destitution is the major cause. In addition, there are older children, who—as a result of death, desertion or any one of the many other disasters which may afflict children in poor communities—become separated from those who might care for them and are the responsibility of no one in the community. There are, then, very many reasons why children must be cared for by organized services, substituting for family and community care and support. As we shall see later, there are, in addition to these considerations, particular special needs, such as those of disabled children or children who are the victims of abuse, neglect and exploitation.

That the response of organized welfare services should be in terms of residential institutions owes a great deal to the history and growth of such services (MacPherson, 1982). It has already been noted that social services in general have relatively low priority and that a remedial approach has dominated provision in most developing countries. It is hardly surprising therefore that, in general, social services for children are minimal. Contemporary services continue to be very heavily dominated by non-government organizations, many of the larger of these having histories of provision going back into the colonial period. Legislative provision very clearly reflects the importation of Western values and approaches; the specific form of residential child care institutions follows this pattern, as it is largely governed by these laws and regulations.

Provision of substitute care for children in the form of residential homes, of whatever type, represents a profound dilemma for social policy in poor countries. The needs are enormous, and in virtually every poor country the numbers of children in need of care are growing. With continuing urbanization, far-reaching social change and worsening economic conditions, there can be no argument that there is a profound need for provision to assist children. These children are victims of social disruption, and cannot in any way be held responsible for their situation. If they are seriously deprived and without family support of any kind, there must be action, and that action must be immediate. The pressure to provide alternative substitute care is therefore enormous; in a profoundly real sense, services of this kind are rescuing the most needy children of all. The need is undeniable. An increasing proportion of the world's children are growing up in poor urban settlements. By the year 2000 about 40 per cent of people in developing countries will live in cities, and in some regions the proportion will be much higher; 75 per cent in Latin America and 73 per cent in East Asia, apart from China. The cities are growing faster, with estimates suggesting that by the turn of the century there will be over 2 billion people in urban areas in the Third World, with at least half of them below the absolute poverty line. Hundreds of millions of children must grow up in appalling marginal conditions. Very often women are left to care for their children alone and economic forces mean that children must look after themselves and their younger brothers and sisters (UNICEF, 1979).

But, although the scale of need is so great as to deny adequate comprehension, and the situation of each individual child so horrendous as to demand immediate action, policies and programmes for the welfare of children cannot be dominated by the provision of substitute care. This is the dilemma. Child welfare programmes and policies have been geared towards the organization and administration of remedial and residual services and in particular for residential children's institutions. Such provision can only, at its very best, assist a handful of children. As we have seen elsewhere, policies which seek to meet the needs of the majority of children must be policies for families and communities. In the poorest urban areas, and in rural areas, which are not exempt from these problems, conventional approaches to social policy have been seen to be inadequate. Seeking to meet child welfare needs through the extension of conventional services is doomed to failure. As we have seen in relation to other aspects of child welfare, the costs of such services are prohibitive. But beyond that, policies and programmes which do not genuinely involve communities in their own welfare and development do not succeed. We shall see later that there are examples of child welfare policies and programmes which are built on the involvement of poor communities. But the dilemma remains; even if conventional substitute child care is no longer dominant in child welfare policy as a whole, it will remain in existence. In practical terms the argument is that very much more attention can and must be paid to preventive social welfare action, and to policies and programmes for child care which do not necessitate the transfer of children to institutional care, however imaginatively provided. The parallels with earlier discussions on health aspects of child welfare are clear; children's needs and problems, in the context of Third World poverty, demand new approaches. But just as sophisticated hospital facilities remain a vital part of any health service system, however firmly dedicated and oriented to primary health care, so too residential child care will remain as part of social service responses to child welfare needs.

The nature of residential child care institutions varies enormously. There are still a large number of huge, barrack-like, impersonal children's homes run on strict authoritarian lines and subject to very much criticism (Khandekar, 1979). At the other extreme there are residential institutions barely recognizable as such; small-scale, closely integrated with the local community and providing an environment very close to that enjoyed by children with families to care for them. But these are extremes; the majority of residential child-care institutions are quite large, somewhat separate from the local community and for these and other reasons somewhat rigid in their administration. Typically, they are grossly under-resourced, poorly staffed and under enormous pressure. They are nearly always operated by voluntary organizations, although most commonly on an agency basis, taking children on behalf of state authorities.

RESIDENTIAL CHILD CARE IN INDIA

India again provides some very useful examples, as with other aspects of child welfare. Given the scale of population and the extent of child poverty in India, together with the wide range of conditions within that huge country, there is considerable variation. The particular nature of Indian society, taken together with the very long period of colonial rule, initiated a concern with social welfare policies pursued with some vigour since independence. This has produced a very extensive and complex pattern of child welfare provision in India as a whole. We can take residential child-care provision in one state to illustrate aspects of this picture. Maharashtra is the third largest state in India, with Bombay as its main city. The population of the state as a whole is well in excess of 50 million, with about 40 per cent of the total population under 14 years old. A rather higher proportion of the population lives in urban areas than for India as a whole—about 35 per cent. There are nearly 3 million children under 16 in Greater Bombay alone. It is further estimated that about half of the total population live in slums, with a further 2 million living in dilapidated tenements built for factory workers at the turn of the century, each room housing an entire family (Datta-Ray, 1984). At the end of the 1970s Maharashtra had about 150 residential facilities for children, which altogether looked after about 13,000 children, of whom 75 per cent were destitute and the rest 'delinquent' (Khandekar, 1979: 210). In addition, some 2,000 children lived in more than twenty orphanages not covered under the Children Act. Housing destitute children and delinquent children together is very common, in India and elsewhere. There are many routes to residential child care but few destinations.

RESIDENTIAL CHILD CARE IN BOMBAY

The Children's Aid Society of Bombay began to take vagrant children into residential care in 1927 and in 1948 the state passed a Children's Act giving juvenile courts the power to place children into residential care until the age of majority. These were children who were abandoned, orphaned, destitute, delinquent or who were ill-treated by their parents. In 1958 the Bombay Women's and Children's Institutions Rules laid down standards regarding accommodation, health, education and training (Economic Commission for Asia and the Far East, 1973). Three different residential children's institutions in Bombay, all run by the Children's Aid Society, a voluntary organization, were studied by the Economic Commission for Asia and the Far East. The three institutions, a remand home, a home for neglected and deprived children, and a reformatory, were judged to offer an average level of provision. Each accommodated between 300 and 500 children, the remand home being for girls, the other two for boys. One of the institutions had accommodation in cottages, the other two dormitory accommodation; rooms were used for several purposes, for example dormitories were used as classrooms during the day. In none of the institutions did children have shelves or lockers where they could keep their own belongings. Cooking was done by the children under supervision, as was sweeping and cleaning. The standard of health, nutrition and education was found to be high but the lack of involvement in the community was noted for all three institutions.

It has been suggested in many other comments, that most child-care institutions do not reach standards of those run by the Children's Aid Society and studied by the commission. Reports in the local press have been highly critical of many of these institutions, arguing for example that care is minimal and children do not get either physical care or sufficient affection. Rao suggests that in many state-run orphanages, adoption is discouraged because the monthly allowance received from the state authorities means that it is financially advantageous to the institution to have as many children as possible (Rao, 1979). In a similar report, Gandhi suggests two reasons why many of these residential child-care institutions are badly managed. Management committees are frequently populated by women seeking social status, with little interest in the activities of the institution, and that staff are so poorly paid that they may syphon funds to maintain their own families (Gandhi, 1978).

A MISSION CHILDREN'S HOME

The Pandita Ramabai Mukti Mission is a Christian institution in the Pune district of Maharashtra. Many residential child-care institutions in India are like this, as are very many in other poor countries. It is part of what is essentially a complex of facilities, which includes a mission hospital and schools in addition to the accommodation for children; in all, the mission houses over 500 babies, girls and women. The children are there because they are orphaned, destitute, in moral danger or handicapped. There are about 300 children, and most of the adults have duties connected with the activities of the mission (Howson, 1983). There are usually between ten and twenty babies at any one time, both male and female, but after the nursery stage only girls are housed. Of the 220 girls at the end of 1982, twenty-three were blind and six mentally handicapped. Children come to the home for a number of reasons; they are often brought because they have been orphaned and have no one willing or able to care for them, other times they may have only one parent and are brought because that parent is simply unable to care for them. A mother of five, whose husband died, was in poor health and could not cope with caring for two boys and three girls, aged between 4 and 13 years old, so in May 1982 the girls were brought to the mission (Howson, 1983: 15). A common cause of admission is illegitimacy, which is greatly stigmatized in this part of India, with some unmarried mothers coming to the mission before having the child, giving birth in the hospital and then relinquishing the child to the children's home. There is some evidence to suggest that the general prejudice against girls is a factor here. This is also seen to be important in admissions where children are considered to be in physical or moral danger. Some commentators have argued that girls are abused more than boys.

The children's home is organized into separate 'family groups' each of which has its own house, but toilet, washing and kitchen facilities are shared. Older girls cook for themselves, and the mission has approximately 160 acres of farm land which is used to provide some of the food needed. Most of the school-age girls go to the mission school, with some being sent to boarding school. In general terms there is a considerable level of self-help within the institution, and conditions are felt to be comparable to those in most ordinary homes. This, together with access to education and other benefits, in fact means that girls in this institution are very much better off than poor children outside the institution. Whatever the defects of large institutions of this kind, and there are clearly very many, they do offer a safe, secure environment, with adequate food, health care, access to education and basic training. But they can offer this only to a very tiny number of children relative to the enormous scale of the problem of child poverty.

Another approach to residential child care, mentioned earlier, is the 'children's village'. In 1967, SOS Villages were initiated by the Indian government specifically to provide an alternative to large institutions for destitute children. The specific form of these villages varies, but in one example 180 children are housed in twenty cottages each consisting of a family group of children with a house mother (Khandekar, 1979: 192). There are both boys and girls in each family group, the children's ages vary, and siblings are kept together; in principle, once a family group is formed it lives as any other family. The children only leave when they marry or can support themselves. Even though an approach such as this cannot entirely avoid all features of an institution, the contrast with traditional residential provision is very great. If the worst aspects of such provision are done away with and a home-like atmosphere approached to some extent, this is a significant advance. Some brief examples from elsewhere will indicate the dominance of residential child care, and in particular that of the large-scale formal institution run on conventional lines.

EXAMPLES OF RESIDENTIAL CHILD CARE PROGRAMMES

In a discussion of social policy in Ghana, Brown argues that the need for social welfare services in that country arose out of 'the recognition of the inability of the family to manage some of the social problems of its members' (Brown, 1982: 76). The Department of Social Welfare in Ghana has three main divisions: Social welfare, community development and rehabilitation. Social welfare services are concerned primarily with urban areas, although the population is primarily rural. The programmes for welfare focus on juvenile delinquency, marital breakdown and child neglect; there are probation and delinquency services in relation to young offenders, and all nine regional capitals and twenty-three urban centres have been provided with facilities for court services, including probation. The Social Welfare Department runs children's homes in three major cities, for abandoned children and orphans. It also supervises the operation of orphanages run by Roman Catholic Missions, the Salvation Army, Anglican Missions and others. From an analysis of both expenditure and specific activities, Brown concludes that 'it is obvious ... that the welfare programme of the Department focuses its main attention on the urban privileged to the neglect of the rural majority who really need these services' (p. 77). He goes on to suggest that in Ghana there has not been sufficient recognition of the role that social welfare programmes can play in national development and especially in rural areas. He argues that priority should be given to the development of social welfare services, particularly in rural areas 'in order not only to correct the urban bias in resource allocation but also prevent or, at least, mitigate the emergence of social problems' (p. 77).

In Colombia, neglect and abandonment of children are among the worst problems, particularly in urban areas. It is estimated that there are about 400,000 abandoned children in Colombia, and just over 400 institutions take care of 56,000 of them—about 14 per cent of the total. The Institute of Family Welfare was established in 1968 'to protect children, especially those of the low-income classes, and to guarantee and preserve the stability of the family' (Acosta, 1976: 232). The institute has tried to supervise the residential child-care institutions and has laid down minimum standards for the services. Acosta argues that the gross child welfare problems of Colombia are the product of severe deprivation affecting low-income families and that 'in recent years the problem has become worse in Colombia, because the concentration of economic power has resulted in a greater social polarization and consequently in a great concentration of political power. These circumstances explain why social welfare programs have failed to reach the vast poor majority' (p. 238).

In the mid-1970s, the population of Egypt was just over 30 million with nearly 45 per cent under 15 years of age. Badran argues that the conceptual framework for the Egyptian social service system was, until the 1960s, 'a mixture of the early charity orientation and the values underlying the American social work system' (Badran, 1975: 31). Following the dramatic political changes which took place in Egypt in the early 1960s, there was considerable discussion regarding the place of social services:

Social workers, sociologists, economists and planners took part in debates, and it was ultimately recognized that reforming political and economic institutions does not automatically create a Utopia. Whatever the ideology of the society, social services contribute to the welfare of individuals, as far as such welfare is a major concern. The question now is no longer the necessity of a social service system, but rather how this system will be adapted to meet the needs of Egyptian society [Badran, 1975: 28].

In the mid-1970s it was reported that in Egypt the voluntary sector was still very active within the social service system, despite confusion about its role. The Ministry of Social Affairs had responsibility for organizing the voluntary sector through legislation, supervision, technical assistance and financing; most residential institutions for children were operated from within this sector. In 1975 there were 176 such institutions serving about 14,000 children over 6 years of age.

Sri Lanka has a population of around 15 million, of whom just under 40 per cent are under 15 years old; the country is predominantly rural with over 70 per cent of the population living outside towns. The importance of the extended family in child care was very great, but this has been found to have broken down considerably in new settlement areas and particularly in urban areas. In the early 1980s there was no comprehensive law with regard to child welfare; but both statutory and customary law were important. State policy recognized several indigenous systems of law, the majority of the population being governed by a mixture of Roman, Dutch and statute law. As late as 1982 the legislation governing the welfare of children in need of care and protection was an ordinance of 1939 revised in 1956. The Department of Social Services is responsible for child welfare and has overall supervision of residential children's homes. There are 150 of these, 142 of which are run by voluntary organizations with state assistance. In 1980 a total of 995 children were in care following abandonment and a further 175 children were referred as new cases. The total number of destitute and abandoned children in Sri Lanka was not known (Sri Lanka Federation of University Women, 1979). In addition, 460 children were referred in 1980 by the courts as juvenile offenders. Offences were usually theft or a minor infringement of the law such as travelling without a train ticket. Some of these children were also destitute and all of them were from very deprived backgrounds.

These examples illustrate the general pattern. In poor countries residential child-care provision is tiny in proportion to the scale of need, generally institutional, almost always run by voluntary agencies, and most often urban. In the past the work of such institutions came to dominate child welfare policies and the work of social services agencies concerned with children. This is no longer true, although residential child care still has a very great influence on such policies and programmes. Substitute care for children in the context of Third World poverty can rescue only a fraction of the victims of that poverty and deprivation. There are very young children who simply will not survive without substitute care. There are others whose lives will be tragically marred and stunted if left to fend for themselves or to be abused by adults; such children can be given an infinitely better chance and an infinitely better life in residential care. There are bad institutions, and all efforts must be made to improve them, and there are forms of institutional care which approach more closely the lives led by children in families. Above all, perhaps, the good work that is done by residential child-care institutions should be recognized for what is is and not criticized for what it is not. Such programmes cannot under any circumstances meet the needs of the vast majority of the poorest children. We have already seen that the tide of need is huge and growing greater with urbanization, social change and worsening economic conditions. Social policy, in the context of poverty and development, must above all seek to keep children out of residential care—while recognizing the inevitability of such care.

7 Social Policy and Children with Disabilities

The predominance of residential care in child welfare programmes was discussed in Chapter 6. For children with disabilities conventional approaches to social service provision have also been overwhelmingly focused on institutional care. Most commonly linked to hospital facilities, responses to the needs of disabled children have almost always revolved around centralized, professionalized, urban and relatively inaccessible services for people with disabilities. Contemporary policies for children with disabilities attempt to shift concern away from the provision of services to people, towards approaches which involve communities themselves, and people with disabilities themselves, in the creation of relevant programmes. There are close parallels with current debates on the role of health-care services in the achievement of health in the context of development.

'The Declaration of the Rights of the Child', discussed earlier, acknowledged the particular needs of disabled children but only in very general terms. In practice those rights are almost universally denied to the poorest children. Recent efforts to produce a convention on the rights of the child have involved responding to disabled children in particular. Article 12 of the draft convention recognized that disabled children should enjoy 'a full and decent life' in conditions which ensure digity, promote self-reliance and facilitate active participation in the community. Typical of these attempts to establish universal rights was the addition in 1983 of several paragraphs to Article 12:

Recognising the special needs of a disabled child, assistance ... shall be provided free of charge, whenever possible, taking into account the financial resources of the parents or others caring for the child, and shall be designed to ensure that the disabled child has effective access to and receives education, training, health care services, rehabilitation services, preparation for employment and recreation opportunities in a manner conducive to a child's achieving the fullest possible social integration and individual development, including cultural and spiritual development [International Children's Rights Monitor, 1983: 9].

Although statements such as this clearly embody awareness of the needs of disabled children, genuine concern, and the wish to encourage all societies to respond to children's needs, they bear very little relation to the conditions faced by the vast majority of poor, disabled children. Above all, there is a serious restriction generated by the emphasis on service provision rather than on approaches to policy.

The problems are immense in scale, complexity and impact on the lives of children. At the end of the 1970s a global study of disabled children in poor countries was carried out by UNICEF and Rehabilitation International (Hammerman, 1980). That study found that many millions of children are severely disabled by impairments that could have been relatively easily prevented. In many cases the impairment itself may be relatively minor, but the extent of ensuing disability is often multiple, and more functionally handicapping than the impairment alone would have dictated. In this the inter-relationships between child disability and poverty were found to be even more extensive and damaging than had been anticipated. Not only were the principal causes of disability—inadequate nutrition, difficulties at birth, infections and accidents—far more likely to affect children in poor communities, but their effects were much greater. Children were very often not identified early enough in their lives for appropriate action to be taken, which could have altered their progress towards severe disability. Given that only a minority of people in the poorest countries have access to organized health services, very few have access to services relevant to disability. For the great majority of poor disabled children there is simply no access to social services, services for rehabilitation or any other relevant services. Added to this, the birth of an impaired child, or the onset of disability, places enormous additional demands on limited resources and pushes the family deeper into poverty.

It is generally accepted that a minimum estimate of the magnitude of the disability problem is that at least one in ten children is born with, or acquires, a physical, mental or sensory impairment. This estimate is very crude indeed; many of the poorest countries have almost no detailed knowledge of the extent of child disability. However, the major international organizations have accepted this figure, as a compromise.

Too often children, and adults, are defined in terms of their impairment; the functional limitations of the impairment may be viciously compounded by social attitudes and practices. Impairment is any loss or abnormality of psychological, physiological, anatomical structure or function; it can be a missing or defective body part, paralysis or even near-sightedness. In some situations reactions to impairment in children may be severe, often as a result of lack of understanding of the particular conditions. Children may be hidden from sight, kept in dark rooms, deprived of stimulations and normal social contact, and ostracized. In many cases the consequences of this for children will be much worse than the disability which might arise from the impairment itself. Disability is defined as any restriction or lack of ability to perform an activity in terms considered normal in relation to age and the community in which the person lives. Disability, then, is the extent of restriction due to impairment. Not all children with impairment will be disabled, although as noted earlier, compounding impairment with poverty makes disability more likely.

Severely limiting disability, especially physical disability, is much more common in poor countries and poor communities. Recent estimates suggest that probably one out of every twenty to thirty children in developing countries has a disability severe enough to create serious hardship for both family and child. In these terms there are more than 100 million disabled children in developing countries. For these children special re-habilitation measures can often make a critical difference, but their needs are almost always neglected by organized social services. Emphasis on the results of disability raises the concept of 'handicap'. This is most commonly defined in essentially social terms: Handicap is a disadvantage for a given individual, that limits or prevents the fulfilment of a role that is normal for that individual. Thus disability may or may not result from impairment, and handicap may or may not result from disability. There is no simple connection between impairment and handicap; it is the effects of functional limitation that are the concern of rehabilitation. In a great many cases rehabilitation of communities, in terms of attitudes and responses to impairment, is as important as work with those who are impaired. Disability is to a considerable extent a social phenomenon; handicap is entirely a social phenomenon. The essential point here is that the physical and mental impairments suffered by many of those labelled as disabled need not incapacitate them from becoming full members of society (Mulitso and Mbukarni, 1981).

If social policy is to respond in appropriate ways to the needs of disabled children it must be based on an acknowledgement of the concepts of 'impairment', 'disability' and 'handicap'; appropriate social policies and programmes can prevent the relentless escalation from one condition to another, which is the fate of so many poor children with disabilities. For impairment, prevention can take a number of forms. As we saw earlier, vaccination against communicable diseases such as polio can have dramatic effects; so too can primary health care directed at women giving birth. In social and economic terms the clearest links are between impairment and poverty; policies which alleviate the worst poverty, the worst malnutrition and give the poorest people more command over their own health, will reduce the incidence of impairment. For some kinds of impairment, for instance congenital deafness, the movement from impairment to disability is inevitable; but for very many others this can be prevented by early intervention, or even reversed in older children.

An example of medical intervention may be seen in the case of trachoma, which is one of the world's most widespread infectious diseases. A high proportion of the 500 million cases are children, of whom 2 million are completely blind. The spread of this infectious disease is closely connected with poor socio-economic conditions, water and sanitation being among the most important. Early medical intervention in the case of trachoma can prevent loss of sight. Similarly, in the case of blindness which results from vitamin A deficiency, early recognition of the problem can prevent the translation of an impairment into a devastating disability. A high proportion of children who go blind from this cause die as vitamin A deficiency is usually accompanied by protein energy malnutrition and increased risk of other infection. But very many do not, and if the vitamin A deficiency is severe enough to cause irreversible blindness, they are disabled for life. In Bangladesh about 17,000 children go blind each year for this reason; in Indonesia between 30,000 and 50,000 children under school age are blinded every year through lack of vitamin A; in India some areas have recorded proportions as high as 30–50 per cent of pre-school children with eyesight impaired by lack of vitamin A (Singh, 1980: 11). The onset of blindness from vitamin A deficiency is most often indicated by a white blemish in the eye; the child's sight can be saved if the vitamin A deficiency is remedied before irreversible blindness occurs. Thus in this, as in many other cases, early medical intervention, a part of primary health care, can limit the disabling impact of impairment. In social terms, perhaps the most dramatic impact is in changing social and cultural attitudes towards impairment.

Measures which prevent the escalation of disability to a condition of handicapping can also be thought of as curative and rehabilitative. A number of devices, interventions and techniques can be used to prevent a disability interfering with the development of the child's ability to do what is normally expected. As we shall see, it is very often the case that dramatically simple interventions can allow children with disabilities to do very much what children who are not disabled can do, and more. In individual terms this may mean physiotherapy, speech therapy or other interventions of that sort; it may also mean the provision of prostheses and orthoses, and other devices to enable functioning. In social terms community involvement and public education will again be of major significance. But so too are special education, and stimulation for young children; the availability of specialized services; deliberate creation of employment opportunities of particular kinds; perhaps above all, policies centred on ensuring that the self-esteem of disabled children is nurtured and developed to its full potential.

There is, as already noted, a crucial connection between vaccination, immunization and childhood disability. The diseases that are preventable by vaccines disable at least as many children as they kill. But the relationship is more complex than it appears. In terms of social policy it is important to recognize that for very many years to come there will be huge numbers of disabled children, and in many cases continually increasing numbers. Disability from poliomyelitis is a tragic example of the consequences of partial success. Estimates of the numbers of children in poor countries who are paralysed by this disease each year are unreliable; the most recent, which err on the low side, suggest that the figure is around 250,000 (Wilson, 1987: 14). The number of cases is increasing in many developing countries and especially in the poorest communities. Endemic in an insanitary environment because an immunity develops in early life, polio only becomes epidemic when public health standards rise and children are not naturally immune. It has been noted that once infant mortality drops below 75 per thousand live births, prevalence increases without wide-scale vaccination (World Health Organisation, 1975). Thus as natural immunity is taken away by rising public health standards, there must be universal immunization. In poor communities where natural immunity has gone, immunization coverage is very often extremely low and rates of disability consequently very high.

As earlier discussion showed, polio, like smallpox, could be globally eradicated. But, although there has been tremendous progress in vaccination, eradication is a long way off. In the meantime more children than before will survive with the crippling paralysis which results from polio. Social policy must face the fact of a growing level of need among disabled children, in a situation where hardly any of the current needs are being met. The statistics of child disability 'are numbing. But each person is disabled individually' (Hammerman, 1980: 4). Both the scale and the nature of childhood disability in the poorest communities demands radical new policies and programmes. As the last chapter showed, child welfare policies in many countries have been dominated by institutional responses and approaches to social service, imported from the West. This is as true in relation to the needs of disabled children as it is for other groups. The vast scale of need cannot be made the excuse for failing to devise social policy responses which are relevant, appropriate and useful to children. The reality for the vast majority of poor, disabled children is that there will be no help unless such policies are produced and action taken. It has been suggested that at the present time 90 per cent of disabled people in developing countries are without trained help and have no prospect of rehabilitation therapy (Hutchinson, 1985). Organized social services in poor countries are highly centralized, under-resourced and infused with Western approaches. Services for children with disabilities are very scarce indeed and, where they exist, are almost always in urban areas with access for poor children being particularly difficult. In general, they are characterized by a very great emphasis on institutional care, and are marginal remedial services which cater for tiny groups of children (Sebina and Kgosidintsi, 1981).

The example of India, already referred to on a number of previous occasions, serves to illustrate the inherent limitations of conventional social service approaches. Paul noted that the care, education, training and rehabilitation of handicapped children was a priority programme in the national policy for children adopted by the Indian government in 1974 (Paul, 1979). Special programmes were laid out for blind, deaf, orthopaedically handicapped and mentally handicapped children. There was only the vaguest estimate of the magnitude of the problem; in India it was thought that there were between 35 million and 40 million handicapped people at the end of the 1970s, but the number of handicapped children was not known. With the resources available to organized social services (both voluntary and state-run) being so low, it is not surprising that 'despite sincere intentions to help the handicapped fit into society as productive self-supporting individuals, the state had not been able to even touch the fringe of the problem. For example, less than one per cent of the handicapped children known are in schools today' (Paul, 1979: 189).

COMMUNITY-BASED REHABILITATION

Policies and programmes for disabled children have focused on hospitals and other institutions. In terms of the provision of equipment, of physiotherapy and of other interventions, emphasis has tended to be in the direction of increasing professionalization and expertise. The impact of professional intervention for individual children can indeed by very great; in many cases individual lives could be totally transformed by access to facilities, devices, training, encouragement and the opportunity to grow and develop. But until very recently, the numbers so helped were tiny, and very often the child was condemned to an institution for life. Too often the skills and equipment used in institutions were inappropriate to life in poor communities; but it is in such communities that most children live.

In general terms, policies began to change during the 1970s, away from narrow specialization and towards a more holistic approach. Linked with the emergence of Primary Health Care, there were moves towards a wider concept of rehabilitation in the mid-1970s. Rehabilitation was increasingly seen to include all measures which reduced the impact of disabling and handicapping conditions and enabled the disabled and handicapped to achieve greater social integration. In the late 1970s and early 1980s considerably more emphasis was put on accessible technology for rehabilitation and on programmes and projects which would allow this technology to be used by the poor communities. There was increasing acknowledgement of the need to provide children with access to the tools which would enable them to integrate meaningfully into the communities which were the centre of their lives. Vocational rehabilitation, for instance, needed to emphasize agricultural and other skills relevant to predominantly rural communities and not be based exclusively on workshop production in urban centres as was so often the case. Paralleling this there was considerable pressure to integrate disabled children into mainstream formal education and not to separate them out in special schools.

The International Year of Disabled Persons was 1981, and 1983 to 1992 is the International Decade for Disabled Persons.

The concept of 'community-based rehabilitation' (CBR) essentially crystalizes many recent trends and involves all those measures taken at community level to use and build on the resources of the community, including impaired, disabled and handicapped people themselves, and their families. UNICEF began active support of CBR programmes in the poorest countries at the beginning of the 1980s; these have concentrated on disabled children and most but not all are linked with general child health services and organized social services.

The essential problems of disabled children are the same whether they live in towns or in rural areas. But just as the vast majority of poor children live in rural areas, so too do the vast majority of disabled children. Programmes are needed for all disabled children, but the majority will be in rural areas and in poor urban communities. For these children the only realistic approach to policy is community rehabilitation. David Werner argues that responses to the problems of children with disabilities should be a high priority in social welfare policy. Without rehabilitation, of the child and the community, the disabled child is likely to become an unhappy, unemployed and possibly completely dependent adult: 'With rehabilitation, often that same child will become a more fulfilled, more independent adult, who actively contributes to society' (Werner, 1986: 2).

Werner tells the story of one 7-year-old boy in Mexico to illustrate some of the basic features of community-based rehabilitation (Werner, 1986). Gabriel was born with arthro gryposis; some of his joints are stiff and straight, others stiff and bent. He lacks most the muscles in his arms, legs and hands and cannot sit alone or lift a hand to his mouth. When he was born doctors told his parents that nothing could be done for him, so they grew used to doing everything for him. As he grew older, they continued to treat him like a baby, though he no longer was one. Seeking ways that surgery or special medicine might improve his condition, his parents took him to a hospital for disabled children, but the specialists said they could do nothing for him. But workers at a community rehabilition project explained that there was a lot that could be done, not to help Gabriel walk, but to help him do more for himself—within his possibilities. Work began with the family, to help Gabriel become more independent and now he is able to meet some of his basic needs for himself. He feels less like a baby and more like a young man. He has stopped using nappies (diapers); he asks when he needs to go to the toilet. He has learnt to use his mouth like a hand to hold and do things. He has learnt to feed himself by swinging his arm onto the table using his neck muscles and hooking his hand over a spoon. Using the edge of the table and the rim of the dish to push against, he see-saws the spoon to his mouth. His family has joined an organized group of families of disabled children. Gabriel attends school now in a specially adapted wheelchair that he can move himself. He is learning to read, write, paint pictures, and to play with other children. Most children with arthro gryposis are very intelligent: 'If given a chance many can learn to do a lot of things for themselves, even with severe disability ... there is much more that Gabriel and his family will be able to achieve, now that they all see how much he can do for himself. Gabriel is happy and eager to learn more' (Werner, 1986: 5).

The majority of disabled children in poor countries are much less impaired than the boy in this example. But unlocking the potential of all children, and releasing children from the prison of disability is surely a central test of welfare. For the poorest children, disability will often have appalling consequences. Rehabilitation can make a dramatic difference. For poor disabled children in poor countries, it is unrealistic to expect any substantial change in economic conditions or the financial priorities of social policy as a whole. Social services for the disabled, including rehabilitation, will remain a relatively minor aspect of organized social programmes, especially in rural areas. It is partly for this reason that in recent years it has been increasingly argued that child welfare policies and programmes must attempt to achieve as much as possible with very few financial resources, essentially maximizing the contribution of the single greatest asset of rural communites, the people themselves:

Although rehabilitation is a big field (as is health care), it has been shown that villagers with very little formal education can become effective rehabilitation workers, covering a range of basic skills. The challenge is similar to that of primary health care: to simplify and de-professionalise. We need to take the magic and the big words out of 'physio-therapy' and 'orthopaedics', decide what is basic and find ways to put that basic knowledge into the hands of the people [Werner, 1986: 2].

There are several arguments in support of community-based rehabilitation, in addition to the pragmatic one that there is no alternative. Proponents of this approach argue that the essence of rehabilitation is social, as suggested earlier, and not medical. In very real ways this approach may be seen as 'primary social services'; the deliberate comparisons with Primary Health Care underline the essentially similar characteristics. Rehabilitation aims to achieve the greatest possible self-reliance for children—but also for their families and the communities in which they live. Whether organized social services exist or not, the main rehabilitation workers are almost always other family members and other members of the community. Health workers and social workers can do a great deal to offer guidance, information and access to scarce resources. But if the goal of rehabilitation is self-reliance, then family and community-based rehabilitation may be more effective in helping the child do more for herself or himself, and others.

In comparison with the health sector, social service training and organization has not in general taken such approaches on board. Although, as we shall see, there are very many specific examples of successful community rehabilitation programmes, in general training for social service workers does not at present include work of this kind. Training reflects the dominant organizations, and these continue to be very heavily weighted in the direction of centralized, professionalized and remedial services.

It has already been suggested that a second essential element in policies and programmes for rehabilitation of disabled children lies in the re-education of the community. In very many countries children with impairments were frequently treated in quite different ways from other children. Bhinyoying reports that in Thailand 'a child with a mental or physical impairment was hidden away in shame within the family, or else pampered for fear that he or she could not withstand competition against others' (Bhinyoying, 1980: 19). In all societies a major barrier to disabled children lies in the attitudes which people have towards disability. But in many of the poorest communities it may be that there is more appreciation of the strengths of people with disabilities and not just awareness of weaknesses. In comparison with industrialized countries, there may be much more personal interaction and more acceptance, although this is by no means universal.

The possibilities for some change in community attitudes might appear to be greater in poor communities if rehabilitation is genuinely a community activity. Personal interaction with children who have disabilities, not least by other children, is one of the surest ways of overcoming superstition, fear and hostility. There is clearly a great danger in overemphasizing the tolerance of poor communities in developing countries; in many, hostility to impairment and disability is very great. Even where there is a level of tolerance it may be that the disabled are tolerated and accepted in positions of the most extreme inequality. Socially legitimated begging by disabled children in many poor countries stands as clear testimony to the fact that tolerance is by no means equal to integration. Greater knowledge of the causes of childhood disability and knowledge of the means by which some, at least, of this can be prevented, together with greater knowledge of what may be done to dramatically change the lives of disabled children, can provide the beginnings of a shift in community attitudes, expectations and actions. Linked with this are wider questions of the priority given to disabled children within social welfare policies and programmes as a whole. It is obviously the case that societies do not shift in their treatment of disadvantaged groups, at least to any significant extent, unless there is pressure for them to do so. If there is organization of families with disabled children, and their communities, such change may be more possible as organized groups can make demands as well as working by themselves on a self-reliant basis.

Although the emphasis in recent approaches to the needs of disabled children is on self-reliance and community involvement, the role of health workers and social service workers is of fundamental importance. Werner argues that, as in health care, the main responsibility of such workers in the area of rehabilitation is as educators (Werner, 1986). For the great majority of disabled poor children, who are far away from urban-based facilities, rehabilitation must mean that their families should be helped to learn how to provide basic therapy, make simple aids, and help their children become as self-reliant as possible. As with primary health care, it is felt that community rehabilitation programmes should be started and staffed largely by locally recruited and modestly trained 'rehabilitation workers'. Where these workers are themselves disabled, there may be significant advantages; they can more personally empathize with the problems of children and they also serve as positive role models.

In terms of aids for the disabled, commercially produced items are very often so expensive that they economically handicap the family. But very many low-cost alternatives are possible (Caston and Thompson, 1982). A whole range of aids can be made out of accessible materials, at a very small fraction of the commercial cost. Even more important perhaps, it is argued that when the family and the community are involved in making such aids, these aids can be adapted to the particular needs of individual children; they can be repaired or changed as necessary and the family and community will have a fuller part in the care of the children. Caston and Thompson suggest that, where possible, children themselves can be involved in making their own aids; using local materials, very often at almost no cost. Groups of disabled children can produce highly functional aids and gain a tremendous degree of involvement, confidence and self-respect. In the rest of this chapter, examples of community rehabilitation programmes and projects from a number of different poor communities illustrate some of the themes discussed so far.

COMMUNITY-BASED REHABILITATION IN PRACTICE

Perhaps the best-known community rehabilitation programme is Project Projimo, in Western Mexico (Hutchinson, 1985).

The project developed out of a successful villager-run health-care network; many children were found crippled by polio and other diseases and most were too poor to afford expensive corrective surgery available in Mexico City. A number were sent for treatment to the United States, but it was clear that in the long run this could not offer a solution. In 1975 a disabled village health worker was sent for training. As a centre began to be established, disabled children were brought in increasing numbers. It was clear that only a few of them required surgery; most could benefit enormously from artificial limbs, supervised exercises, and wheelchairs. Relatively simple equipment and treatment could radically transform their lives. The community rehabilitation programme was begun by village health workers in co-operation with local people. The project set out to 'de-professionalize rehabilitation' and found that a very great deal could be accomplished by harnessing local skills. By the mid-1980s the project team consisted of fifteen workers, three-quarters of whom were disabled. Based on the principles of community rehabilitation discussed earlier, the project has set out to help families of disabled children 'to become as independent as possible, by helping their children in ways that are both inexpensive and enjoyable' (Hutchinson, 1985: 20).

Families are involved in learning therapy exercises, making, maintaining and repairing equipment, and building up the confidence of their disabled children. A major success of the project has been the development of a range of effective aids at low cost. These include walkers, chairs, crutches, trolleys and swings, all made from cheap, local products. The example of leg supports demonstrates clearly the approach this project has followed. When purchased commercially through government-run rehabilitation centres, low-quality plastic leg braces cost the family of a disabled child US $200; the project produces braces moulded from cut up plastic buckets which cost about US $4. The same principle applies to other fundamentally important aids. In the case of wheelchairs, many disabled children need reliable, easy-to-maintain chairs, but commercial wheelchairs are too expensive and are not designed for the rough conditions. The project began to design a rough terrain wheelchair cheap enough for poor families to buy yet strong enough for the conditions.

Community education is seen as an integral aspect of the project and during their stay most of the disabled children live with local families, some getting part-time jobs temporarily in the community. The rehabilitation playground is used by all local children and the disabled workers themselves are now permanent members of the community. As Hutchinson suggests, 'people often fear what is different, when they do not understand it' (Hutchinson, 1985: 21). For this reason the project attempts community education by all possible means, including the staging of plays and shows.

Linked with efforts to change the attitudes of the community to be more supportive of disabled people, there is a preventive campaign aimed at changing views about injections and their 'magic properties'. As in very many other poor communities, people demand injections because doctors and health workers so often prescribe them, frequently because people demand them. It was found that dirty needles not only caused abcesses and infections but in many cases injections could cause polio paralysis. Most children infected with the polio virus do not become paralysed, but it appears that injections of any medication may trigger the virus to cause paralysis. Most children with paralysis from polio had received an injection within a period of fourteen days before the onset of paralysis. The project reports very great success as a result of its campaigns locally to warn people of the risks of unnecessary injections.

The project has had tremendous success, but as Hutchinson reports, although many problems have been solved, new problems are emerging. In particular, although a great many technical difficulties have been solved in producing low-cost aids from local materials, different problems have come from the pressures to expand the range of work. The project has concentrated almost entirely on children with physical disabilities and recognizes that there are still no adequate services for children who are mentally handicapped or disturbed, or for those who are deaf or blind. The reputation of the project has spread. Children are now coming from very great distances:

PROJIMO has developed approaches to rehabilitation in a rural context, but already the poor of the cities are making demands on its resources. The financial target of the project is to be self-sufficient after three years when the initial launching grant would expire. It will be difficult to achieve self-sufficiency as poverty is now so widespread in Mexico. It is for the poor that PROJIMO exists—and as the recession in Mexico deepens, so, more families will be unable to pay for the services obtained [Hutchinson, 1985: 24].

It is estimated that the services and equipment produced by the project would have cost eight times as much in Mexico City, by conventionally organized services. Similar services in the United States would cost fifty-six times as much. The project seems to have been extremely successful in developing an approach to rehabilitation cheap enough for villagers to afford and not dependent upon experienced professional workers and equipment. In the short run it seems that one problem the project must face is the danger of being overwhelmed by the demand which has resulted from its success.

An example of a community rehabilitation programme working with mentally handicapped children is reported by Wong and Tunay (1980). The project began at the beginning of the 1980s in two villages in the Philippines with a combined population of 585 families, and an under-6 population of 568; of these, 119 children had one or more disabling impairments. The project focused on children under the age of 6, both because they are most vulnerable and because prevention and necessary intervention for impairments should take place as early as possible in a child's life. The project was concerned to pioneer new approaches to the early detection of impairment in young children, and to establish measures which could stop impairment degenerating into disability and handicap. On the basis that to be replicable the project had to be kept simple, a set of non-technical indicators was drawn up for detecting impairments, which could be applied by the people themselves. Interventions were kept on a low-cost basis and used local materials and resources.

Initial surveys of the two communities found first of all that there was a crucial relationship between malnutrition and disability; 33 children had only one impairment and none of these was malnourished. In contrast, 80 per cent of the remaining children, who had multiple impairments, were malnourished. The project as a whole involved co-operation among Ministries of Health, Social Services, Agricultural Extension, and others. In addition, programmes of training were put on for both parents and workers of all kinds. From the beginning the intention of the project was that local people should be made aware of its cause and should plan and carry out the project largely by themselves 'because ultimately the solution for a child's impairment goes beyond the immediate family' (Wong and Tunay, 1980: 22). Early results from the project suggest considerable success, with nearly 46 per cent of children showing improvement. This was due to early detection of problems, correction of nutritional deficiencies and therapeutic interventions of a very simple kind, particularly for children with psycho-social and motor problems. It was also noted that a major impact of the project was on community attitudes to impaired and disabled children, with the Philippine experience echoing points made earlier:

'Disabled' in rural areas is practically synonomous with 'sub-normal' if not 'sub-human'. At best the disabled child could normally expect to be the object of pity and over-protection; at worst of ridicule and utter neglect. These attitudes, which inhibit or destroy the chance an impaired child has of developing normally, play at least as important a role in the progress of that child towards permanent handicap as the actual impairment itself [Wong and Tunay, 1980: 23].

A programme with similar goals is reported from Jamaica (McIntosh, 1980; Thorburn, 1981). The Jamaica Council for the Handicapped began the Early Stimulation Project in 1975 for handicapped children under 6. The organizers of the project argued that two misconceptions stood as the main obstacles to development of services for handicapped children. These misconceptions, it was argued, were held as much by social welfare professionals as by members of the public. The first is that handicapped children must become dependent, non-productive adults and are therefore not worth devoting resources to. The second is that work with handicapped children requires highly trained, highly paid specialists working in teams on a one-to-one basis and is thus extremely expensive. Early stimulation is now generally accepted as essential for handicapped children, and the Jamaican project is based on the premise that lack of stimulation is most often due to lack of knowledge and poverty rather than deliberate neglect. In Jamaica, as elsewhere, poor families are always under enormous pressure, and if mothers are in employment, they must leave their children with relatives. Child minders and day-care centres were found to have negative attitudes towards handicapped children and most often refused them.

Taking as a model the community health aides, the project recruited 'child development aides'. These were women with little or no formal education but with the maturity and understanding which would enable them to assist mothers in training their children and developing their skills and capacities. Women were recruited for these positions from the Government Special Employment Programme. After five years the project is assisting 200 children in the capital and eighty others in a nearby rural area. The child development aides visit children in their homes every week and other aides are employed to work in residential and day-care centres. In 1979 the progress of thirty-six children who had been in the project for two or more years was assessed. Mildly and moderately handicapped children were found to have gained almost as many skills as would be expected of a normal child. The more severely handicapped had gained more than twice as many skills as would have been expected with no stimulation.

The extension of the project to the neighbouring rural area in 1978 was much more difficult than the urban programme. Economic deprivation was much worse, as was malnutrition and correspondingly children's handicaps were worse, with as many as 43 per cent suffering multiple handicap. Of these, one-third had a combination of mental and physical handicaps related to prenatal, birth and neonatal complications. Although the project has demonstrated considerable cost-effectiveness and has disproved the notion that services for the handicapped must be extremely expensive, funding has remained a continual problem (Thorburn, 1981). Those responsible for the project are concerned to expand what it can offer, integrate it more closely into health and child welfare services and use the mothers of handicapped children as child development aides, particularly in remoter areas. They are also concerned to develop preventive work. The economic circumstances in Jamaica make all this extremely difficult, but it is felt that the project has brought tremendous improvement, not least that parents of children helped by the project report that attitudes to their children have improved.

In 1982 a community-based programme for disability prevention and rehabilitation began in Burma. It had two main aims, to make rehabilitation part of a comprehensive health system and to change public attitudes to the disabled (Pe, 1984). Prior to the introduction of this programme, services for the disabled in Burma followed the conventional pattern discussed earlier. There were two schools for the blind, two for the deaf, a psychiatric hospital and two leprosariums. There is a hospital for the disabled providing medical care and orthopaedic appliances. Some disabled men are able to use technical skills learnt at a rehabilitation centre in employment at a producers co-operative in the capital. All these facilities are recognized as extremely valuable, but they meet the needs of only a tiny fraction of disabled people in Burma. Located exclusively in urban areas, they are expensive to operate and are not readily accessible to the vast majority of people who live in rural areas. There was no possibility of seriously expanding these services given the demands on social programmes as a whole.

In the first year of the community-based programme, 1,000 copies of the World Health Organisation manual *Training Disabled People in the Community* were printed in Burmese and ten doctors and physiotherapists were shown how to use it. Initially, the programme covered fifteen villages, each with a population of between 500 and 1,000 and 'a hard working community health worker'. The volunteer community health workers, together with midwives and other health staff, sought to implement the programme in co-operation with local community leaders. In each village the project began with a house-to-house survey. By the end of the first six months the community health workers had found 153 disabled people, about 1.5 per cent of the population, the majority of whom had difficulty with mobility. The basis of the project was assisting families to train disabled people with training packages and the assistance of community health workers. Supervisory visits are used to check that the disabled and their disabilities have been correctly identified and that families are using the right therapies and methods.

Pe gives an example of the success of the programme (Pe, 1984). Hla was 9 and the oldest of four, the son of a labourer. At the age of 4 muscular dystrophy began to take away the functions of his legs and arms. At 6 he could not sit up from a lying position, though if lifted up he could move slowly about on his haunches indoors. Everything but feeding had to be done for him. As part of the community-based rehabilitation programme Hla's mother received training packages and was helped to give him appropriate training. She did this twice every day and the community health worker visited every week. Two months later he could sit up from a lying position by pulling on a rope. A month later he had learnt to stand up by holding onto different objects. He can now walk around outside the house, for short distances, using a bamboo pole. 'Both his parents are very happy with his progress and expressed great surprise on learning that their son still had the capacity to do these things' (Pe, 1984: 10). The Burmese programme is run by the Ministry of Health with United Nations assistance. If this project is successful it is planned to extend community-based disability prevention and re-habilitation services to other states in Burma by 1995.

As has been pointed out several times, social services in general and services for disabled children in particular cater only for a tiny proportion of those who need help. As with other aspects of child welfare, poor disabled children are even more disadvantaged than disabled children in general. Most of these children live in rural areas of developing countries and, as we have seen, specialized facilities are almost exclusively located in urban areas. Mia shows this to be the case in Bangladesh, where available facilities are tiny, relative to the level of need (Mia, 1983). Poor countries cannot establish professionally staffed, sophisticated centres to cater for all their disabled children. In the Bangladesh case, as elsewhere, conditions demand an alternative approach. As in the Philippine example cited earlier, Mia suggests that pro-grammes which involve the poor community can both shift attitudes to disabled children and raise awareness of the causes of disability. To the extent that this can be done, there are much-improved chances of preventing childhood disability.

Earlier in this chapter it was noted that the conventionally organized and administered social services in India were severely restricted and could not meet the needs of disabled children. Recent experience in that country, as elsewhere, suggests the vital necessity of a comprehensive approach which includes prevention, early detection and community-based rehabilitation as essentially the only viable answer for the mass of poor disabled children. Rao describes the involvement of non-government organizations in community-based rehabilitation programmes for disabled children in India (Rao, 1983). Beginning in 1982 the Indian government gave priority to projects generating community awareness of the causes and prevention of disabilities, training community workers and families in early detection and extending low-cost rehabilitation services to disabled children in the poorest communities. Particular attention was paid to projects benefiting children under 6 and to those which used available local resources of all kinds.

As we saw earlier, about 80 per cent of India's children live in rural areas; of over half a million villages scattered throughout the country, over half have populations of less than 500. Although the total number of children disabled and in need of rehabilitation is enormous, the numbers in any one place may be small. For this and other reasons, the Indian programme concentrated on generating multi-purpose rehabilitation skills in the community and the child's family. It was felt that the most appropriate first-level intervention should be identified; professions should be demystified and 'training of field workers must cut across existing specialist boundaries and disciplines'. The Indian experience suggested that while community-level volunteers and parents can be extremely effective in the rehabilitation of disabled children, they need support with appropriate information and technical expertise to ensure that their intervention is suitable and effective. The interaction of specialists, voluntary organizations, communities, and families themselves, is fundamental. Rural workshops were organized to train carpenters and families in the production of low-cost aids. It was found, as in the Mexico case discussed earlier, that production was certainly possible, but the selection of appropriate aids and training in their use required inputs from physiotherapists.

Rao describes two projects which illustrate the approach followed in the Indian programme for community-based rehabilitation. They both use other basic services and existing infrastructures. The first project was carried out by the Indian Red Cross with a major hospital and aimed to extend preventive, early detection and simple community-based rehabilitation services to five large villages. Using a junior Red Cross counsellor as the focal point, information is provided to parents and village workers. Preventive services are provided via immunization, nutritional rehabilitation, detection and treatment of disabling conditions such as vitamin A deficiency and trachoma. The preventive services cover about 1,200 children under 6 years old and provide direct benefits to about 240 disabled children aged up to 14.

Another project is operated by a voluntary organization concerned with health-based community development pro-grammes in rural areas. The basic objectives of the project are to strengthen ongoing activities for disability prevention, to introduce early detection techiques and to promote community-based rehabilitation of disabled children. The major focus of the project is training of workers at the village level. Specific activities of the project include a survey for the detection of disabled children, the training of those children in simple self-help skills, and the integration of disabled children into those existing pre-school programmes which already exist. The project also provides referrals to specialized agencies for further treatment where necessary. About 1,800 disabled children are expected to benefit from the project. Re-habilitation services include provision of simple aids and appliances, and provision of village-based vocational training which will enable children to acquire useful skills (Rao, 1983).

SOCIAL SERVICES FOR POOR CHILDREN

Earlier chapters have shown that the conditions in which hundreds of millions of poor children live are such as to make conventional approaches to the provision of social services inappropriate and irrelevant. The basic conditions of children's lives will be affected in the long run by social and economic changes taking place great distances from where they live. It was clear from discussions of child health that appropriate policies can, even in the most adverse circumstances, significantly affect child welfare. The same can be seen in relation to the needs of disabled children. Disability has a profound effect on the lives of children, an effect which in the vast majority of cases is life-long. The poorest children not only suffer disability in greater numbers, but feel its effects even more harshly. Conventional social services cannot meet the needs of disabled children, but new approaches to community-based rehabilitation demonstrate that there are alternatives which can succeed. Echoing in so many ways approaches to social policy in relation to other aspects of welfare, in particular primary health, these policies and programmes for disabled children stand as an example of the possibilities of social services for poor children.

As we have seen, the concept of community-based rehabilitation has two distinct elements to it. First, it necessitates family and community involvement in planning, implementation and successful continuation of the programmes. Second, because there is a need for technical expertise, the approach demands that families must have access to trained workers in the community. Community involvement in this case, as in others, can take a number of forms, from effective utilization of services to contributions in labour, money or otherwise. But poor communities have very few resources indeed which are not already fully committed. For this and other reasons successful community involvement means that programme objectives have to be perceived by communities and families as real and immediate priorities, in the context of their own goals and aspirations. In this regard mobilization for the welfare of disabled children is no different from other attempts at community organization, mobilization and participation. All programmes in this field stress the importance of raising awareness of prevention, causes and effects of disability in children. But raising awareness should not be equated with the simple transfer of information. It is only if information is shared and discussed within the context of local priorities and realities that it will be internalized and used as the basis of action.

New approaches and services must be, and be seen to be, a significant advance over what is already available. It is not the case that families and communities do nothing for their disabled children. That children with disabilities survive at all in the conditions of most poor communities is testament to the continuous efforts of poor families. If these families are to invest even more time and effort, the welfare of their children must be significantly improved as a result. Community-based programmes are advocated on grounds of cost effectiveness, but also because of the inherent value placed on participation. The costs to be borne by families participating in such programmes are often not sufficiently noted. Although long-term benefits may be more than sufficient justification for the immediate costs to be borne by these families, this may be not just unrealistic, but unreasonable. For families whose major preoccupation is with immediate problems of physical and economic survival, long-term goals may have little perceived importance. Put simply, in many cases there is a limit to what families, and especially the women in them, can do; they cannot do more at present even with the sure knowledge that things will be easier in the future. For community-based rehabilitation to be successful, it is not only that interventions must be perceived as relevant and necessary. If burdens are to be reduced, in the future, support in the present is necessary. For community-based programmes to succeed, it is clearly vital that many agencies are able to respond. As illustrated by several of the earlier examples, in the area of childhood disability, early detection is extremely important. But early detection alone will be of relatively little use if it is not supported by appropriate interventions from health and other agencies.

An element common in community-based approaches, illustrated by the Burmese example, is the use of existing community-level workers. Most such workers already carry very heavy burdens of work, much of it perhaps contributing to the reduction of childhood impairment and disability. It is not always possible simply to add more functions to those already being carried by these workers. More workers may be needed, allowing new functions to be taken on by whole groups of, for example, Primary Health Care workers, or new groups of workers may need to be recruited. In general terms, it would seem from the experience of programmes in many countries that orienting and training workers of all kinds on the causes and prevention of disabilities in children is of vital importance. Not least it helps to highlight the importance of their present work and promote more effective delivery of their services.

The potential of community-based rehabilitation is enormous in advancing the welfare of the most disadvantaged of poor children in developing countries. As an approach to social provision, it illustrates very clearly a dramatic contrast with conventional services. As we have seen, it is not so much a means of service delivery as an approach to social development. To the extent that such programmes are successfully implemented and carried through, their outcomes are not restricted to the vitally important problem of effective service delivery to needy children beyond the reach of conventional services. Their long-term significance lies in their potential for community organization and community development as much as in the possibilities for affecting the performance of social service agencies.

8 Abuse and Exploitation of Children

Principle: The Child Shall Be Protected Against All Forms of Neglect, Cruelty and Exploitation
[from 'The Declaration of the Rights of the Child', UN General Assembly, resolution 1386 XIV, 1959].

Earlier chapters have shown that the welfare of many millions of young children in developing countries is threatened by poverty. When poverty is linked with the patterns of rapid social change common in poor communities around the world, the consequences for child welfare are extremely severe. Social policy and social welfare services must, as we have seen, be formulated and implemented in ways which recognize these fundamental forces. Just as disability and handicap are essentially products of poverty, so too is virtually all the abuse and exploitation of young children. The UN 'Declaration of the Rights of the Child', and most national child welfare legislation, does not recognize the problems of child abuse and neglect. It is only relatively recently that policy has begun to come to terms with the need to protect children from adults, not just from strangers but from those closest to them. In the new 'Convention on the Rights of the Child' there is specific reference to the need for protection of children against 'all forms of physical or mental injury or abuse, neglect or negligent treatment, maltreatment or exploitation' (International Children's Rights Monitor, 1983). Most social welfare systems in developing countries have only recently begun to recognize this need for protection. That many millions of children are abused and exploited by adults has only slowly been acknowledged. Abuse may be direct, as in the case of physical and sexual abuse, or more indirect, as with child labour or leaving children to fend for themselves.

All these are extremely complex topics and are not dealt with fully in this chapter. Only a few aspects of these vitally important subjects are discussed here, and particular reference is paid to the possibilities of positive action in social policies and programmes. Some aspects of child abuse and neglect are discussed briefly, as are the main features of the abuse of child labour. The latter part of the chapter is devoted to a discussion of the problems of 'street children' and the emergence of new approaches to policy. We are concerned here with the poorest children in the poorest communities in developing countries. As with other aspects of child welfare discussed earlier, the incidence and consequences of abuse and exploitation are worst for these children. It is not possible to avoid discussion of these topics on the grounds that the numbers affected are very much lower than the numbers involved in discussions of other aspects of child welfare. All dimensions of the welfare of poor children are interlinked; many of the conditions described earlier can equally be seen as neglect, cruelty and exploitation. In discussing some of the more specific issues in this chapter, attention is focused on the principle of protecting children from harm. To the extent that social policy fails to protect children, it not only fails those children, but all children. The extent to which adults abuse children, and the degree to which other adults fail to prevent that abuse are both measures of social policy's effectiveness in child welfare.

CHILD ABUSE AND NEGLECT

Virtually all research on child abuse and neglect—a topic which has been seriously studied for only about twenty-five years—has been in industrialized countries. Definition is an important and complicated matter. As child-rearing practices vary between cultures, so those behaviours which may be regarded as neglect or abuse will vary. Korbin, in the introduction to a unique collection of studies on child abuse and neglect across cultures, argues that culturally appropriate definitions must be adopted:

there is no universal standard for optimal child rearing or child abuse and neglect. This presents us with a dilemma. If we do not include a cultural perspective, we will be entangled in the ethnocentric position of considering our own set of cultural values and practices preferable, and indeed superior, to any other. At the same time, a stance of extreme cultural relativism, in which all judgements of human treatment of children are suspended in the name of cultural sensitivity, would be counter-productive to promoting the well-being of the world's children [Korbin, 1981: 5].

Child maltreatment must be considered within the context of particular cultures, and child abuse must principally be concerned with behaviour that departs from that which is acceptable within given cultures and societies. The notion of 'culturally acceptable practices' is in itself an elusive and difficult one, particularly in situations of rapid social change, including migration from rural to urban society. In the conditions obtaining in the poor countries of the world, there is increasingly less clarity as to what culturally accepted practices are. None the less, for the present discussion child abuse is identified as the hurt that adults do to children outside what is normally accepted in the community. Thus, however shocking normally accepted practice may be, we are here concerned specifically with behaviour which is idiosyncratic in the harm that it does to children. As Korbin points out, it is important to note that in no culture is there sanction of the extreme harm done to children in what has come to be known as 'the battered child syndrome' (Korbin, 1981: 206).

A number of authors point to the links between rapid socio-economic change and child abuse and neglect. Particular consequences of this change are identified, for example social isolation and greatly increased consumption of alcohol. Increased stress on individual parents in the context of poverty and poor environmental conditions is seen to be associated with an increase in child abuse and neglect. Although children in traditional societies, and the majority of poor communities at the present time, suffer considerable physical hardship and pain, the extent of idiosyncratic child abuse and neglect appears to be very low. There is of course considerable difficulty in assessing the meaning of findings such as these. It is now very well understood that the reported incidence of child maltreatment increases dramatically as public and professional awareness is enhanced.

On the basis of studies from a number of societies, Korbin suggested four general principles which were seen to have particular impact on the incidence of child abuse and neglect (Korbin, 1981). The first of these was the cultural value of children; where children are seen as important in the maintenance of tradition, the perpetuation of the family and in the household economy, they are likely to be treated well. Second, beliefs about particular groups of children will be especially important; a community may value most children highly but not all. Some may be considered inadequate or unacceptable and so not receive the same standard of care given to children in general. Although idiosyncratic abuse and neglect will still be rare, this may put certain children at much greater risk. As earlier chapters have suggested, adopted children, illegitimate children, orphaned children, female children, children with impairments, and others who do not fit normal expectations, may be more likely to suffer abuse and neglect. Third, in many developing countries cultural beliefs about age capabilities and the developmental stages of children are such that children are usually not considered competent until perhaps 7 or 8 years of age. Where this is the case, punishment before that age would have no point. As Korbin suggests, this is 'in direct opposition to the age-inappropriate expectations of very small children and infants that are so often implicated in child abuse and neglect in western nations'. Fourth, and perhaps of most significance for child welfare policies and programmes, it is clear that the embeddedness of child-rearing in kin and community networks is crucial. The existence of a network of concerned individuals beyond the immediate nuclear family is a very powerful deterrent to idiosyncratic child abuse and neglect.

Shared responsibility for child care and child-rearing reduces the likelihood of child maltreatment in many ways. A number of studies have shown that where there is a wide network of individuals concerned with the well-being of children in the community, general standards of child care are more likely to be high and to be maintained. With an extended network, it is very much more likely that an adult will intervene when standards of child care are violated.

Furthermore, to the extent that child care is a matter for the larger group, that group provides alternative caretakers, relieving either or both parents of the entire burden of child care. As was seen in earlier discussion of adoption and fostering, these devices are very frequently used outside the provisions of the formal legal system, as a means by which children can be redistributed, in some cases in situations where they cannot receive a high enough standard of care. Having said that, very many studies in industrialized countries, and some from developing countries, have noted that children who are adopted or fostered, particularly not with kin, run an increased risk of abuse.

In terms of the principles outlined above, Papua New Guinea is marked by cultures which regard children very highly and in which idiosyncratic child abuse and neglect is unknown. Langness suggests that one reason for the virtual absence of child abuse in Papua New Guinea is that people are not driven by the same motives to 'succeed' or faced with the same insecurity as those in the so-called developed countries (Langness, 1981). He also suggests that 'whatever pent-up rage or hostility adults build up towards their children can be channelled into culturally constituted mechanisms that allow for its release' (p. 29). The fact that we can even articulate and comprehend a concept such as child abuse says very much about the societies of the West. Langness suggests:

Had I tried to explain to Bena friends and informants in 1962 that some people in the United States beat small children until they are seriously damaged, lock them in closets, starve them, deliberately burn them, or whatever, I doubt seriously they would have believed me. That type of 'savagery' would have been entirely beyond their comprehnesion [Langness, 1981: 30].

But as Townsend notes, what was believed to be the first case of the battered child syndrome was reported at the main hospital in Papua New Guinea in 1974 (Townsend, 1985). A fifteen-month-old girl presented a typical picture of malnourishment, bruising and evidence of previous fractures, her foster father denying that she had been assaulted. As Townsend suggests, 'probably other cases would come to light if medical workers were trained to differentiate persistent child abuse from other injuries, but it does not appear yet to be a major problem, because of the value placed on children and the frequent availability of alternative caretakers' (p. 61).

In a survey of child abuse and neglect in sub-Saharan Africa, Le Vine and Le Vine put considerable emphasis on the contraints of the traditional social system (Le Vine and Le Vine, 1981). They argue that 'it is when that social system starts to fall apart that we begin to come upon instances of abuse and neglect which the old order largely prohibited' (p. 38). The cultural variation is considerable in terms of what would constitute abuse—although sexual molestation or excessive physical punishment would be commonly regarded as such. In their view idiosyncratic child abuse and neglect is still very rare but seems to be increasing. Particularly as a result of increasing social disorganization, parents are less protected than in the past from emotional and physical stress, and instances of child abuse and neglect seem to be rising. The same point is made by Mumba in relation to Zambia (Mumba, 1981: 198) and by Okeahialam, who discusses child abuse in Nigeria (Okeahialam, 1984).

Considerable emphasis is put in the latter case on rural-urban migration and in particular on the stress associated with urban poverty. As noted earlier, these themes are common in discussions of child mistreatment in poor countries. The importance of this for child welfare policy, and for social policy in general, is the relationship between traditional child-rearing patterns, in both their negative and positive aspects, and contemporary strategies for social welfare. In a discussion of child abuse in Polynesia, Ritchie and Ritchie discuss the experiences of Polynesians in New Zealand in contrast to societies in other parts of Polynesia (Ritchie and Ritchie, 1981). They point out that city environments are grossly deficient in child-care provisions from the Polynesian point of view. In addition, 'the strain placed upon adults by unaccustomed, unremitting child care can create either the preconditions or the flash point for actual child abuse' (p. 200). From the experience of migrant communities, they argue that what appear to be the universal preconditions of the battered child syndrome can arise very quickly in any community which has ceased to maintain good standards of child care: 'Large families, poor living conditions, an intolerable degree of isolation, marital instability, strain, and alcohol—all compound in a generation to create the pre-conditions for child abuse' (p. 200).

Earlier discussion has emphasized the degree to which contemporary social welfare policies and social service provisions embody alien concepts and approaches. Many poor countries continue to pursue child welfare policies which are inappropriate and to a considerable degree irrelevant to their most urgent child welfare needs. We have seen this in terms of health policy, child care legislation, policies for the disabled, and other aspects of child welfare. In terms of the prevention of child abuse and neglect, we are concerned principally with social service provision and perhaps especially with the work of social workers or their equivalent within such services. As we have already seen, professional boundaries often act as a major inhibitor of innovative and productive policies and programmes; as earlier discussion has suggested, child welfare demands approaches which transcend conventional boundaries and go far beyond questions of service delivery. As before, we are ultimately drawn towards questions of community self-reliance, supported by and stimulated by outside intervention. Ritchie and Ritchie believe that in the Polynesian context, 'reconstruction' is not only possible but the only way forward. They argue that although child abuse and neglect may generally be associated with the social disturbances of migration, rapid urbanization and other change, this is not a natural or inevitable association. To accept it as such is in their words 'to admit helplessness'. Their argument for reconstruction is a powerful one, and one which may be applied with similar force in very many other poor communities:

We believe that the Polynesian heritage rests upon Polynesian child rearing. We believe that conscious and deliberate conservation of that pattern would prevent child abuse. In the Polynesian context a pre-existing child rearing tradition is a major resource upon which people can draw to handle culture change constructively and creatively. ... Little really needs to be done to bring a preventive perspective into the problem of child abuse and neglect among Polynesians [Ritchie and Ritchie, 1981: 201].

EXPLOITATION OF CHILDREN

In every poor country there is legislation, sometimes extensive, to prevent the direct exploitation of children. But children are easier to exploit than adults and many millions have their childhoods destroyed by exploitation:

Children are a valuable commodity in the transactions between rich and poor; their exploitation demonstrates the vulnerability of the poor to abuse by those more powerful and rich. The exploitation of child labour, the commercial exploitation of children for pornographic or sexual purposes, and the traffic in children and babies, are all directly or indirectly the outcome of the growing need for the poor to earn income, the contraction of the labour market and the increase in contact between privileged and disadvantaged sectors of society [Boyden and Hudson, 1985: 7].

In recent years very much has been done to raise questions of child exploitation and abuse in employment, where virtually all such exploitation takes place. Damage done to children by employment is clearly a central concern of child welfare legislation, and most developing countries have provisions forbidding employment of certain sorts, almost always allied with regulation of hours worked and the ages of children who work. It is, however, quite clear that in the majority of states, existing legislation is inadequate or inappropriate to prevailing conditions. Beyond this it is also clear that in very many cases existing legislation is not enforced (Mendelievich, 1979; Goddard and White, 1982; I.L.O., 1986).

It is not work itself that is the cause of concern but exploitation. In all developing countries children of all ages have always taken part in productive and economic activities central to the life of the family. It is only with the extensive penetration of the cash economy that child labour in the form of systematic exploitation of children by employers outside the child's family became common. Although in conceptual and analytical terms the boundaries between acceptable and unacceptable child work may seem difficult and elusive, in practice this is rarely so. The child's part of domestic economy is also part of a general process of learning in which the child gradually acquires necessary skills; non-formal education is a rich and varied experience. Clearly, there are difficulties if a very great proportion of children's time is spent in such activities—most significantly in lost opportunities, for instance for formal education and outside experience. At a more general level, the nature of the traditional process may be seen as destructive of full individual development, where for example socialization of girls is into restrictive, dependent and submissive roles. But in comparison with the excesses of formal paid child labour, such activities rarely brought ill-treatment and exploitation.

In the poorest communities of developing countries there is extensive use of paid child labour in industrial and service employments, both in urban and rural areas, much of it in unregulated, informal sectors. In very many countries even extremely young children are working for long hours for very little, under damaging conditions, deprived of opportunities for education and development. The worst examples are most commonly found in the most marginal sectors of poor economies, primarily but not exclusively in the cities. Banerjee discusses the problem of child labour in India, and argues for concentration on the problems of children employed in urban areas (Banerjee, 1979).

In India over 10 million children under 14 are estimated to be child workers, under 1 million of them in urban areas. One-third of those in urban areas are employed in manufacturing, in direct contravention of legislation restricting the employment of children under 14. Banerjee's case is that:

In spite of poverty and lack of education facilities and normal recreation, these [rural] children are at least assured of parental attention during their chores. In contrast, the children working in the manufacturing sector in the urban areas are left to the mercy of their employers [Banerjee, 1979: 5].

Although it may be the case that a smaller proportion of children working in association with their families suffers extreme exploitation, it is certainly not true that exploitative relations do not exist within families. Especially in urban areas, children may make a deliberate choice to work outside the home for some money, rather than inside it for none. In many situations families may engage in productive, paid work on an 'outwork basis' where production is done at home on behalf of an outside employer. Where this kind of arrangement prevails, closer regulation of employers may simply transfer exploited child labour to the home. It will be less visible and certainly less easy to control to the extent that this happens.

Two contrasting case studies illustrate aspects of this problem in relation to social policies for child welfare (Banerjee, 1979). Banerjee reported on the brick manufacturing industry in India. A typical brick-kiln, about 20 km from Delhi, employed around one hundred families; wages were paid to families, not individuals, on a seasonal contract basis. On average each family, of about five or six people, produces between 2,000 and 3,000 bricks a day. The case-study family had three working children, two daughters aged 9 and 10 and a 13-year-old son:

Thakurdas and his family are engaged in preparing raw bricks from the clay. He digs out the clay, piles and adds water to wet it. His children carry the wet clay to his wife and help her to mould the bricks. ... After a day or two these bricks are turned the other way round, so that they are dried from all sides. The tasks are interchangeable, the children sometimes digging up the clay and wetting it and the father moulding the bricks [Banerjee, 1979: 29].

Of the 400 children on the site, only four or five are attending schools; there was no provision of drinking water for the families, they used the same water as for moulding the bricks; the most common disease resulting from this work was silicosis. Child workers were likely to be affected within three or four years; there was no provision for medical insurance or medical treatment. There are no fixed working hours; the bricks are made at speed during the hottest part of the year. A great deal of work is done during the night, by both adults and children, as daytime temperatures are too extreme. The entire area is permanently enveloped in dust and families live on the site. Banerjee reports that workers are totally ignorant of rights and prevailing legislation, and largely because they are migrant workers from different parts of the country, they do not come together and organize as a group. Varied rural backgrounds and the seasonal nature of the work are seen to militate against any community organization on the site.

Ennew and Young studied the problem of child labour in Jamaica (Ennew and Young, 1981). In that country, as in most others, it is the informal or casual sector which has the highest incidence of child labour. Those who work in the formal sector do so on an informal basis, and their conditions are therefore largely unregulated. Ennew and Young conclude that such children are extremely vulnerable to exploitation. In the casual sphere, they found many children working within households, very often so that their mothers would be free to earn money outside the home. In addition, very many young children work in a variety of street jobs and 'many of them grow up before their time. They become proto-adults adept at surviving in the midst of poverty and unemployment' (Ennew and Young, 1981: 59). They give an example of street vending, by quite young children, which is common in poor urban areas. Selling newspapers in the street can in principle be fitted into a school day, but Ennew and Young found that it tended not to be. In 1978, as the result of a study of the conditions of work of these children, an approach was made to the major daily newspaper to see if schooling could be provided as a condition of their employment. The newspaper denied any responsibility for the literacy of these children and as the newspapers are sold in large quantities to dealers who in turn sell them to the children, such approaches seem unlikely to succeed. Evening papers were sold by the youngest boys, morning papers by older boys in their late teens. These boys have a precarious existence:

A boy over fifteen can no longer use his youth, which was virtually his only saleable asset, to wheedle casual coins from motorists. ... His future is almost certain to remain within the limitations of the casual sector, where the highest returns are bound to be in criminal activities. Unless he is lucky enough to come into contact at an early stage with one of the few government and quasi-government self-help rehabilitation programmes which have had a good success rate within the slum areas and which teach some practical skills and provide some employment opportunities, his future is bleak [Ennew and Young, 1981: 56].

Ennew and Young conclude that there can be no radical improvement in the child labour situation in Jamaica without fundamental social and economic changes directed at eradicating poverty. It is poverty and the lack of support services which force families to use child labour in order to survive. None the less, they argue that a variety of small-scale actions could considerably improve the situation of child workers without fundamental economic and social change. None of these, they suggest, require major legislative changes but a change of attitude and a shift in priorities, so that institutions are produced in a form appropriate for the children they exist to serve (p. 59). In particular, they recommend that education policies should be more flexible in order to allow a combination of school attendance with part-time or seasonal work; more flexible attitudes generally within formal education, which acknowledge the realities of child labour for children. They also argue for more community-based nursery and crèche facilities, which could be developed by strengthening the present systems of informal sharing of child care and by providing nursery and crèche facilities for very young children at schools, enabling older children to attend school together with the younger siblings left in their charge. They also argue that legislation should be reviewed and amended in order to end what they see as the present discrepancy between the minimum school leaving age and the minimum age for admission to employment.

Such small-scale incremental changes are typical of those suggested in many poor countries in order to improve the situation of children forced to work. They acknowledge the realities of social and economic life in poor communities and attempt in realistic ways to improve child welfare. As noted earlier, inappropriate legislative provision does not provide an adequate basis for appropriate policies and programmes. But even appropriate legislation has severe limitations in circumstances such as this. We have seen that bad conditions have got worse for many of the world's poorest children, due to national and international economic forces; consideration of child labour and exploitation demonstrates the very severe limitations of social policy. As Ennew and Young say, 'Legislation, however well intentioned, cannot compensate for an economic situation which makes it imperative for a child to work' (p. 11). Further consideration of so-called 'street children' will illustrate some of the very difficult problems and issues of child welfare policy in relation to children in the most extreme situations.

STREET CHILDREN

In all the great towns and cities of the developing countries, street children are a common sight. They work, beg, steal, and live in many cases, on the streets. Their numbers are greatest in the huge fast growing cities of South America and Asia, but the problem is increasingly reported from all continents. Precise data is almost completely absent for this problem, but current estimates put the world population of abandoned and street children at between 100 million and 200 million (Jupp, 1984). In Latin America, more poor people live in cities than in other developing countries, and more work has been done with abandoned and street children. It has been suggested that a realistic estimate of the numbers of street children in all Latin America and the Caribbean would be between 40 million and 50 million. Although detailed numbers are not available, Jupp cites survey evidence from Africa, the Philippines, Thailand, Bangladesh and India, all of which suggest that the numbers of abandoned street children are very much higher than previously believed (Jupp, 1984: 32). In common with other commentators on this issue Morch (1984: 1–2) discerns three distinct groups among these children which may be relevant to social policy strategies in response to their needs. The first group, the 'children *on* the street', is the largest by far of the three categories and consists essentially of working children who still have regular family connections. These children earn a living, however meagre, on the street, but still their focus is the family home; many of them attend school, although perhaps irregularly, and most return home at the end of each working day. These children spend the greater part of their lives on the streets, because their work is there. But most will have close connections with the local community in which their family home is situated. Jupp estimates that this group may account for about 60 per cent of all street children (Jupp, 1984: 32).

The second category, about one-third of all street children, is 'the children *of* the street'. These children see the street as their home, and it is to the street that they primarily relate. They seek shelter, food and a sense of belonging among companions on the street. They may have some sporadic contact with their families, but have made their own decisions, for whatever reasons, to live independently. The remaining children, about 7 per cent, who form the third group, are those children who have themselves been abandoned. In terms of daily activities they may be practically indistinguishable from the second group, but because all ties have been severed with their families, they are entirely on their own, for material and psycho-social survival (Tacon, 1984).

Appropriate policy responses are clearly different for these different groups of children. For children who are abandoned and alone, child welfare programmes must seek to provide substitute care—essentially a new family of some sort, but of a form and nature which is realistic and relevant. Most abandoned children are between 10 and 14 years old, with considerable experience of life on the streets. As earlier discussions of social service provision for children suggested, conventional approaches to institutional care are largely irrelevant in the context of poor developing countries. For these children institutional care of the kind most frequently found in the urban areas of poor countries may bear little relation to the lives they are used to leading. For children *of* the street, links with their families is a major priority, but will in practice be extremely difficult in many cases. If it is not possible for the family to again become the focus of the child's life, then for this group also some form of substitute care will be necessary.

But child welfare policy and practice should not too easily assume the failure of families to provide for their children, and should recognize the enormous pressures on the poorest families in the worst conditions. The Fourth World Movement has argued that policies for street children should not ignore the existence of their families and what the families mean for the children (Fourth World Movement, 1986: 9). Examples are cited of the extent to which even the very poorest of families wish to stay together. A study in Bogotá, Colombia, concluded that 'all the children ... hoped that their families could improve their living conditions; they wished to remain on good terms with them and, when things got better at home—when they could find greater security at home—they wished to stay there, help their families, study and improve their situation' (p.

9). The experience of a project in the capital of Burkina Faso brought similar conclusions from work with street children. The project is with children as young as 7 and involves the children themselves in what is essentially a vocational school (Action for Children, 1986). From experience with many other projects, the Fourth World Movement argues that projects, and advocacy, for destitute children must take their families into account. The point is also made that the fathers of very poor families are often accused of abandoning them; very few remedial services acknowledge men in the community who may thus be excluded and abandoned themselves: 'A street child or an exploited youngster is essentially the son or daughter of a family that has been struck down, humiliated, or forgotten' (Fourth World Movement, 1986: 9).

As noted earlier, the largest group, perhaps two-thirds, are those children *on* the street, for whom the street is a source of work and income but who still live with their families. For these children child welfare policies and programmes should essentially be preventive. To prevent children moving into the groups of those who see the street as their major focus, or further, joining those who are completely alone, initiatives must see children as members of families, which in turn are parts of communities. Conventional social service provision has generally responded to a tiny number of children by offering substitute care and little else. Many now argue that, while seeking to change basic social and economic conditions, programmes for child welfare must recognize the context in which children live:

Such projects must also seek not to take away the child's work, but to give it as well as the child a new dignity. Work need not be damaging, exploitative and abusive, if it is made appropriate to the child's age and development, adaptable to educational and recreational opportunities, accessible for health and nutritional services, and directed towards training for a happy and useful future, which of course includes sound employment [Morch, 1984: 2].

In child welfare policy terms, what has emerged in recent years is the concept of the 'model programme'. Jupp argues that this has resulted from two pressures: first, a move away from traditional institutional care; second, an acknowledgement of the need for an integrated approach which deals with the whole range of social and economic factors (Jupp, 1984). Clear links can be seen here with very many of the policies and programmes discussed in earlier chapters. In seeking a child welfare policy which is both service-oriented and wide-ranging implies an integrated network of programmes. Such a network will have a number of different but closely relating goals. For those children suffering acute damage from life on the streets, programmes must provide short-term residential shelter. Day-care facilities can provide medical services, nutritional help, legal assistance and facilities for recreation; such facilities may be seen as essentially providing a refuge for children. Linked with these provisions, child welfare services must attempt to build systems which can locate families and, by working both with children and their families, seek ultimate reintegration and reconciliation.

But in very many of the poorest communities this is simply not possible; a network of programmes must also involve the provision of alternatives to the family. These may include foster care and other conventional approaches; but in the context of the poorest urban areas, the network of programmes is more likely to involve group living schemes or independent living schemes, particularly for older children. Many projects attempt to provide some educational and skill-training opportunities for children, but these are not only very difficult to provide but may be of relatively little relevance. Given the circumstances in which so many of the very poorest urban children live, action with regard to their economic activity is the subject of considerable controversy. On the one hand, there are many who argue that existing legislation forbidding child employment should be more rigorously enforced and children systematically protected from the inherent abuse and exploitation of street employment at a young age. But there are very many others who suggest that the welfare of children would not be served by such policies, not least because they bear virtually no relationship to the realities of life for the very poorest children. Many now argue for child welfare policies which accept as a fact that children are working and which seek to build a network of child welfare policies and programmes around this. Jupp proposes:

the provision of appropriate economic activity for the children concerned, by the *protection* of street children in their existing occupations, the provision of a job location programme or network within the community, or the development of a new, local entrepreneurial economic base for either the child, the family or the community [Jupp, 1984: 32].

Such approaches to the welfare of the very poorest abandoned urban children demand quite serious shifts in the orientation of social services as well as significant changes in the extent of community involvement. In relation to the first of these, we have noted on a number of occasions that conventional services are severely restricted in the extent of their provision and cannot be made to meet the full range of children's needs if they remain in conventional form.

It is generally the case that poor children forced into an independent existence on the streets will, by virtue of almost any aspect of their lives, commit offences against the law. Given that their life-style itself is 'illegal' in so many ways, the confusion between child care and criminal justice noted earlier is inevitable. It is reported from the vast majority of poor countries that almost always children are not dealt with at all until they commit offences, and are then treated harshly. Almost always this process ends by putting children into institutions, very often of a rigid and repressive kind, where little attempt is made to diagnose the nature of the child's problem in the wider context, and where the experience the child receives is irrelevant at the very best, and deeply damaging at worst (Lorne Stewart, 1980).

In the very worst cases, children are held in adult prisons, almost always with terrible consequences (Tomasevski, 1986). The lives of these young prisoners are most often appalling, in terms of their suffering and degradation many times worse than conditions of life on the streets:

While the great majority of these children are victims of severe poverty, many of them street children forced to violate laws in order to survive, they are incarcerated as criminals. The desperation which drove them to unlawful acts and the social marginalisation which they already suffer are reinforced by imprisonment. Often cast out by the communities and even their families, these boys and girls are in profound need of care, protection and understanding—not further alienation and stigmatisation as delinquents [Grant, 1986: ix].

That, as in these cases, it is the state itself that exploits, abuses and neglects children most systematically and dramatically, is a terrible comment of child welfare policy as a whole. That, in the vast majority of cases, children are in prison because there is no alternative, vividly underlines the need for a network of child welfare policies and programmes, not just for abandoned and street children but for all poor children. Recent attempts to produce alternative and appropriate policies and programmes have focused on work in Latin America. The numbers of street children are very high in that continent, the problem has gained recognition, and the general trend of activity is towards the construction of more effective and more caring approaches to the needs of abandoned children which will keep those children within the community. A project in Brazil serves as an example.

Street children in Cachoeira Paulista
In 1982 the Ministry of Social Assistance and Welfare in Brazil initiated a two-year project which sought 'more appropriate community-based solutions for street children than had been provided by traditional institutionalisation' (Morch, 1984: 3). After two years of the programme, 200 communities were involved, with varying levels of success. In Cachoeira Paulista, a town of 30,000, it was found that about a quarter of all children did not attend school because they were working in the streets to supplement family incomes. Many drifted away from their families and into trouble. By the mid-1980s the town's programme reached about 1,300 children, between 3 and 18 years old. It was estimated that there were about 2,500 street children altogether in the town. Of those involved in the programme, about 300 were children *of* the street with the rest categorized as children *on* the street, working children with relatively stable family lives. The programme consists of a number of separate projects: Day care for very young children, recreation and some education for older children, free meals twice a day for all children, and other activities. Income generation is seen as fundamental to the project, especially for 7 to 11 year olds; it is recognized that between these ages the child's income becomes more and more important to the family. A large number of different income-generating

activities were established, with all children taking some part. It was expected that the programme would be self-financing within a relatively short period.

Early experience of the programme suggested that children usually enter by way of the free meals; emphasis is then put on education, income generation and on the children's relations with their families. It is argued that community participation is crucial to the success of this project:

It is the whole town that has been mobilised to care for its own children. Everybody is working together in support of the programme. Decisions are being taken at grass-root level by street children, their families, and social workers, and they are being backed up by municipal authorities, private business, and voluntary organisations [Morch, 1984: 5].

A number of features may make this example untypical: It is a relatively small town, the municipal authorities have resources which they are willing to make available for a project of this kind, there are opportunities for income-generating activities for young people, and a large number of agencies are able to co-operate. For these, and many other reasons, examples of this kind may stimulate action elsewhere, but cannot be copied. What clearly distinguishes projects such as this from conventional approaches to child welfare is their integrated approach, the involvement of children and families, and perhaps above all the acknowledgement that the employment of children is an essential feature of the life of poor communities. It is in the recognition of this reality, the enhancement of rewards for employment, and attempts to build education, recreation and reconciliation with families around employment activity, that projects such as this demonstrate the potential of alternative approaches in child welfare.

500 MILLION CHILDREN: SUMMARY AND CONCLUSION

In this chapter, and those which have preceded it, a few aspects of the welfare of poor children in developing countries have been explored. In attempting to illustrate some themes and approaches to child welfare, emphasis has been put on three dimensions: survival, protection and development. It is still the case that for a very large proportion of the world's poorest children, survival itself remains a massive struggle. Individual families, local communities and societies as a whole are diminished to the extent that children's lives are lost in circumstances where saving them is possible, feasible and achievable.

The social, economic and political dimensions of policies for child survival have been seen to be as important as any technological or professional input. Consideration of ways of realizing the potential of elements in the 'child survival revolution' forces consideration of the nature of social policy as a whole, in the context of development and under-development (MacPherson, 1982; MacPherson and Midgley, 1987).

Although massive gains can be wiped out in a very short time by economic devastation and other forces, significant progress has been made. The imperatives of child survival programmes as part of primary health care were seen to be social and not medical. Primary health care, as with other aspects of social welfare, was seen to be an aspect of development and not an approach to service delivery. In health as elsewhere, the successful implementation of programmes, policies and projects which genuinely advance child welfare, but which do so as part of a total approach to social development, was seen as vital. It is now a truism that the injection of technical improvements into unequal situations tends to increase inequality and works against the interests of the poorest. This is as true in relation to health and physical survival as it is in agricultural production or other aspects of development. In child survival technological interventions can have dramatic impact, but can only do so in the long run, when there is a shift in social conditions which allows this impact to be realized and sustained. Although absolute changes may be achieved in the rates of survival of the poorest children, their relative position will ultimately depend on changes in economic, social and political relationships, which will remain at the heart of social development issues. Successful child survival programmes were seen to be those which affected such relationships and most especially those which began to give some power to the poorest communities.

Beyond survival, the welfare of children demands that they should be protected from abuse, exploitation and cruelty, and given the opportunities for development. Child welfare legislation and organized social services seek to do both these things but in many of the poorest countries have had very little impact. Laws may be irrelevant and inappropriate to the conditions of the poorest children, and the institutions established to enforce those laws weak or inaccessible to the poor. Conventional approaches to social service delivery may also be seen as inappropriate in many cases. New approaches to policies for child welfare in poor communities have gone beyond the boundaries of conventional legal provision and social service organization. Having a great deal in common with programmes for child survival, and very often linked with such programmes, these approaches emphasize relevance, low cost, community involvement and generally modest objectives. In day care, work with disabled children and with neglected, abused and abandoned children, there are examples of the practical expression of development action. In very many ways, they demonstrate powerful general principles, but not easily transferable models.

An essential but frequently neglected feature of welfare is that it consists, at its heart, of irreducible problems. A 'reducible' problem is one to which there is a solution, and that solution can be passed on intact to others so that the same problem can be solved elsewhere. Problems in human welfare are not of this kind. For 'irreducible' problems there is no one answer; there may be some possible and partial solutions, but these very often cannot be checked and may anyway change over time and certainly with place. Solutions, or more properly responses, to human welfare problems will consist of parts which do not necessarily fit together and may even be contradictory. By definition, responses, if they add up at all, will add up 'to something which is messy, incomplete and elusive' (Adamson, 1980: 27). We can attempt to advance understanding of the problems with which we are faced, and it is hoped that some of what has appeared in preceding chapters has done that. We can furthermore attempt to identify general principles which might inform successful responses to welfare problems and to elucidate the position of those responses in relation to wider social, economic and political forces. What we most certainly cannot do, given the fundamental nature of child welfare problems, is offer centralized solutions which may be imposed in all situations. It is this, perhaps more than anything else, which is clear from even the partial examination of child welfare in this book. Social policies and programmes cannot be worked out by a few and applied to the many:

If the problem of development is ultimately a problem about relationships then it need not be the preserve of experts, the conventionally educated and conventionally intelligent, who are not noticeably better at forming and sustaining just and loving human relationships than are the poor and the illiterate. In the area of human relationships, in the heart of the matter, there are no experts [Adamson, 1980: 29].

Bibliography

Abed, F. (1983) 'Household teaching of ORT in rural Bangladesh', *Assignment Children* 61/63, 249–65.

Acosta, J. (1976) 'Colombian élites and the underdevelopment of the social welfare system' in Thursz and Vigilante (eds), pp. 221–40.

Action for Children (1986) 'Fourth World Movement pilot project for street children in Burkina Faso', *Action for Children*, 1/2, 1, 7.

Adamson, P. (1980) 'Development: a design for the 80s', *UNICEF News*, 27–9.

Ahmad, I. (1975) 'Adoption in India', *Indian Journal of Social Work* 36/2, 181–90.

Anandalakshmy, S. (1980) 'Day care centres' in Barnabas (ed), pp. 115–26.

Anti-Slavery Society (1984) *Children in Especially Difficult Circumstances: The Exploitation of Child Labour*, London: Anti-Slavery Society.

Aries, P. (1962) *Centuries of Childhood*, London: Jonathan Cape.

Azicri, M. (1980) 'Cuban family code: some observations on its innovations and continuities', *Review of Socialist Law* 6, 183–91.

Badran, H. (1975) 'Egypt's social services system' in Thursz and Vigilante (eds), pp. 28–68.

Baig, T. (1975) 'The End of the Queue', *Assignment Children*, 29, pp. 72–87.

Baig, T. (1980) 'Overview of child welfare' in Barnabas (ed), pp. 3–16.

Bandiare, A. (1977) 'L'enfant dans le société nigerienne', *Revue Juridique et Politique* 31 (2), 371–9.

Banerjee, S. (1979) *Child Labour in India*, London: Anti-Slavery Society.

Barnabas, A. (ed.) (1980) *Profile of the Child in India*, New Delhi: Ministry of Social Welfare, Government of India.

Benjamin, A. and Biddulph, J. (1980) 'Port Moresby infant feeding surveys, 1979', *Papua New Guinea Medical Journal* 23 (2), 92–6.

Bhatia, S. and Cutting, W. (1984) 'Teaching millions individually', *Diarrhoea Dialogue* 19.

Bhinyoying, S. (1980) 'Disyabhan: measuring his steps', *UNICEF News* 105/3, 19.

Black, M. (1986) *The Children and the Nations*, New York, UNICEF.

Boyden, J. and Hudson, A. (1985) *Children: Rights and Responsibilities* London: Minority Rights Group.

Brown, C. K. (1982) 'Social policy, social welfare and rural poverty: the case of Ghana', *Development and Peace*, 3/2, 71–83.

Bukenya, K. (1982) 'ORS in Uganda', *Ideas Forum*, 1, p. 3.

Burkina Faso, Ministry of Health (1985) 'Vaccination Commando in Burkina Faso', *Assignment Children* 69/72, 301–27.

Caro, M. (1979) 'From the child to community participation', *Assignment Children*, 47/8, 143–65.

Caston, D. and Thompson, J. (1982) *Low Cost Physiotherapy Aids*, London: AHRTAG.

Chambers, R. (1983) *Rural Development: Putting the Last First*, London: Longman.

Chaturvedi, T. (ed) (1979) *Administration for Child Welfare*, New Delhi, Indian Institute for Public Administration.

Chen, L. C. *et al.* (1980) 'Anthropometric assessment of energy-protein malnutrition and subsequent risk of mortality among preschool aged children', *The American Journal of Clinical Nutrition* 33 (8), 1836–45.

Chen, L. C. (1983) 'International Conference on ORT, *Assignment Children*, 61/62, 93–101.

Chetley, A. (1983) 'Our campaign has just begun', *Ideas Forum* 14, 3–5.

Chetley, A. (1984) *The Baby-killer Scandal*, London: War on Want.

Clavano, N. (1983) 'The promotion of breastfeeding' in UNICEF, 86–92.

Cole-King, S. (1983) 'Oral rehydration therapy and its linkages with other programmes', *Assignment Children* 61/62, 103–18.

Datta-Ray, S. (1984) 'Bombay: city at bursting point', *People* 11 (2), 8–17.

de Souza, A. (1979) *Children in India*, New Delhi: Manohar.

Economic Commission for Asia and the Far East (1973) *Regional Survey of Social Welfare Trends*, New York: United Nations.

Ellerbrock, T. (1981) 'Oral replacement therapy in rural Bangladesh with home ingredients', *Tropical Doctor* 11/4, 179–83.

Elliott, K. (1983) 'Oral rehydration therapy: the Jamaican experience', *Diarrhoea Dialogue* 14.

Ennew, J. and Young, P. (1981) *Child Labour in Jamaica*, London: Anti-Slavery Society.

Fanon, F. (1967) *The Wretched of the Earth*, Harmondsworth: Penguin.

Fourth World Movement (1986) 'Position paper on street children', *Action for Children* 1 (5), 9.

Foxley, A. and Raczynski, D. (1984) 'Vulnerable groups in recessionary situations: the case of children and the young in Chile' in Jolly and Carnia (eds), pp. 53–76.

Galeano, E. (1987) 'Being' in UNICEF, *State of the World's Children 1984*, Oxford: Oxford University Press.

Gandhi, A. (1978) 'The urgent need for adoption', *Eves Weekly*, 23 December 1978.

Goddard, V. and White, B. (1982) 'Child workers and capitalist development: an introductory note and bibliography', *Development and Change*, 13 (4) 465–77.

Gokhale, S. (1979) 'Administration of child welfare services in India' in Chaturvedi (ed), pp. 59–68.

Gokhale, S. and Sohoni, N. (1979) *Child in India*, Bombay: Somaiya.

Goriawalla, N. and Raghunath, M. (1979) 'Legislative provision and child welfare' in Gokhale and Sohoni (eds), pp. 258–73.

Grant, J. (1983) 'Foreword' in Pappas (ed), pp. XI–X.

Grant, J. (1986) 'Foreword' in Tomasevski, pp. IX–X.

Green, R. and Singer, H. (1984) 'Sub-Saharan Africa in depression: the impact on the welfare of children' in Jolly and Carnia (eds), pp. 113–27.

Grillo, R. and Rew, A. (1986) *Social Anthropology and Development Policy*, London: Tavistock.

Gunatilleke, G. and Kurukulasuria, G. (1984) 'The global economic crisis and the impact on children in Sri Lanka' in Jolly and Carnia (eds), pp. 139–46.

Gupta, J. P. *et. al.* (1979) 'Integrated Child Development Services Scheme: a Study of its Health Component in a Delhi Anganwadi' in Chaturvedi, pp. 202–217.

Hammerman, S. (1980) 'A strategy for reaching the unreached', *UNICEF News* 105/3, 3–5.

Harrell-Bond, B. (1977) 'The influence of the family case-worker on the structure of the family: The Sierra Leone case', *Social Research* 44 (2), 193–215.

Hoggett, B. (1984) 'Adoption law: an overview' in P. Bean (ed), *Adoption*, London: Tavistock.

Howson, G. (1983) '*Child care in Maharashtra*', unpublished dissertation, Department of Social Administration, University of

Nottingham.

Hutchinson, A. (1985) 'Project Projimo: A villager-run rehabilitation programme for disabled children in Western Mexico', *Ideas and Action*, 160: 18–24.

International Children's Rights Monitor (1983) 'Draft convention on the rights of the child', Spring, 8–9.

International Labour Organisation (1986) *Child labour: A Briefing Manual*, Geneva: ILO.

International Society on Family Law (1979) *The Child and the Law*, Berlin, ISFL.

Inter-Parliamentary Union (1983) 'Policies, programmes and legislation for children in Africa', *Inter-Parliamentary Bulletin* 1, 10–36.

Jagannadham, V. (1979) 'National policy for children', in Chaturvedi (ed.), pp. 1–16.

Jain, S. (1979) *Child and the Law*, Bombay: Tripathi.

Jolly, R. and Cornia, G. (eds) (1984) *The Impact of the World Recession on Children*, Oxford: Pergamon.

Jupp, M. (1984) 'From needs to rights: abandoned and street children', *NGO Forum*. December, 29/32.

Kapoor, S. (1979) 'Integrated child development services scheme' in Chaturvedi (ed), pp. 168–76.

Katumba, R. (1985) 'ORS: becoming a household name in Uganda', *Ideas Forum* 22, 85/3, 23.

Khandekar, M. (1979) 'Residential child care: some conceptual and organisational issues' in de Souza (ed), pp. 182–216.

Kielmann, A. A. and McCord, C. (1978) 'Weight for age as an index of risk of death in children', *Lancet* 1, 1247–50.

Korbin, J. (ed) (1981) *Child Abuse and Neglect: Cross-cultural Perspectives*, Berkeley: University of California Press.

Kothari, R. (1984) 'Communications for alternative development: towards a paradigm', *Development Dialogue* 1–2.

Krishnamurthi, K. and Nadkarni, M. (1983) *Integrated Child Development Services: An Assessment*, Delhi: UNICEF.

Kulkarni, P. (1979) 'Some issues in national planning for children' in Gokhale and Sohoni (eds), pp. 89–106.

Ladjili, J. (1980) 'Recherche d'une responsabilité égale des pères et mères dans la garde de l'enfant mineur en droit Tunisien', *Revue Tunisienne de Droit*, 225–40.

Lambert, J. (1978) *National Nutrition Survey*, Port Moresby, Papua New Guinea Department of Health, mimeo.

Lancet (1978) Editorial, Lancet, 11, p. 300.

Langness, L. (1981) 'Child abuse and cultural values: the case of New

Guinea' in Korbin (ed), pp. 13–34.

Le Vine, S. and Le Vine, R. (1981) 'Child abuse and neglect in sub-Saharan Africa' in Korbin (ed), pp. 35–55.

Lorne Stewart, V. (ed.) (1980) *Justice and Troubled Children around the World*, New York: New York University Press.

Lovel, H. *et al.* (1984) 'How mothers measure growth', *Assignment Children* 65/68, 275–90.

Lowie, R. (1930) 'Adoption: Primitive' in E.R. Seligman and A. Johnson (eds) *Encyclopaedia of the Social Sciences*, New York: MacMillan.

Luthra, P. (1975) 'The Child in India's Fifth Plan', *Assignment Children*, 29, pp. 26–41.

Luthra, P. (1979) 'The child in India: policy provisions and practices' in Gokhale and Sohoni (eds), pp. 51–64.

Macedo, R. (1984) 'Brazilian children and the economic crisis' in Jolly and Carnia (eds), pp. 33–52.

McIntosh, S. (1980) 'Something positive to offer', *UNICEF News* 105/3, 12–15.

MacPherson, S. (1982) *Social Policy in the Third World*, Brighton: Wheatsheaf.

MacPherson, S. (1986) *Legislation and Child Welfare: An Annotated Bibliography*, Geneva: World Health Organisation.

MacPherson, S. (1987) 'Social security and social assistance in developing countries', *Social Policy and Administration*, Spring, 1–13.

MacPherson, S. and Midgley, J. (1987) *Comparative Social Policy and the Third World*, Brighton: Wheatsheaf.

Mahadevan, M. (1975) 'Children without childhood', *Assignment Children* 29, 26–41.

Mattai, J. (1983) 'The Brazilian national breast-feeding programme', *Assignment Children* 61/62, 225–47.

McKeown, T. (1976) *The Role of Medicine*, London: Nuffield Provincial Hospitals Trust.

Mendelievich, E. (ed) (1979) *Children at Work*, Geneva: International Labour Organisation.

Meyer, P. (1983) *The Child and the State: The Intervention of the State in Family Life*, Cambridge: Cambridge University Press.

Mia, A. (1981) 'Situation of handicapped children in Bangladesh', *Assignment Children* 53/54, 199–214.

Mia, A. (1983) 'Community participation: the needed approach to primary and secondary prevention of disability and re-habilitation of the disabled in rural communities', *International Social Work* 26, 26–34.

Midgley, J. (1981) *Professional Imperialism: Social Work in the Third World*, London: Heinemann.

Midgley, J. (1984) *Social Security, Inequality and the Third World*, Chichester: Wiley.

Midgley, J. *et al.* (1986) *Community Participation, Social Development and the State*, London: Methuen.

Minority Rights Group (1985) *Children: Rights and Responsibilities*, London: Minority Rights Group.

Morch, J. (1984) 'Abandoned and street children', *Ideas Forum*, 18, 1–5.

Mulitso, K. and Mbukani, K. (1981) 'Aspirations and integration of the disabled in the Kivu, Zaire', *Assignment Children* 53/54, 186–95.

Mumba, F. (1981) 'Adoption in Zambia', *Child Abuse and Neglect* 5, 197–9.

Mundle, S. (1984) 'Recent trends in the condition of children in India: a statistical profile' in Jolly and Carnia (eds), 127–38.

Mungoshi, C. (1983) 'Chizuva' in UNICEF, *The State of the World's Children 1984*, Oxford: Oxford University Press.

O'Collins, M. (1984) 'The influence of western adoption laws on customary adoption in the Third World', in P. Bean (ed) *Adoption*, London: Tavistock.

Okeahialam, T. (1984) 'Child abuse in Nigeria', *Child Abuse and Neglect* 8, 69–73.

Pappas, A. (ed) (1983) *Law and the Status of the Child* (2 vols), New York: United Nations Institute for Training and Research.

Paul, R. (1979) 'The Child in India: formal programmes' in Gokhale and Sohoni (eds), pp. 173–91.

Pe, H. (1984) 'A good start in Burma', *World Health*, May, 10/11.

Rao, A. (1980) 'The Balwadi programme in Pondicherry' in Barnabas (ed.), pp. 352–9.

Rao, A. (1983) *Community-based Intervention for disabled children*, New Delhi: UNICEF.

Rao, A. and Choudhry, G. (1979) *The Balwadi Programme in the Union Territory of Pondicherry: A Brief Report*, New Delhi, National Institute of Public Cooperation and Child Development.

Rao, E. (1979) 'Let's give them a family', *Illustrated Weekly of India*, 6 May 1979.

Ritchie, Jane W. and Ritchie, James (1981) 'Child rearing and child abuse' in Korbin (ed), pp. 186–204.

Rohde, J. (1981) 'Therapeutic interventions in diarrhoea', *Food and Nutrition Bulletin* 3 (4), 34–8.

Rohde, J. (1983a) 'Why the other half dies', *Assignment Children* 61/62, 35–67.

Rohde, J. (1983b) 'Oral rehydration therapy' in UNICEF, *The State of the World's Children 1984*, Oxford: Oxford University Press.

Sebina, D. and Kgosidintsi, A. (1981) 'Disability prevention and rehabilitation in Botswana', *Assignment Children*, 53/54, 135–52.

Seers, D. (1972) 'What are we trying to measure?' *Journal of Development Studies* 8 (3), 21–36.

Sharma, U. (1986) *Women's Work, Class and the Urban Household*, London: Tavistock.

Sicault, G. (ed.) (1963) *The Needs of Children*, New York: Free Press.

Singh, D. (1980) 'Mobile Crèches', in Barbabas (ed), pp. 359–68.

Singh, H. (1981) 'Under one roof', *UNICEF News*, 20–21.

Smith, W. (1983) 'Delivering the goods', *Diarrhoea Dialogue*, 14.

Sri Lanka Federation of University Women (1979) *Survey of Child Care Needs in Low Income Families*, Colombo: Konrad Adenauer Stifting.

Swaminathan, M. (1979) 'Children of the urban poor', *Social Action* 29 (3), 221–34.

Tacon, P. (1984) 'I know that my father's here somewhere', *Ideas Forum* 18, 5.

Tandon, B. (1981a) 'Integrated Child Development Services in India', *Indian Journal of Medical Research* 73, 374–84.

Tandon, B. (1981b) 'ICDs in India: evaluation of delivery of nutrition and health services', *Indian Journal of Medical Research* 73, 385–94.

Tandon, B. (1981c) 'A co-ordinated approach to children's health in India', *Lancet*, March, 650–3.

Tandon, B. *et al.* (1984) 'Management of severely malnourished children by village workers in Integrated Child Development Services in India', *Journal of Tropical Pediatrics* 30, 5, 274–9.

Tchibinda, J. and Mayetela, N. (1983) 'The rights of the child in the People's Republic of the Congo', in Pappas (ed.), pp. 183–230.

Thorburn, M. (1981) 'In Jamaica, community aides for disabled pre-school children', *Assignment Children* 53/54, 117–34.

Thursz, D. and Vigilante, J. (1975) *Meeting Human Needs: An Overview of Nine Countries*, London: Sage.

Thursz, D. and Vigilante, J. (1976) *Meeting Human Needs 2: Additional Perspectives from Thirteen Countries*, London: Sage.

Tomasevski, K. (1986) *Children in Adult Prisons*, London: Frances

Pinter.

Townsend, P. (1985) *The Situation of Children in Papua New Guinea*, Port Moresby: Papua New Guinea Institute of Applied Social and Economic Research.

Tremlett, G. *et al.* (1983) 'Guidelines for the design of national weight-for-age growth charts', *Assignment Children* 61/62, 143–75.

UNICEF (1979) *International Year of the Child: Discussion Paper*, New York: United Nations.

UNICEF (1982) *The State of the World's Children 1982–83*, Oxford: Oxford University Press.

UNICEF (1983) *The State of the World's Children 1984*, Oxford: Oxford University Press.

UNICEF (1984) *The State of the World's Children 1985*, Oxford: Oxford University Press.

UNICEF (1985a) *The State of the World's Children 1986*, Oxford: Oxford University Press.

UNICEF (1985b) *Within Human Reach*, Geneva: UNICEF.

UNICEF (1986) *The State of the World's Children 1987: A Summary*, New York: UNICEF.

UNICEF (India) (1984) *Integrated Child Development Services in India*, New Delhi: UNICEF.

United Nations (1980) *Adoption and Foster Placement of Children*, New York: Economic and Social Affairs.

United Nations (1983) *The Exploitation of Child Labour*, New York: United Nations.

Van Ginneken, J. and Muller, A. (eds) (1984) *Maternal and Child Health in Rural Kenya*, London: Croom Helm.

Vittachi, V. T. (1985) 'The dialectics of survival and development', *Assignment Children*, 69/72, 19–34.

Weisberg, D. K. (1978) 'The concept of the Rights of the Child', *Review of the International Commission of Jurors* 21, 43–5.

Werner, D. (1986) 'Disabled village children', *Contact* 91, 1–8.

Wilson, J. (1987) 'Vaccines versus disability', *World Health*, January/February, 14/15.

Wong, W. and Tunay, T. (1980) 'A few miracles for the many', *UNICEF News* 105/3, 22–3.

World Bank (1985) *World Development Report 1985*, Washington, DC: World Bank.

World Health Organisation (1962) *The Care of Well Children in Day Care Centres and Institutions*, Geneva: WHO.

World Health Organisation (1975) *WHO Policy and Programme for Disability Prevention and Rehabilitation*, Geneva: WHO.

World Health Organisation (1981) *Global Strategy for Health for All by the Year 2000*, Geneva: WHO.

World Health Organisation (1981) *Expanded Programme on Immunisation, Progress and Evaluation Report*, Geneva: WHO.

World Health Organisation (1982) *Manuals on Child Mental Health and Psychosocial Development (I–IV)* New Delhi: WHO.

World Health Organisation (1983) *Training Disabled People in the Community*, Geneva: WHO.

WHO/UNICEF (1983) *The Management of Diarrhoea and Use of Oral Rehydration Therapy*, Geneva: WHO/UNICEF.

Yorac, H. B. (1981) 'Child custody determinations: a reappraisal', *Philippine Law Journal* 56, 367–94.

Name Index

SUBJECT INDEX